KOOKS & DUKES
COUNTS & NO-ACCOUNTS

William C. Heine

KOOKS & DUKES
COUNTS & NO-ACCOUNTS
Why Newspapers Do What They Do

Hurtig Publishers
Edmonton

Hurtig Publishers Ltd.
10560 - 105 Street
Edmonton, Alberta
Canada T5H 2W7

Canadian Cataloguing in Publication Data

Heine, William C., 1919-
  Kooks and dukes, counts and no-accounts

  Includes index.
  ISBN 0-88830-302-5

  1. Heine, William C., 1919-   2. Journalists
– Canada – Biography.   I. Title.
PN4913.H45A3   1986   070'.92'4   C86-091291-4

Printed and bound in Canada

For Vivian
who kept the home fires burning

Contents

Acknowledgements

The editorial-page staff of the *London Free Press* in recent years included, at various times and in several roles, Tony Bembridge, Jack Briglia, John Elliott, Craig Fess, Eric Finch, Don Gibb, Cheryl Hamilton, Merle Tingley, George Hutchison, Norman Ibsen, Rory Leishman, Bill Morley, and Gordon Sanderson, though seldom more than five or six on any day. They'd often interrupt a discussion with raucus and ribald comment and a question, "You gonna put that in *Kooks?*" I'd grin and make a note to myself after discussion broke up. They contributed, for which many thanks, more than they realize.

Peter G. White, president of the Blackburn Group, kindly released copyright to all articles and editorials I'd written for the paper. As there are direct quotes from some of those articles in this book, I am appreciative.

Tony Bembridge, features editor, read an early draft of portions of the book and offered helpful criticisms. Merle Tingley, "Ting" to all, generously agreed to some of his cartoons being used as illustrations. Kenneth Smith, photo supervisor at the *Free Press*, allowed reproduction of photographs from his files. Ron Steele, consumer reporter for the *Free Press*, was kind enough to read the chapter on advertising to verify the accuracy of his involvement. Jack Briglia, then managing editor, wisely persuaded me to delete a few sections in which I was unreasonably snarky. The late John Elliott, my predecessor as the newspaper's editor, discussed an outline of subjects to be covered and offered a number of innovative ideas.

Several years ago Joe Hirsch wrote in the *Daily Racing Form* a reference to "dukes and kooks, counts and no-accounts, stars and czars" having added to the legend of Sarasota, New York. Later I noted his phrase in an article about Sarasota in *The Smithsonian*. The rhythm of his words ran around in my head like a familiar tune. In a way, because they were appropriate to so many aspects of my daily work, they led to this book being written. Modified somewhat, his words became the title, for which due thanks.

My wife Vivian patiently numbered pages, shuffled inserts, renumbered them more than once, read early drafts, suggested deletions she thought a little shrill, encouraged other references I'd forgotten, and showed commendable patience while I juggled long and short chapters into varied sequences down the length of her ironing board. My debt to her, after forty-one years, cannot be measured.

W.C.H.

Behind an Editor's Recollections — Friction Makes the Wheels Go 'Round

To an editor, the world sometimes seems to be made up of two kinds of people — those fighting to get their names in the paper and those fighting to keep their names out. Most of the time, however, people are indifferent, content to appear in print for a reason but not hung up about it either way. Those who are hung up, either because they're about to appear in court or because they want their good deeds recognized, call the editor. That can be tiresome, frustrating, downright obnoxious, even frightening. It can also be wonderfully stimulating and exciting.

An editor's responsibility is to serve, as best fallible humans can, not just the caller on the line but all readers. A distraught man might call to demand (easy to handle) or plead (more difficult) that despite his having been arrested for diddling a six-year-old child, his name be kept out of the paper. Yet the man lives on the same street or in the neighborhood of hundreds of people who have small children, and he's out on bail. Which right is greater, the accused to privacy or the neighbour to information? To me, there's no contest. Unquestionably, the public's right to know in a democracy must be paramount; that's the price we pay to preserve the free flow of information. Shut off that flow and democracy is eroded and disappears, as some 110 dictatorships of the left and right demonstrate among the world's 160-odd nations.

Equally strong pressure can come from advertisers who believe their dollars entitle them to favoured treatment when they have a strike or are charged with tax fraud. They usually begin by telling the editor they buy a lot of advertising "on your goddam newspaper." My approach was to pretend I thought they wanted to buy more advertising, put them on hold, and transfer the call to the marketing manager.

1

Along with advertisers are special interest groups — among them pro-life and pro-choice on abortion, Arabs and Israelis on the Middle East, "life is sacred" and "hang 'em" factions on capital punishment. Call them bigots, partisans, dedicated believers, or saints waiting a call to paradise, they can be difficult.

Is the reader to assume that an editor's chair is a constant battlefield? Yes and no. Yes, it is potentially; no, it isn't all that often once the ground rules are clear to management, staff, and the public. Yet the intensity and frequency of confrontation was enough to make me swallow my quip in early years that "I don't get ulcers, I give 'em." Well, maybe I gave a few but in time I got them and ended up in Queen Alexandra's Nursing Home in Bangkok (of all places) with radiologists trying to pin down my stomach's bleeding.

Essentially, the first duty of the editor of a newspaper is to serve, to the best of his ability, the interests of the public who read the paper. Given human fallibility, that's an impossible objective. None of us knows with absolute certainty what is in the best interests of the public, sometimes least of all the public. Nevertheless, the name of the game is to try. If an editor is doing his job properly there will be times when he must risk his job putting the public interest ahead of the publisher's interest. That can result in unemployed editors. And who knows? The publisher just might have been right. The unemployed editor might then have the courage to admit he was wrong, though doing so is unlikely to see him running things again on that paper.

Maintaining the concept of ultimate responsibility primarily to the public not only risks the editor's relationship with the publisher/ owner but also poses problems in working with marketing and production colleagues. Even more acute difficulties crop up in dealing with the score of editors, photographers, columnists, reporters, artists and others in the newsroom who have (if they are any good at all, as were most of those with whom I worked at the *London Free Press*) an equal commitment to the public's right to factual information on news pages and vigorous opinion on the editorial pages. Differing interpretations of what is the public interest create challenging confrontations with the public, various levels of government, the business community, and the newspaper's own staff, as some of the following chapters reflect.

I was immensely fortunate to have Walter Blackburn as publisher. He believed his first responsibility was to serve the newspaper's reader; if he did that, the newspaper would be financially stable because advertisers would want space in it. In almost three decades of working closely together, we had few significant disagreements. Where they existed, only a few times a year, sometimes I convinced him of my point of view, as often he persuaded me to his. The rest of the time we compromised on a position neither of us really liked. In all those years one hand would serve to count the number of times I finally had to say: "Well, I disagree but it's not a matter of principle. I can live with it. I'll show you an editorial later today."

Walter had his peculiarities, so did his editor. When he added "in chief" to my title as editor, I commented that if I was a good editor the "in chief" wasn't necessary. If I wasn't, being "in chief" wouldn't save me. He was not amused. Nevertheless, it was nice of him, even if it was his effort to gloss over my not having been chosen as general manager.

As editor for seventeen years I had between 130 and 150 on my staff. All deserve special mention but I've pruned the list to three. The selection drops past several presidents, vice-presidents, and general managers to A. J. (Jack) Briglia, then managing editor, and N. I. (Norm) Ibsen, editorial-page editor. For well over a decade, few significant news stories or editorials were published without discussion among at least two, usually the three of us. There were times when Jack and I thought Norm was sadly off base; others when Norm and I were convinced Jack was out of his tree; and times when both of them thought I was two bricks short of a full load — and we never hesitated to say so. Yet we were tuned into the same wavelengths and together led the newspaper in understood directions. The third was Marjorie Holliday, a warm, caring person who, for my entire term as editor and for a good many years earlier, dealt with a wide variety of callers (telephone, letters, and in person) with unfailing courtesy and grace beyond the call of any secretarial duty, as well as keeping up with a voluminous correspondence and making sure I turned up for appointments and speeches.

What this book attempts to do is illustrate how one newspaper functioned in its relations with staff, management, advertisers, and the entire spectrum of society. There's some of the milk of human kindness here, but the thrust essentially is negative. For that I make no apology.

In a senior officers' class at the Ontario Provincial Police college near Aylmer, I compared the relationship between police and press to the clutch on a car. The only way the engine can move the wheels is to create friction. The two faces of a clutch (or multiple discs with automatic) provide that friction. Police have their job to do, which includes keeping information to themselves until they are able to solve a crime and make an arrest. Journalists also have a job to do, which in a democracy, among other things, is to keep people informed about what their police are doing. Inevitably, friction develops, which is healthy as long as it doesn't (to carry the analogy a bit further) burn out the clutch by ruining a police investigation or failing to serve the public.

That police/press relationship applies in virtually every other aspect of modern democratic society. On religious news, for example, the average person assumes it should be positive and non-controversial, with stories about people doing good to others, as frequent stories about Calcutta's Mother Teresa testify. Newspaper readers, however, really don't want the good news (those who do should read the Bible, though there's considerable murder and miscellaneous mayhem there, too). What readers want, and get, are newspapers which report an Anglican bishop's opposition to full funding for Catholic schools as well as a Catholic bishop's demand that full funding be implemented immediately — and readers will be strongly critical of a newspaper which doesn't report such controversial religious news.

Essentially, this book is a highly personal account which reflects such concepts and convictions and how, in a medium-sized city of a quarter million people, one newspaper editor tried to cope with that inevitable friction.

To Name, or Not to Name:
Police versus the Public and Media

As editor of the *London Free Press*, I was in contact with the police mainly through Walter Johnson, chief of police. A pleasant, relaxed, outgoing man, Walter and I got along fine in every aspect of our "friction" relationship except one.

Walter was determined, one way or another, to refuse to identify persons arrested until they appeared in court. His approach was that until an arrested person appeared in court, he or she should not be considered to be facing the charge for which they were arrested. At the *Free Press* we were determined that the names of persons arrested and/or detained by police were to be released on arrest. The reason was simple: if police could lock up unidentified individuals until they appeared in court there'd be more cases of police keeping people in cells without good reason. The administration of justice had to be open; otherwise, abuse was inevitable. The investigation of crime, as distinct from arrest, however, demands secrecy.

Our argument, aside from the practical and common-sense elements, to say nothing about centuries of legal precedent, was based on a 1949 royal commission report by Mr. Justice Rand. He stated that a citizen detained by police becomes, at the moment of arrest, a ward of the court. In Canada courts are open. From the moment of arrest, persons detained have a right to have their arrest known. More important, the public has a right to know about every arrest. Anything less leads inevitably to police secrecy and, in time, secret police.

The major effort to turn London's police activities secret developed in 1976, when Inspector George Bruton, drawing heavily on one side of the argument in a publication of the Ontario Press Council, *To Name Or Not To Name*, proposed to his chief and to the London Police Commission that "this force... adopt a system of reporting to the news media, on a daily basis, the *number of persons brought to the detention area*... [including] the number of charges, sex, age and municipality where the accused [reside]." There was more such garbage, but that was the bottom line. We vigorously opposed the decision in editorials, especially after learning that these rules had already been introduced. The initial editorial ended by noting that "The public should fight vigorously against such restriction of their right to know what goes on in their judicial system... from the moment of arrest." Within a week the police commission chair-

5

man, Judge Gordon Killeen, directed London police to revert to established practice in press-police relations. Bruton's report was never formally implemented (we'd have fought it to the Supreme Court) but the problem didn't go away. Walter continued to try to run a closed shop.

Most people, of course, feel that if arrested they don't want anyone to know. That's where they are sadly short-sighted. For my part, either as a person involved in a major crime or as a person well known in the community, if I'm ever arrested and detained with or without a charge, my phone call (assuming I'm allowed only one) will be to a newspaper. If my detention is on public record, police will be very careful indeed how they handle me. They might even let me then make a second call to my lawyer and a third to my family.

There was an incident where a girl was murdered and found in a ditch near London Hunt and Country Club (which unfairly caused considerable glee among some non-members). For reasons never revealed, local police picked up a youth then living in a group home. When he didn't return, staff phoned police, described the boy, and asked police help. Twice during the night staff phoned again asking if police had found their missing charge. Three times police said they knew nothing about the youth, who was then being questioned in police headquarters. When we heard about it, the story was prominently displayed and a strong editorial protest followed. Taking full responsibility as police chief, Walter Johnson publicly accepted the criticism and regretted the police error. Good for him; end of that story. He still didn't seem to realize, however, that his own attitude towards public awareness of detention contributed to such errors by his officers.

Then there was the black driving home with his young daughter and a friend who was stopped and questioned over a defective licence-plate light. Detained unreasonably long, he apparently began arguing with the officer, whereupon he ended up in the cells. Police offered to drive the girls home but, terrified, they ran there on their own. All evening and into the small hours the man's wife phoned police asking where her husband was. The reply was they knew nothing about him. About 2 A.M. he was released. No apology or even comment followed.

During those years the *Free Press* was also critical of the London Police Commission. Its members included a provincial court judge, the mayor, and a citizen (appointed by the provincial government). The judge, in our view, was in an automatic conflict of interest as one of the administrators of the London police force while hearing testimony from local police on cases in his court. The mayor to a lesser and more indirect degree was also in a conflict of interest by his interest as mayor in police salary scales. Our editorials argued that one citizen-at-large was not enough, that the police commission should have five members, and that provincial court judges should not be one of them. In time those changes were made by the province. We were faced with a police commission inclined to consider Walter's proposals, open and covert, not to name people until they appeared in court. At every opportunity our editorial page hammered away at the theme that arrest had to be accompanied by a charge, that arrest put every individual under protection of the court, and that in Ontario courts were open.

Walter wasn't the only one with confused ideas about how police and courts should function. In the September 1981 issue of *Saturday Night* editor Robert Fulford, in an article titled "Trial by Headline," concluded that police should be authorized to withhold from newspapers names of arrested persons until they are brought to trial. November's issue carried my letter agreeing with Fulford — but only if Canada enjoyed perfect police, from the greenest rookie to the head of the RCMP, each of whom made certain that the rights of every individual, no matter how obviously guilty, were always fully protected:

> Unfortunately, Canada suffers from imperfect police forces ... only in dictatorships are police ... considered perfect. They bury their mistakes ... there have been (and continue to be) many reported instances across Canada of people being improperly detained, denied access to family and legal advice ... .
>
> Some journalists abuse their responsibilities just as some police abuse theirs. Exposing journalists' abuses is entirely proper and desirable. Using journalists' mistakes to put police work behind closed doors is to deny the sacrifice of millions of men and women who fought and died to preserve open government and an open system of justice, both responsible to the people.
>
> Whatever injustice is suffered by those arrested and tried in an open system of justice it is a small price to pay not to suffer as do those detained (by the secret police) in Argentina, Chile, Iran, Libya, Uganda, the Philippines ... in a free society, the rights of individuals are far, far better protected by openness.

Both London's chief of police and *Saturday Night*'s editor would have been wise to heed the advice of Sir Robert Mark, sometime head of London's Metropolitan Police Force. He outlined his policy of full information to the media, and thereby to the public, at a Commonwealth Press Union meeting in Toronto: "If a society is to be judged by the preservation of justice and logic under the stress of brutality and emotion, I think that Britain in recent years need not fear the light of exposure. The press, all the press, are better able than anyone to ensure that propaganda and rumour are dispelled by facts and by truth … a free press is no less essential than laws and government to the achievement of a just society."

I wasn't above shafting Walter by making sure he read such speeches as Sir Robert's, nor was there any hesitation in comparing London police with those in other cities. In August 1981, after two people were charged with murder, I wrote Walter noting the co-operation Woodstock police had given: "Our coverage made the public aware how effectively and efficiently [Woodstock] police work … reporting risks police took in the arrests … indicated that police work is dangerous and demanding." Also, by "releasing names at once … police … were operating according to law and doing so openly with full protection of the rights of the accused." That snarky letter ended that it seemed "you're missing out in significant opportunities to demonstrate to the public of London the kind of police force operating in London … by the kind of guidelines offered recently to our city staff … it's a pity, Walter … you and your police forces are the losers."

That was around the time our police reporters again suddenly found their access to information about arrests largely cut off. I decided the issue was too important to fool around locally any longer and took the problem to Toronto. In discussions with John Hilton, deputy solicitor general, and Shaun MacGrath, chairman of the Ontario Police Commission, Shaun handed me a small printed plastic card carried by OPP officers. It outlined what officers were expected to give the media (that is, the public) about any arrest:

Name, age, address, charges, circumstances of the arrest, court appearance date. Photographing a suspect in a public place is neither encouraged nor discouraged, but the accused should not be posed and "facial identity" should be protected.

The names of juveniles are not to be released.

Police are required not to prejudice future trials by discussing evidence, disclosing any confession, referring to the accused's character, or discussing the accused's previous record.

There followed a note: "The public has a right to know about the services we are performing on their behalf and for the protection of their community. This information will be disseminated as consistently as sound police practice will allow." Perfect. That was what the public was entitled to in a democracy and what the *Free Press* was entitled to have on the public's behalf. If Walter could be persuaded to hand out such cards to his constables, and most importantly to his sergeants and inspectors, the public interest would be well served.

The Ontario Police Commission chairman decided to invite Walter to attend a meeting in Toronto to discuss my complaints and asked me to be there as well. In due course Walter phoned and invited me to the Toronto meeting. If I remember correctly, Walter joined me for the drive down. Discussion was lengthy and animated. My most vivid recollection is the point where Walter was insisting that police had the right to detain people without laying a charge. I turned to Shaun and said something along these lines:

"Look here. My understanding is that if I'm walking down the street and a police officer stops me and asks me to go with him, to the police station or anywhere else, I have a right to ask him what is the charge. If he refuses to tell me the charge under which he is detaining me, I have the right to ignore him and walk off. If he then physically detains me and doesn't charge me and keeps me in a city cell without either laying a charge or bringing me before a magistrate, I'm in a strong position to sue him personally, the police force and the city."

Shaun nodded.

"I'm right on that?"

"Yes."

"Then how be you explain to Walter that if I'm a ward of the court at the moment of arrest or even at the moment of improper detention, he can't close Canadian courts."

Well, they didn't put it quite so strongly but there was general agreement that the matter would be thoroughly reviewed. Walter stayed on after I left. What they said I don't know, but until he retired a few years later London police ran a reasonably open shop.

When he retired, our personal relations were as amicable as when the "fortress east" (as *Free Press* staff called the new police station) closed-shop mentality first began to appear. In wishing him well in his retirement, there was a happy note. Mentioning an accident in which I slid on an icy street into an intersection and smacked a car which had the green light, I complimented the young officer who was "courteous ... and firm," managed details most efficiently, and "equally courteous in quite properly handing me a 'failed to stop' ticket," adding it was nice to see a relatively young officer "handling things so smoothly." Walter replied with thanks for both comments and a copy of the memo quoting my letter which he sent to the file of the young officer.

T'was a nice way to end a quarrel.

It Wasn't All Quarrelsome between Police and Media

There were times when media-police co-operation was something they and we could remember with pride. It began with the body of a young teenager being found in a green garbage bag along a creek south of the city. City and provincial police were even more worried than usual because there'd been a rash of sexually related murders in the city, involving both young females and males, without the crimes being solved. I decided to run a strongly worded page-one editorial. In seventeen years as editor there weren't more than four or five of them. This seemed to warrant special concern. "All they need is one good break," the editorial ended. "Somewhere in London there must be a person who knows enough to crack the case wide open ... if anyone knows anything which might be of value to the investigation ... tell the police." Nothing happened for a week, then police charged a man with manslaughter.

A week or two later London city police turned up in my office, being cagey as good policemen should, but pleased as punch. A woman in Lambeth had called police "with additional information"; two women spontaneously searched hospital records for evidence about treatment for injuries; and a hospital patient phoned with useful information. My visitors were saying, without fingering anyone or jeopardizing trial evidence, our editorial had yielded information which helped solve the case.

When the case came to trial the guilty man turned out to be a janitor at the girl's school; he'd been molesting the girl and when she pulled away on the basement stairs she tripped and was killed. Panic-stricken, he stuffed her body in a garbage bag and dumped it. He was convicted of manslaughter.

Basically I like policemen. There are grade A bastards among them just as there are among reporters, and of course editors, but most of them are decent fellows.

Years ago, rushing down Highway 22 towards Sarnia for a luncheon speaking engagement, a police officer flagged me down; a spotter aircraft had been operating overhead. "Sorry, I was late for a speaking engagement in Sarnia," I muttered, and handed over my driver's licence.

"That's tough," he said, and made out a ticket.

Paperwork done, he handed over the ticket and leaned over confidentially.

"Sir," he said with a grin, "there's no more speed traps between here and Sarnia."

Another time, rushing back from the Toronto installation of Cardinal Emmett Carter, an old friend from his days in London, to a dinner and performance at Stratford, I was stopped for speeding. Again I handed over driver's licence and said I was sorry, I was rushing from an installation ceremony in Toronto to a performance at Stratford.

"Oh," said the officer, "that Cardinal Carter's ceremony?"

I nodded.

"What was it like?"

I briefly described the service, the singing, and the packed cathedral. The pencil went back into the pocket and the charge book closed with a snap.

"Well, sir, you weren't too much over the limit. If you'll drive more carefully the rest of the way I'll skip a ticket this time."

"That's decent of you indeed, officer. Thank you."

"That's all right." A grin spread over his face and he leaned over as confidentially as his colleague on the road to Sarnia.

"Ah, you see, I'm a Mick myself, sir."

The Guilty Deserve Full Press Coverage but the Innocent Need It Most of All

Of all the misunderstandings which existed about the role of newspapers in a democracy, none was greater than the relationship among courts, newspapers, and the public.

The problem surfaced in classic form over the trial of a London school teacher on morals charges concerning school children. The teacher was acquitted by a jury which went out of its way to make clear to the accused, the court, and the public its sympathy with the accused. In fact, several lawyers suggested to me it was a case in which the Crown should never have laid charges. Also, at least one juror volunteered he held the same opinion.

Nevertheless, once charges were laid, the court proceeded according to precedents and laws which are centuries old, which have stood both the test of time and of transplanting from Britain to this continent.

What astonished me was not the reaction of teachers to the trial, but of the Board of Education. Apparently without understanding how essential it is that our courts administer the laws in the open, the board deplored the coverage given the trial, and directed their chairman to write to the *London Free Press* expressing their views. John Ferris's letter read:

> The board of education for the City of London wishes to register strong objection to the manner in which the trial ... was reported in *The London Free Press*.
>
> We, as trustees, respect and acknowledge the right and duty of the news media to report the facts of a trial or of any situation in which the public has an inherent interest. However, we also respect the right of an individual to the protection of his character from injury which can result from innuendo and unproved accusations made widely public. The news media, because of its recognized pervading power over public opinions, also is obligated to the protection of simple natural rights.
>
> We believe the articles concerning the trial ... which appeared in *The London Free Press* drew the attention of the reader strongly to statements of minors which in all likelihood, by the style of language used, would result in an emotional response on the part of the reader which could not help but be damaging to [his] character. We cannot agree with your contention that it is proper to make all aspects of such a trial public. It is interesting to note that the other senior media representative, CFPL-TV, chose

to carry no coverage during the trial and simply announced the result at the trial conclusion. The news media cannot ignore the damaging effects of statements made in isolation to their accepted rebuttal.

We regret the necessity of this letter and trust that your newspaper will show sincere consideration for the rights of an individual when any further such situation arises.
John P. Ferris
Chairman, for the Board of Education

My reply was somewhat longer:

Dear Mr. Ferris:
It is easy to understand the sympathy the board of education would feel toward a teacher in their employ who had been acquitted on morals charges involving school children. The board would know that every teacher in the city could say that under certain circumstances it could happen to anyone.

However, I feel that the board does not adequately appreciate the degree of responsibility that rests with a newspaper to provide comprehensive coverage of court proceedings and to keep the community as fully informed as possible of matters affecting its interest.

Full coverage is, of course, a qualified term. Short of verbatim reports of all public proceedings, coverage is a matter of judgement, which is often made in difficult circumstances, in the face of deadlines and without the knowledge of how a trial, or any continuing event, is going to turn out. That is one reason why this newspaper is particularly conscious of the need to maintain balance in coverage, especially when a personal reputation may be at stake.

Open courts are even more important than openness in other public bodies. In the courts a person may be sent to prison for offences under the Criminal Code. Taking away a person's liberty by locking him in a cell for months or years is an extremely serious matter. Every trial must be able to bear full scrutiny.

In a democracy where all citizens cannot themselves see justice done, a system of press reporting of the courts has evolved. Many thousands of people with children in the school system of London would have had a right to complain to this newspaper if we had failed to provide a comprehensive account of the trial. Laws have been passed governing such coverage and one of Canada's laws requires that reports of trials be a fair and balanced summary of evidence.

In the case about which the board has complained, the teacher involved was entitled to have made known to the public his defence against the charges. In my opinion, his defence was fully and effectively presented. By providing that coverage of the defence, however, we are obligated legally and ethically to present equally fully the prosecution case against the defendant.

To do less for one aspect of the case would be a denial of balanced coverage to the other, and of our responsibility.

This newspaper does not relish such trials, any more than we relish any other trials held in London courts, but we have a responsibility to the entire community, in this instance the community of parents who have thousands of children in city schools, to report fully the evidence given in court.

It happens that the man accused in this instance was acquitted. We reported that also, noting that the jury quickly reached their decision and that jury members smiled broadly at the accused as the verdict was announced.

To have done nothing, to have reported only the verdict at the end of the trial, would have been to deny the people of London their right to comprehensive reports of such trials and would have been a failure of our responsibility to provide a fair account of what happens in the courts.

As for the testimony of minors, to which you make specific reference, I have to point out the entire case for the prosecution rested on the evidence given by the minors involved and that the judge who conducted the preliminary hearing — at which public reports were barred — decided that their evidence justified ordering the defendant to trial.

In our experience, Canadian courts exercise great responsibility in such situations. If you or other members of the board of education disagree with the Judge's decision in admitting the testimony of minors in this trial, I feel you should direct your views to the judge or to the attorney-general of Ontario.

As to the publication of the evidence by minors, once accepted by the court, I repeat it is our responsibility to report the accused's full defence and that requires a full presentation of the prosecution case.

I believe with the utmost sincerity, as I said in commenting on your objections when they appeared in our newspaper, that the best interests of the teacher involved in this unfortunate case were served by comprehensive coverage of the trial and of the verdict of acquittal. Anything less would have left a swirling current of rumour and innuendo circulating indefinitely because the facts of the trial were not known.

In retrospect, I think that our coverage of the trial is open to criticism only to the extent to which we reported and repeated details of the evidence given by the young girls. Every morals trial raises questions of good taste and balance — including the question of how much prominence is warranted — which must be weighed against the need for fair presentation of both prosecution and defence. A preoccupation with sexual detail in coverage of any morals case is a danger *The Free Press* recognizes. We continually re-examine our policies in an effort to ensure that testimony published in such cases does not for purely vicarious reason go beyond that required for fair and comprehensive coverage.

On the evidence, it is my conviction that the jury quite properly brought in a verdict of not guilty. Obviously, you and your board feel the same way, as do, I understand, an overwhelming majority of the teacher's colleagues.

I believe those full and accurate reports of the trial are the reason you and your colleagues on the board, as well as the teaching profession in London, and the general public, have so overwhelmingly accepted the jury's verdict. Given less than full reporting, a great many people might be asking a great many unanswered and unanswerable questions.

If you, or a group of members of your board, or the board itself would like to discuss this response with me, I'd be happy to make myself available at any time at your convenience.

William C. Heine
Editor

There was no response to my invitation.

A few weeks later, I was in the Arctic for three days with fifty London and Western Ontario teachers. I invited informal discussion on the issue. Several took the opportunity. I was delighted that every discussion was on the merits of the views expressed. Not once did our talks, on buses, boats, and at barbeques, degenerate into emotionalism.

It's hard to say what was the total reaction but several teachers were realistic enough to say they now saw the problem differently. At one point I asked if they'd read press accounts of the Peter Demeter murder trial, which was held in London. Everyone had, in detail.

"Why," I asked, "if you believe so strongly that trials should not be reported until the accused is acquitted or convicted, did you not protest to the newspaper at the time of the Demeter case?"

A teacher replied she guessed it was because one was a contractor and the other was a teacher — a rather good summation.

People Have Trouble Adjusting to Computers

The lady was shrill at first, the easily recognized voice of a soul in torment. She announced, without introduction or even a howdy-do, that she was going to sue us. Before she could be asked why, she told me she knew we had computers on our second floor.

"Yes, ma'am, we sure do — but what..."

"Every morning when I read the paper," she interrupted, "I see stories I thought about yesterday. So I know you're using those computers to tap my brain. It's not right. I can't sleep at nights worrying about it and I'm going to sue you."

What do you do with that one? Call a local headshrink — the police — try to calm her down — or just hang up?

Well, the answer came in a flash of blinding light: "You caught us out!"

Long silence. Then, aggressively, "Yes, I certainly did."

"We had a meeting about that just last week and we were worried whether we were doing the ethical thing, but we were getting so many good news stories that way, we put off a decision for a week."

Now the silence was longer, so the trowel was loaded with another sticky pile of goo.

"Tell you what; I'm going straight upstairs and I'll turn off those computers. We just shouldn't do it any more."

The voice was sweet as pie. "Really, you mean that?"

"Yes, indeed, right away." She was profuse in her thanks and hung up.

Next morning there was another call from the lady. She just wanted to say how appreciative she was — she'd had the first good night's sleep in months. Then she added that "others are still doing it," which was a bit of a contradiction given her good night's sleep.

"Oh?"

"Yes, there's a radio station in town tapping my brain, too."

Well now, a fellow doesn't get an opportunity to hammer the competition like that very often (there are several radio stations in town). I gave her the call letters of a radio station, the name of the manager, the station's phone number, and stressed she should refuse to talk to anyone but the station manager.

She was most grateful. She didn't phone back. Nor did the radio station manager call. Sometimes life is good.

Covering the Parade
and Marching in the Band

Becoming involved in even the most innocuous local, national, or international organizations can create downright schizophrenic situations for newspapermen. Sooner or later, reporters and editors who take office, or in some instances merely join social, cultural, business, or political groups, find themselves facing serious conflicts of interest. Sitting on a board of directors, no matter how deserving of public support, journalists can be put under subtle but strong pressure to tilt coverage of events to favour the board's objectives or to participate in a cover-up. The more involved in such organizations a journalist becomes, the easier it is not to raise the awkward questions and to forget that the primary objective of any good newspaper and of its reporters and editors is to inform the public what is happening. Publishers should also take note.

John Delane, the nineteenth-century editor of the London *Times*, wrote that "the first duty of the press is to obtain the earliest and most correct intelligence of the events of the time, and instantly, by disclosing them, to make them the common property of the nation ... the press lives by disclosure." Newspapermen who join boards are under substantial pressure to withhold information until, as I've heard more than one president say, "we're ready to release ALL the information."

It took some time but eventually I learned the hard way that a former associate at the *Free Press*, Max Macdonald, was right: "You can't cover the parade if you're marching in the band." Sooner or later someone wants you to march to their music. As a reporter or editor you should be marching to a different drummer.

The year I became editor I was slated for two non-professional jobs: president of London's United Community Services, which allocated the funds raised by the United Appeal, and chairman of the Division of Communications of the United Church of Canada, which in effect was chairman of the board of Ryerson Press. Both involved significant community service and a great many fine people. Also, selfishly, they provided administrative experience in fields other than newspapers.

Both tasks were discussed with the publisher, Walter Blackburn. He was engaged in many community activities, as editor Arthur Ford had been. As publisher, Blackburn hovered above the fray. He didn't have reporters pounding on his door demanding an account of his extracurricular activities as did his editor. The problem never occurred to him — and I wasn't smart enough to see what was coming.

With the UCS, no sooner was I banging the gavel at luncheon meetings than a major organizational problem developed. The former president, Allan Cohen, a retail merchant in London who'd taken his Ph.D. in social science, had been much concerned about some of the accounting practices of the "Y" in allocating funds for youth activities. London's YM-YWCA treasurer, Kenneth Lemon, a senior partner of Clarkson Gordon, the prestigious accounting and tax consulting firm, stoutly insisted his allocation of costs and revenues and UCS grants was entirely fair. Both Ken and Al had a well-developed capacity to call a spade a spade, and indeed to extend the description. Before long, despite my best efforts and those of the board, the "Y" was threatening to pull out of UCS and the United Appeal, raising its own funds. The "Y" could do it, too. There was substantial support in the community for the YM-YWCA — and United Appeal campaigns, getting larger and larger every year, didn't always make annual campaign objectives. Attitudes were complicated by the knowledge that many people didn't understand why the "Y" got a large segment of UCS funds while charging what some considered relatively high rates for the children of anyone with money to pay. The "Y" had a great many dedicated supporters; it also had some vocal critics.

If the "Y" had left the United Appeal there would have been serious repercussions. Many men and women who would otherwise work hard for the annual United Appeal might shift their efforts to a separate YM-YWCA campaign. Other agencies might be encouraged to do so. Worst of all, the city might revert to a multiplicity of campaigns, about one every two weeks the year round, if the United Appeal went down the drain. Yet there were dedicated supporters of both the United Appeal and of the "Y" who were deeply concerned with the financial arrangements.

Being president of an agency facing break-up was difficult, as were meetings where Al and Ken argued in rather blunt terms. What was worse was having information which reporters on the staff of the *London Free Press* would dearly love to know. As president of UCS I had to respect the privacy of Board of Directors meetings. As a newspaperman I felt the public should know, directly or through a reporter, about the conflict between the "Y" and UCS.

It was a clear and disturbingly difficult conflict of interest. If I told what I knew, my colleagues on the UCS board would say I'd failed to represent UCS best interests. Going public was almost guaranteed to freeze both sides of their postures, which in turn would cause the "Y" to leave UCS and precipitate a possible, indeed probable, breakup of the United Appeal. If I didn't tell what I knew, my colleagues at the *Free Press* rightly would say that I'd failed the elementary test of any good newsman to publish information about the public's business. Since the public contributed every dollar to the UCS, this was certainly the public's business. I fudged it.

When reporters came to my office to ask questions about rumours circulating on the issue, I said that as UCS president I wasn't in a position to comment on information I had in confidence and that it would be improper to break confidence. To the managing editor I was equally reticent but added that if newsroom got any story developing in UCS from other people, from other directors or anyone else involved, we would run the story. One way or another, most of the story appeared in print.

In the end a compromise was worked out, as usual in such matters. The "Y" came up with additional financial information, though not enough to satisfy UCS militants. Doing so, the "Y" said, would cost more money than the information was worth. For the remaining year or so of my two-year term I kept the lid on an explosive situation and managed to turn over the office without UCS being broken up. There were generous compliments from more than one director about my efforts, but I remained uneasy about the conflict of interest.

Meanwhile, Ryerson was another simmering mess. The publishing house was a 140-year-old Canadian institution which began when Egerton Ryerson printed Methodist religious tracts, the first of a long series of religious magazines. Over the years it had also become a secular publishing house, a refuge for Canadian writers who were appallingly poorly paid. Among them were L. M. Montgomery, Robert Service, Bliss Carman, Arthur Lower, and a host of others. It was a national institution. It was also a millstone around the neck of the United Church. When I became chairman, Ryerson was losing about half a million dollars a year. There had been a time when Lorne Pierce was editor, when Ryerson Press provided the building (299 Queen Street West) out of which United Church headquarters operated. It also subsidized a long list of missionary and other publications for the church. Profitable though it was for many years, it could hardly be said to be run in a business-like fashion. By the late 1960s, when I first joined the board, Ryerson was heading for trouble, one of the major errors being a new press which did not have the flexibility to meet the constantly changing printing needs of the church. A revised series of teaching aids for Sunday schools, called the New Curriculum, stirred up considerable controversy over what many thought were excessively liberal theological concepts. They were, in fact, merely a recognition of the most thoughtful post-war developments in religious thinking, but also involved the church and Ryerson Press in what at first appeared to be a highly profitable venture which, when sales fell off sharply, helped create additional losses and drained away the firm's surplus.

Presiding over this secular and religious publishing empire was an autocratic, precise, and aloof Victorian figure, Dr. Heber Dickinson. Board meetings heard relatively little from successive chairmen, or from board members for that matter. Each subject on the agenda was referred to Dickinson, who told the board what he felt they should know; then it was time for the next item of business. The whole operation was ridiculously paternalistic, run along the lines of a nineteenth-century counting house, though it must be remembered that in Lorne Pierce's day it was Canada's single most powerful, prestigious, and prosperous publishing house.

After I joined the board, several members demanded and got, with assistance from United Church headquarters (by then moved to a new building on St Clair, to the great satisfaction of many anxious to escape from 299 Queen), a consultant study of Ryerson operations. The study had been precipitated by the annual losses which were reaching substantial proportions and by a realization that the expensive new press was not the best for the job. The consultants eventually brought down a report which drew attention to all the obvious problems, in language which was carefully calculated not to disturb those who chose not to read between the lines, as is the custom of business consultants. They supplemented that by providing selected board members with a frank verbal assessment, as is also their custom, which in this instance included reorganizing Ryerson Press from top to bottom.

A few months later, having participated in these changes largely as an observer, I was asked to be chairman. There was of course no salary, though expenses were paid. It was to be a thankless task, literally and figuratively. At the time I had dreams of being able to turn Ryerson around and make it profitable again. There may have been experienced commercial publishers who, given a completely free hand and a large infusion of new capital, could have turned Ryerson around, but I rather doubt it. Certainly I didn't have the experience to do so, though we quickly cut losses from $500,000 a year to less than $250,000. An indication of management irrationality was that there were no fewer than five shipping doors in the building, each sending out great quantities of printed material for different church boards, each staffed with clerks to record shipments.

When it became obvious Ryerson was not going to be made profitable, the church Executive Committee decided it would have to be sold. The Rev. Frank Brisbin, who had succeeded Dickinson as secretary of the division, and I began sounding out potential buyers. It took a year or more before firm offers were hammered out. Among offers which were eliminated were those from some of the management staff and from other small Canadian publishers; they were primarily offers to manage the enterprise and pay the church its equity in the business out of anticipated future profits. Two offers to be considered seriously were from McGraw-Hill, the American book publisher, and Maclean Hunter, the Canadian magazine publisher — both in the $1.5 million range.

If we'd been smart we'd have called the Executive Committee together, got quick approval of a recommendation to sell to Maclean Hunter, passed it to the church's Executive Committee, and been considered fine fellows. There had been no expectation the church would get anything like that sum out of Ryerson. Pessimists thought the whole package would bring less than $500,000, land and building not included.

Frank and I felt strongly we could whipsaw the price higher and went to work on it. I remember sitting in Frank's office one day, talking to McGraw-Hill officers in New York (we'd been down a couple of times to meet them) and saying that, yes, theirs was the best offer so far but that it wasn't enough better to warrant the church selling to an American firm. The church, in Frank's opinion and mine, would sell to a Canadian bidder.

McGraw-Hill came up; Maclean Hunter came up. Then McGraw-Hill really jumped the price. I suspect someone in New York finally said, "Make them an offer they can't refuse." It worked out to about $2.8 million when the offer was boiled down to a bottom line. Maclean Hunter's offer was $1.8 million; they wouldn't go higher.

I called a meeting of Ryerson's Executive Committee, knowing there would be a majority decision to sell Ryerson Press to McGraw-Hill. That's when I wondered if we'd been wise to twist arms for higher prices because, if the difference had been a quarter million or possibly even half a million, the committee probably would have voted differently. With a million dollars at stake the vote almost certainly would be for sale to McGraw-Hill. In the plane to Toronto I pulled out notepaper and scribbled a short note to the moderator, Dr. Robert McClure, tendering my resignation effective immediately.

That's the way it went. There was one negative vote — mine. I handed McClure my resignation, joined him in his office later at his request, declined to reconsider, and caught the next plane to London.

"CANADIAN MONEY OK?"

My problem was not only a personal commitment to some degree to Canadian nationalism, but also that the *Free Press* editorial page fostered Canadian nationalism. Foreign capital should be encouraged to make investments in Canada, but selling the country's oldest and most prestigious publishing house to an American publisher strongly oriented to commercial publishing was not one of them. It wasn't a matter of my job, it was a question of personal ethics. I couldn't with integrity write editorials encouraging Canadian nationalism while participating in the sale of Ryerson to an American firm.

As predicted to Ryerson's board, the public outcry was horrendous. To reporters on my own staff and to radio, television, and newspaper reporters from Toronto I said on the record that I had resigned from Ryerson Press "for personal reasons." To those who asked off the record I told the whole story, except to the *Globe and Mail*. Under James Cooper, then publisher, the *Globe* had (and may still have) a policy of not honouring information received off the record. Its reporters were expected to take off-the-record comments, then use the material. Well aware of this, having had more than one puzzled person telephone about it, I told the *Globe* reporter that if he would obtain from his publisher a hand-written, personal undertaking to repect my off-the-record comments and have it delivered to me in London, I'd talk off the record. There were no further calls from the *Globe*.

Months after the sale had been consummated and public indignation died down, I wrote an article reviewing the background of the decision, my understanding of the reasons the church's leaders voted as they did, and my own reasons for resigning. It was published in the *Free Press* and later in the *United Church Observer*. It read, in part:

> My reasons for saying only that I had resigned "for personal reasons" were simple. The majority decision had been made by men whose church responsibilities were as great or greater than mine. While I couldn't share their view, I respected the honesty and integrity of their decision ... having predicted the volume and intensity of protest against the decision, and being aware of how easily it could be focused into non-productive pressure, I chose not to allow myself to be made into some kind of 30-day "Canadian hero" at the expense of my colleagues.
>
> Those who criticize that specific decision should keep in mind that they might have had equal difficulty making it. Dr. Robert McClure, moderator of the United Church, must have been

deeply conscious of the fact that the difference between the two prices would have kept several medical missionaries — as he was in India — in the field for decades. He may have felt the church has a wider mission than Canadian-American economic relationships. If others, out of ignorance, choose to fault the majority decision, they're free to do so. Though unwilling to participate, I did not and do not criticize it.

Canada will survive the sale of Ryerson Press to McGraw-Hill.

What Canada needs is not anguished screams when individual economic takeovers occur, but carefully-prepared legislation which will mark out those areas of our national life where Canadians feel we cannot tolerate economic domination ... broadcasting, newspapers, basic communications systems, publishing, magazines, oil and gas, hydro-electric power, water and many others ... and where we demand that economic development be under the majority control of Canadians.

If we can do that, and we must if we are to survive as an independent nation, the Ryerson Press sale will be a mere incident in a great country's development.

If we don't act, Ryerson's fate won't matter.

There was virtually no reaction to the article; a few letters from friends, but nothing else.

The public furore over the sale, however, was one of the principal reasons Parliament later established the Foreign Investment Review Agency to rule whether the takeover of a Canadian firm by foreign capital was in the national interest. FIRA legislation was long overdue, though it has since interpreted its mandate so widely that desireable foreign investment has been stifled.

I mentioned the Ryerson involvement was a thankless task. Several months later, visiting Brisbin, I made a casual and rather snarky comment that there hadn't been a single word of thanks from United Church headquarters for whatever contributions I'd made to Ryerson and its sale at a couple of million more than many headquarters brass expected, certainly a million higher than the best Canadian price offered. We both laughed and shrugged but Brisbin must have said something because a letter of thanks arrived from Dr. Ernest Long, United Church general secretary. Considering the circumstances of its receipt, it's hardly among my treasured possessions.

There was one more venture into service organizations before I began declining invitations. The London Art Gallery Association had a consultative role in the art gallery associated with London's public library and wanted a new, larger, separate, and more appropriate art gallery. Anne Lowry, Marion Richmond, and other women in London invited me to lunch one day and asked me to be president of LAGA. They needed to get the organization moving on a specific plan towards raising funds for a new gallery and to begin construction. Despite the UCS and Ryerson experiences I finally agreed, after consulting a number of colleagues and friends around town.

My commitment to LAGA was for one year. It was expected I'd stay for a second year but off on the horizon there were storm clouds gathering. As is usually the case when people want to spend money on art, there were those in the community who opposed it. There'd be public protests and hassles. For the editor of the only local newspaper to be president of LAGA in such a public dispute was asking for trouble. I declined a second year's term and quietly withdrew.

Sure enough trouble came along, both in anticipated opposition and in the efforts of J. H. (Jake) Moore to donate his superb collection of Canadian art to the new gallery. Jake was a free-swinging entrepreneur who had built John Labatt Ltd. into a major corporation before going on to become head of Brascan. In 1977 he met secretly with London's mayor Jane Bigelow and the Board of Control and made a deal that he'd donate his collection to the new gallery if the city would donate a triangular parcel of land at The Forks as a site for the gallery. The deal was made and Jake, with all the corporate apparatus he could deploy, began preparing for a major press event, at which these carefully worked out plans would be announced — the site, plans for the gallery, his collection, provincial and federal funding participation, and much else.

The *Free Press* reporter at City Hall, Don Gibb, knew his way around the political corridors of power and it wasn't long before he sniffed out the deal. Don assumed, rightly, that the public had a right to know public business. The donation of a valuable piece of real estate owned by the city was public business. He turned in a story which ran page one. Jake got downright angry and an angry Jake is something to behold.

If the quotation had been handy I'd have offered him the reply of the editor of *The Times* to Lord Derby. The peer attacked *The Times*, which had published a British ultimatum to Russia before the Russians had received it. How could the editor, Derby demanded, live with his conscience, having published what he knew the government wanted to keep secret? Delane replied publicly in *The Times*: "To accuse this or any other journal of publishing early and correct intelligence ... is to pay us one of the highest compliments we can hope to deserve ... We hold ourselves responsible, not to Lord Derby ... but to the people."

Actually, it was an advantage to the art gallery to have the story break in advance. That way they got two page-one stories. A cynical old newspaper adage has it there are three stories to any event: tell 'em you're gonna tell 'em, tell 'em, then tell 'em you told 'em. No one, least of all Jake, seemed appreciative of that attempt at humour, so I let it ride.

What the gallery had really tried to do, of course, was to manage news. Politicians, businessmen, labour leaders, every organized element of society wants to tell the public what they'd like the public to know when they think it most advantageous to them to do so. The inevitable conflict between those who try to keep the public informed and those who try to manage the news was also sharply delineated by Delane in another joust with Derby over the right of the press to print facts.

"The press lives by disclosures; whatever passes into its keeping becomes a part of the knowledge and the history of our times; it is daily and for ever appealing to the enlightened force of public opinion, anticipating, if possible, the march of events ... and extending its survey to the horizon of the world." *The Times* continued that the statesman does precisely the opposite, an observation which applies equally to all those who have information involving the public welfare, public funds, public concepts and ideas. "He cautiously guards from the public eye the information by which his actions and opinions are regulated; he reserves his judgment on passing events till the latest moment, and then he records it in obscure or conventional language ... the duty of the one is to speak; of the other to be silent."

I was delighted with Don's story, though not because Jake was mad. He has contributed much to London in addition to his art. We broke the story because we had it and because the public was entitled to know what was being done with land which, as taxpayers, they owned. I was also delighted at not being president of LAGA, which came in for considerable criticism over the proposed gallery site, and about which there was a continuing flow of news stories.

A week later came the big day for the formal announcement which many thought was spoiled by our earlier story. Though some gallery supporters were still angry with me, I was invited; as past president of LAGA I could hardly be ignored. People were polite but no one stayed by my side long, possibly because doing so might leave the impression they'd been the one who had tipped off that most ungracious newspaper, the *London Free Press*.

That was enough — I had learned a lesson. Talk shows, speaking engagements, radio and television interviews, turning up at functions for community purposes — these were fine. But I no longer took on responsibility for any community activity whether or not there appeared to be a possibility it might become news. Inevitably it would.

Newspapers Sell Readers; First, You Gotta Get 'Em

Newspaper readers wonder whether newspapers play down or leave out stories their advertisers wouldn't like. People find it hard to believe that newspapers deliberately set about making life awkward for advertisers who spend hundreds of thousands of dollars on newspaper ads. Yet good newpapers do just that and accept sometimes serious revenue losses as a result. Readers understandably ask "Why?"

In the long run it is far more important for a newspaper to retain its credibility with the reader than to keep an advertiser happy over a news story. If a newspaper retains its readers, the publisher of a newspaper will always have advertisers. Merchants desperately want to be in the same package of print as the latest news. An advertiser may get angry if a story gores his particular ox and may sometimes cancel advertising, though usually only briefly. Advertisers don't advertise in newspapers because they like or dislike the publisher, the editor, or a reporter. They advertise because they need to tell people about goods and services they offer. Despite competition from radio, television, magazines, billboards, and direct mail, the daily newspaper is still the most powerful advertising medium available to most local and many national advertisers.

Some newspaper publishers and editors cringe and murmur "yessir" when an advertiser complains, but there aren't many who do so openly and survive for long. Exceptions are found in some small newspapers. They don't yield to direct advertiser pressure; they simply avoid creating situations to which advertisers might object. With the tight budgets some publishers and editors must meet, they have no recourse.

On larger papers the ethical approach is reinforced by professional standards of the editorial staff. There was a time not many decades ago when reporters accepted bottles of rye from sources, cadged free meals, and let those perquisites of the job filter through to the news stories they wrote. No longer. Journalism today is a relatively well-paid field. Educational standards are much higher (usually a bachelor's or master's degree compared to high school or less a few decades ago) and there is a greater consciousness of responsibility towards the reader. These and other factors mean that the reader of most newspapers in Canada and the United States can be reasonably sure that advertisers are not dictating, directly or indirectly, the content of news pages.

That isn't to say some advertisers don't try. Frequently there are sharp arguments. Advertisers often scream over a story about smoking and cancer being placed beside a cigarette advertisement, or a story about an airline crash being placed next to an Air Canada ad for budget flights to Florida. Editors making up the newspaper have no idea what the advertisements are on any given page and don't want to know. That merely complicates things. They just use available space. They also ignore resulting complaints.

The marketing side understandably negotiates with the advertiser and tries to placate him, sometimes running the ad a second time and hoping desperately lightning doesn't strike twice. That's happened a few times to me: marketing ordered a repeat ad for a liquor advertisement which had a story about a drunk-driving trial wrapped around it; when the repeat ad ran, the story happened (honest, purely by accident) to be about a group of mothers organizing to fight drunk drivers.

More often arguments develop with advertisers over the content of news stories considered detrimental to the corporation involved. General Motors won't complain about an accident story involving a defect in one of their cars. They're too smart. A local automotive dealer, however, might well complain about an unfavorable reference to his product in a news story.

Advertisers will make an editor's life miserable — if the editor lets them do it. Coping with them is merely a matter of establishing who's running the newspaper. I got tough from my first day, on the principle that if I were fired in the first six months it would reflect more on the poor judgment of those who gave me the job than on me. The battle isn't easy but it has to be fought with firmness and consistency. Each new editor has to take a strong stand — like a teacher in front of a new class.

Most irritating are those advertisers who begin by insisting on talking to "the guy in charge." Since I usually answered my own phone that wasn't difficult. They begin by saying how unhappy they are with a story involving their firm, refute every fact in the story, and profess to fail to understand how a reputable newspaper could publish such a pack of lies. Then anger takes over.

"I'd like you to know, Mr. Heenee, or whatever your goddam name is, I buy a lot of advertising in your goddam newspaper..."

At that point I had a standard response.

"Sorry, I didn't realize you wanted to buy more advertising. Hold the line a moment, I'll transfer you to marketing."

Invariably there was a moment of shocked surprise and sometimes a protest was cut off by putting the caller on hold. Usually no more came of it. Sometimes he called back; then the conversation was about the facts of a disputed story and there was no mention of advertising.

My policy was clear and unequivocal. If we were wrong, we'd publish a prompt and prominent correction for any reader or advertiser. If the caller had an opinion, we'd publish it as a letter to the editor. If there was new information which altered the story, we'd send a reporter to gather the facts. Otherwise, the story stood.

If the advertiser or businessman or labour leader or politician was really mad he often began talking about his lawyer. Just one reference to "lawyer" or "libel" meant end of conversation. There was no point in talking after being threatened. Any angry man who said he was going to talk to his lawyer was threatening the newspaper and me personally. The caller needed to be disabused quickly of any notion we'd pull a story because he was going to talk to a lawyer.

At one time in the late 1970s there were eighteen libel suits hanging around. Virtually all of them were attempts at intimidation. We were hit hard once, in an odd libel suit over our failure to identify a woman as a "white" witch (no racial factor involved) in an article about witchcraft. She went to court and brought a jury verdict against us which, with costs, ran about $25,000. She's dead now and the dead can't be libelled. Our real mistake was in interviewing her in the first place; she was two bricks short of a full load. In two other cases we settled out of court, once for about $200 and costs, which I would have preferred to fight, over the libel of a local police detective, and another time for about $2,000 and costs when we reported, entirely improperly, what one politician said about another politician who was also a teacher.

As an example of attempted intimidation from an advertiser there was a cliffhanger which ran to within fifteen minutes of press start before being resolved. In 1980 the provincial government announced a 7 per cent reduction in automobile sales tax in an effort to stimulate sales in a depressed industry. Across the province, dealers ran advertisements with prices reflecting the reduction in tax. Two weeks later, Ron Steele, *Free Press* consumer reporter, noted that a local auto dealer had run an advertisement in the *Free Press* after the tax was reduced with prices significantly higher than prices advertised before the tax reduction. In other words, they had increased prices by the amount of the tax reduction. Ron could prove it by comparing numbers assigned to individual cars which appeared in advertisements published before the tax was reduced and those published afterwards.

Ron's story ran in morning editions on February 14. By the time I got to the office that morning the dealer had been on the telephone to more than one person around the building; each referred him to me. At first he sympathized with me that the newspaper had made such a grievous error, which was an approach I hadn't heard before. However, I listened carefully as his sympathy turned to anger and downright abuse. He was arguing that he had acted in good faith.

He insisted this was the sequence of events. The tax reduction was announced the morning of Thursday, January 31. It was reported in the afternoon editions of the *London Free Press* that same day. He published an advertisement on Saturday, February 2, which listed cars, identified by number, at higher prices than in the firm's earlier Ford advertisements. His staff, he said, had prepared the February 2 advertisement on January 30 and had delivered it to the *Free Press* the morning of January 31. The afternoon edition did not appear until 1:30 P.M. on January 31, which was the earliest he would have known about the tax reduction. He had acted in good faith in submitting the advertisement. The *Free Press* was malicious, inaccurate, and dishonest in having published libellous statements about him and his company.

He demanded withdrawal of the story from the afternoon paper and an apology for the inaccuracy of the morning story. He would, of course, be consulting his solicitors. It was a long conversation. When it ended I was worried. If the dealer's staff had indeed submitted copy for the February 2 advertisement prior to the tax reduction becoming known on January 31, the newspaper and its editor could be in trouble. Libel law requires the accused to prove his innocence; he must prove the truth of the alleged libel. Truth being ultimate defence of libel, the defendant is then home free. But proving intention is difficult, almost impossible. At this point in the incident, lack of proof about the dealer's *intention* put me in a most unhappy position.

First step was to verify with our advertising department the accuracy of the dealer's claim his staff had submitted copy the morning of January 31 for the February 2 advertisement. He had indeed. Then I talked to the managing editor and reviewed the facts as we knew them. Jack Briglia noted the dealer had had time on the afternoon of January 31 and all day February 1 to cancel the scheduled February 2 advertisement or to change the prices in it to reflect the 7 per cent tax reduction and had not done so. I pointed out that in a libel action we might well be convicted by a jury hearing the dealer say he had not submitted the advertisement with any intention of taking advantage of the tax cut by raising prices and saw no reason to change. He could also testify he had told me in a telephone call that his intentions had been honest. If we published the story in the afternoon editions, he could argue with some justice that we had refused to accept his version of his intention — which we could not disprove. He insisted he had acted honestly in submitting copy for the February 2 advertisement.

If we killed the story for the afternoon edition we would have had to publish a retraction of the morning story, otherwise there'd be several consequences. Readers would think we had yielded to pressure from an advertiser and pulled an accurate story. Also, the dealer would then be in an excellent position to sue for damages, based in part on our having pulled the afternoon story and published an abject apology. In a libel action an apology may serve to mitigate damages but the action can still go forward. If we did not pull the story and apologize, we were not in a position to prove anything about his intentions the morning of January 31 when he submitted the advertisement which ran February 2. It was a hell of a spot.

Yet we were convinced that Ron's story was accurate for two reasons: confidence in Ron's reporting and a gut feeling about the way I'd been abused on the telephone. The dealer's version was too pat and there had to be something else. Experience and intuition, I guess.

As the morning wore on other information came in, including a phone call from the dealer's lawyer asking what we intended to do in the afternoon paper. Though inwardly seriously worried I told the lawyer that at the moment I was relying on the fact that the dealer had the Thursday afternoon and all day Friday to change his advertisement — adding I wasn't certain what would be the final decision. He expressed his client's deep concern. I said I'd call back.

Finally, about fifteen minutes before deadline, Jack, two or three other editors, and Ron gathered in my office. We might have to run an apology despite being convinced Ron's story was accurate. It wasn't enough, I again reminded them, to believe we were accurate. We had to be able to prove it.

Discussion wandered around every aspect of the situation and there was mention again of the afternoon story in the *Free Press* of January 31. Suddenly, Jack wondered if there'd been a leak. The formal announcement had been made the morning of January 31 in time for our afternoon edition. Had there been an earlier leak in Toronto? We looked at each other hopefully, alert to the possibility that we'd been scooped. Stories like that tax reduction often leaked out of Queen's Park hours or days before being announced. There was a quick scurrying for a copy of the January 31 *Globe and Mail* — and there it was, an eight-column line, top of the page, predicting that a 7 per cent auto tax reduction would be announced by the provincial government.

We all knew the *Globe* had been on the street in Toronto the previous evening between 9 and 10 P.M. That meant the story must have broken in Queen's Park the afternoon of January 30, which also meant the government's intention would be known all over Toronto before the close of business January 30. I could safely assume that someone had got the word. I could have checked further to find out if Toronto radio and television stations had had reports of the forthcoming tax reduction on the air the afternoon and evening of January 30, but I didn't bother. Undoubtedly they had, but the *Globe* was good enough.

Everyone was grinning hugely, Ron most of all. He's an old pro, a responsible reporter who gets it right. He understood why I had felt I might have to pull the story and run an apology, but, like me, he knew it had been a solid story from the beginning. To Jack I said only, "OK. Leave it in."

As they dispersed I was dialing the dealer's lawyer. I told him the further information we had and that the story would be running in the afternoon paper exactly as it had appeared in the morning paper. If his client wanted his story told, all he had to do was call newsroom and ask for Ron, who would arrange an interview. Approached prior to publication of the original story, the dealer had refused comment. He now decided to talk. His version of the circumstances, largely repeating his claim to have submitted his advertisement in good faith, was published prominently and promptly. There was, of course, no legal action.

The most satisfying aspect of the incident, aside from having told readers the score as far as that firm's sales tax deductions were concerned, was the attitude of marketing executives at the *Free Press*. Accustomed for years to having *Free Press* advertising staff blindly endorse anything they were told by an advertiser and critical of newsroom any time the facts were revealed in the news columns, I was delighted to have solid support. R. A. (Sandy) Green, then director of marketing, had only one comment. "They got caught with their hands in the cookie jar."

A far happier incident followed a story in the *Free Press* about a fine levied for misleading advertising against Patton's Place, the city's leading furniture and appliance dealer. Ron Logan and Gord Patton teamed up after University of Western Ontario business school to start a retail furniture store. They've done exceptionally well. They relied on heavy advertising, high volume, good service, and bargain prices to build up a business which has made them both millionaires.

Their very volume trapped them in what the Department of Consumer Affairs deemed to be misleading advertising involving the manufacturer's list price. The government cited a Patton's Place advertisement which had referred to a manufacturer's "regular" price for a wringer washing machine as $229.95. Patton's offered the machine to the public for $129.50, a saving, the ad claimed, of $100. The government showed that the manufacturer did not have such a list price, nor had the washers ever sold anywhere for $229.50.

The magistrate several times stressed that there was "no suggestion at all that the public was not getting value for the machine," adding later that Patton's Place was getting less than $20 profit per machine and that the public got "a bargain." Nevertheless, under the law the advertising was misleading and he levied a fine of $250 plus $100 costs. The story included this evidence and ran under a two-column heading.

At the time, the general manager of the *Free Press* was William Carradine. He was a former manager for Switzerland of Proctor and Gamble who was invited by Walter Blackburn to shift back to Canada. Bill and I got along reasonably well. He is a slim, good-looking, energetic man who knew a lot about soap and, at that time, damn all about the newspaper business. Now senior vice-president of the Southam chain, he probably knows a good deal more than I do. But then, for two of the four years he was with the newspaper, he chivied me for detailed reports on every decision and kept making comparisons with newsroom costs on other newspapers, apparently without recognizing that the *Free Press*, unlike most papers, then published two newspapers daily (morning edition to Western Ontario, afternoon edition to London and suburbs). Two shifts cost more than one.

We had a fairly sharp tiff when he got a note late on a Friday about two years after he arrived. He'd asked for information on some administrative detail. Being more than a little fed up with constant questioning in these areas and feeling he should devote his time to the policy matters which were his responsibility, I suggested just that in language which wasn't very polite. Monday morning there was what the Russians call a full, frank, and free exchange of views. He got the message. The volume of queries fell off considerably.

He was strongly marketing-oriented and had difficulty understanding some aspects of newsroom operations. When the Patton's Place story appeared in the morning paper, one or both owners phoned Chuck Fenn, then director of advertising. Knowing he'd get nowhere with me, Chuck called Carradine who called me. Bill had progressed far enough to know his best approach did not include asking me to take the story out of the afternoon edition. But he did want to know why the story had been run in the first place. After I'd answered Carradine, I offered to pass it on to Ron and Gord at Patton's Place. That appealed to Carradine. The furniture partners were a tough pair and might chew up the editor and spew him out in little pieces all over the shop floor.

At the furniture store, Gord was the aggressor. He's pretty far over on the right-hand side of the political spectrum and sees life in entrepreneurial terms. His question was blunt. "What the hell did you have to do that for?"

I suggested that their sales depended on the credibility of the newspaper. People wouldn't trust the newspaper if it didn't report everything of interest in the community regardless of who got hurt. Their agreement at this point was a little reluctant but it was there. How many people knew about the charge and the fine? We included the store's staff, fifty in the federal departments involved in laying the charge, at least another fifty in the court and among lawyers involved, and every other retailer in town, plus their families — say 400 or 500 total.

If all those people knew, how long would it be before anyone interested knew the story? People would then wonder how credible was the *London Free Press* if it kept out of the paper such a story, which in turn would throw doubt on the credibility of Patton's Place advertising, which in some degree at least would undermine the deserved high reputation the partners had built up over many years. That was aside from the certainty that if the facts weren't printed, gossip would have Patton's Place convicted of crimes they didn't commit and fined thousands of dollars, not $250 — even that the partners had been jailed. It was far better for the facts to be published with the display they deserved, which in this case was a two-column head with part of a column of type, than to have the city's rumour mills aided and abetted by at least some of their competitors blowing up the matter out of all proportion.

It would be inaccurate to say the partners agreed enthusiastically. If they could, they'd have nodded their heads and shaken them at the same time, agreeing in principle but disagreeing with the consequences. But my guess was right. They listened and learned something about the function of the advertising medium they'd been using for many years. Gord grumbled a bit but Ron understood. As I left he put a hand on my shoulder and assured me he'd never complain again. He never did. Blessings on him.

The battle over who was going to control the editorial content of the *London Free Press* began just a few days after I took over as editor. For years, the newspaper had fudged a clear delineation between advertising and editorial. As a part-time reporter attending university I'd had to write movie readers, which were simply rewrites of publicity handouts from local movie houses, under an unethical deal the marketing people had with theatre operators in town: buy an advertisement and get a free reader which ran among other entertainment news as if it were an honest review of the movie. That was not uncommon in the late 1940s and early 1950s in Canadian newspapers but it was dishonest. It put the newspaper's editorial department behind a strictly public relations handout.

In the early 1950s, before moving to the administrative side of the paper for something more than a decade, I was supervisor in the promotion department, where all the junk which was generated to fill special advertising sections was written. The editorial side of a newspaper should contain only legitimate news. The confrontation wasn't long coming.

Most vivid is Forest City Motor Products. A downtown Chrysler dealer, Forest City had decided to reduce costs and, it was hoped, improve sales (it went broke later) by moving to a new plant east of the city. On the new site they built a perfectly ordinary, one storey, concrete block building, with all the attractiveness of an orange crate. Chuck Fenn suggested to newsroom that he'd like a photograph of Forest City's new plant — lovely building, big windows, nice large repair garage, air-conditioned offices where customers can sign contracts, and much else. The trouble was, from my point of view, there wasn't anything our readers would be interested in reading. By my prior direction, Chuck's request for a photograph came back to me. He got a polite note explaining why we were not going to run the picture.

Chuck, bless his bulldozing old heart, was in my office within the hour arguing there was indeed a news story there. A great story, he suggested, characteristic of the entrepreneurial enthusiasm which motivated all London merchants. When we got rid of all the big words, it boiled down to my being an SOB because Chuck, going by the past, had already promised Forest City Motors that their new plant would be suitably promoted in the newspaper. It never was. Chuck was free to do what he should have done all along — run the photograph as an advertisement at the bottom of a page. Eventually he did.

Similar incidents happened many times. I would get nasty and suggest that Chuck's reluctance to publish such inane pictures and equivalent copy must be due to the shame he felt about his advertising — otherwise, why would he try to avoid such material appearing as advertising and want it to look as if it had been chosen by newsroom? That position, taken regularly and obnoxiously and very deliberately, brought snorts of derision which were loud and antagonistic. But I hung in there.

There were mistakes, the Lord knows I made mistakes. Long after Chuck retired, a new Simpsons store opened in a mall south of the city and newsroom sent a young reporter out to cover it. In itself the new store was worth several paragraphs on second front, the page where local news of consequence was displayed. The reporter talked to the public relations man from Simpsons, who quite innocently mentioned all the minor gaffes of the day and the reporter used those bits to make his story, relegating G. L. Burton, chairman of the board of Simpsons, to one paragraph at the bottom of the story. It ran that way in the afternoon edition.

I was so angry I could have spit. We grind no axes for advertisers but this was a legitimate story about a major addition to the city's business life. Burton's comments were worth more than a mention at the end of a story of mistakes. I simmered all afternoon and turned up at the office in the evening to direct a complete rewrite of the story and rather objectionably shoved the revised story down the throats of night editors, who of course had had nothing to do with the original story. Next morning I regretted having given way to anger. What I should have done the previous day was take the rather bitter complaints from the advertiser and marketing, write it off to experience, and stay with the original story.

Within days there were rumblings in the newsroom about my hatchet job on the original story and the somewhat pious pap carried in the story the following morning. The staff was right; I was wrong. At a meeting with reporters I opened by saying I had been wrong and should not have ordered changes in the story.

The reacton was quick and generous, along the lines of "Oh, well, we all make mistakes. Forget it, Bill." I didn't forget.

People Can Be Stuffy —
Sometimes Very Much So

The classic example in my experience happened at least thirty years ago. I was assigned to cover a reading by E. J. Pratt of his poetry. As I didn't have a highly developed sensitivity towards verse, except in a rather simple way of Kipling and Service, the editor who made the assignment was sadly inefficient. But then, he may have been desperate for a body of any kind to fill the slot that evening.

It turned out to be one of the highlights of the year. Pratt was superb and his verse was promptly added to that of Service and Kipling on my reading list.

When the evening ended, reporter and photographer went backstage to get some local colour and a photograph. As with all such efforts, a little juggling was necessary and more people crowded into the photograph than we wanted, five as it turned out. As usual, I walked down the line double-checking each person for cutlines, bypassing Pratt who was well identified, and ending with a tall, portly gentleman on the right end of the line.

"And your name, sir?"

"If you don't know my name," was the arrogant reply, "I'm certainly not going to tell you."

Now that was a new twist for a then relatively young reporter.

Thinking about it for a second, I nodded, turned away, and went back to the office. When the print came up I scissored off the starboard portly figure and wrote cutlines for four people, telling several editors about it. They instantly identified the fellow as Dr. Allan Skinner, a well-known physician, and laughingly refused to paste him back into the picture.

Next morning there was a call from the publisher's office.

"Bill, could you come to my office for a moment, please?"

There sat an angry Dr. Skinner.

To the publisher's query I repeated what the doctor had said. Before either could comment I added insult to injury with an outright lie told with a perfectly straight face.

"I asked around the newsroom but no one knew who he was so I just cropped the print."

The publisher stared for a second, registering that he was faced with a deliberate lie about which he could do nothing, then very quietly said, "Oh, I see. Very well, Bill, thank you for coming up."

What he said to the doctor I never learned but years later a mutual friend told me the publisher had dressed the fellow down for fair and delighted in telling close friends about the double shaft with which his reporter had punctured Skinner's pomposity.

Kent Report Doomed to Failure by Its Own Irrationalities

The report of the Royal Commission on Newspapers was released at 1600 hours, August 18, 1981, having been under lock and key until precisely that hour. The extreme secrecy was understandable given its content, which violated virtually every concept of freedom of speech, freedom of speech in print, and freedom to own property which had evolved under parliamentary government. It was difficult to believe that the report had been written in a free society by people appointed by an elected government.

After an hour reading the summary of recommendations and skimming the report, we reviewed specific sections and I wrote the editorial for next morning's paper. It was twice as long as most editorials, yet touched only highlights.

The lead paragraph noted it "added up to a massive intervention by government in the functioning of the media — and probably of a free press as well." The proposed press rights panel was "radical, complicated and dangerous ... resembles the freedom of information proposals in UNESCO by Third World dictators ... [and would] merely create more jobs for more government supporters and additional civil servants." It included a "mish-mash of divestments, restrictions on further growth of chains, dangerous definitions of how the editor of a newspaper functions, and tax incentives and disincentives which would put government into the country's ... newsrooms .... The government," I concluded, "chose not to act on the Davey committee report a decade ago ... [on] the Kent commission report ... it should not act either."

And, when it came to the crunch, the government didn't act, though for a time it tried hard to find ways to implement parts of the report.

Initialing a quick proof, I caught a plane to Ottawa and a breakfast meeting next day with Laurent Picard, sometime president of the CBC and one of three Kent Report commissioners. The others were the chairman, Tom Kent, sometime editor of British newspapers and for a few years editor of the *Winnipeg Free Press*, and the late Borden Spears, *Toronto Star* newsman for many years and executive director of the Davey committee hearings on newspapers a decade earlier.

I'd known Picard during and since his CBC years. Over eggs he admitted he had thought seriously of writing a minority opinion. Why hadn't he? Well, Kent and Spears had made "so many major changes" to meet his objections that in the end he rather felt obliged to accommodate them.

"Does that mean they'd considered even more drastic recommendations?"

"Yes," he said, they had; having a citizens' committee appoint editors, for example.

There was more, but after a second coffee Picard had to leave for a television interview. He couldn't be persuaded to say publicly what he said privately. Would he go public if the information came from another source. "Yes, you get it elsewhere and I'd consider confirming it."

Two months went by, with several trips to Ottawa and innumerable phone calls from London without result. Then a civil servant appalled at Kent's irrationalities revealed much of what Picard had said and added several items Picard hadn't mentioned. I tracked down Picard at his summer cottage and told him what I'd heard. This time he spoke for publication.

The story ran about three months after the report was released. While "reluctant to comment on whether he had filed and threatened to release a minority report," Picard confirmed he had had a "serious difference of opinion" between himself and Kent and Spears. Appointment of editors by community advisory committees was "clearly unworkable." Picard said the commission had been making significant "changes up to the last minute." Spears and Kent differed; they said Picard's threats were much earlier. Picard disputed that; he said they continued "until the last week." In a follow-up story Kent suggested Picard hadn't been as deeply involved as the other two commissioners (Kent and Spears).

What had distressed Picard, among other things, was that any two members of each city's local advisory committee could call a meeting of the committee. In theory, this privilege could result in daily direction to an editor on how to run the newspaper. As it could be assumed that committee members would all be good Grits (in 1981, or now good Tories, if both are not contradictions in terms), imagine how much coverage the opposition would get.

Picard said that though there had been "some talk of chain breakup," the proposal wasn't "taken seriously." As a result, the Thomson group was to be required to divest itself either of the *Globe* or all of its other forty papers, on the grounds that the *Globe* and local papers in forty cities were owned by one corporation. The Southam group with twelve papers was not to be broken up at all, though a few broadcast stations in British Columbia were to be divested. Yet Kent recommended the Sifton chain (two papers) and the Irving chain (three papers) be divested of one each, using the argument that those chains, respectively, dominated Saskatchewan and New Brunswick. Picard said there was a tone of "self-righteousness ... which bothered me," both about this recommendation and the report in general. Many aspects of the Kent Report reflected "a kind of morality" that suggested "we know better," and that "annoys me." He added the danger was that the remedy "could be worse than the problem."

What was disturbing about Picard's change of heart as early as the morning after the report was released was his unwillingness to stand and be counted. He had accepted responsibility for making recommendations he could support, not necessarily those of his fellow commissioners. He would not answer questions directly, saying only it was better to have a unanimous report. It wasn't a point on which to press him hard; it was enough to have on record his unhappiness.

The more I read and studied the Kent Report the clearer it became that it had been poorly researched, casually debated, slapped together to meet an impatient government's deadline (nine months), and was highly unlikely to stand the test of court challenges. The essence of my position was that if, under the Kent Report, newspapers and newspaper editors were required to report to local community advisory committees, which in turn reported to something euphemistically termed a National Press Rights Panel (a better name would have been National Press Control Panel), newspapers would end up in the same category as radio and television stations which must report to the Canadian Radio-Television and Telecommunications Commission on their content — what kind of music is played, what nationality is the composer and the singer, how much music is played compared to voice programs — all measured by the minute and carefully added at taxpayers' expense in a vast new CRTC building in Hull. Not only could the National Press Rights Panel lead to every line of type being measured for Liberal, Conservative, and New Democrat bias, but also to square-inch measurements of headlines on all such stories — and God help the editor who gave Brian Mulroney more space than Pierre Trudeau or, now, John Turner more than Mulroney.

Kent confirmed that view, probably unwittingly, in a radio broadcast defending his commission's recommendations against a chorus of bitter opposition from newspaper reporters, editors, and publishers: "There is no interference ... or intervention in the affairs of newspapers," he said. "There is the setting of a framework within which the *proper motives will operate*, instead of the purely pecuniary motives that operate now. There will be a real motivation to perform public service. That's all." (my italics)

As I wrote in an article published in *Editor & Publisher*, an American publication received in every Canadian and American newsroom, "Kent's concepts are precisely what is proposed by the United Nations Education, Scientific and Cultural Organization; 'proper motives' for journalists. Third-world members [of UNESCO] have consistently argued it was improper of western journalists to try to gather and report facts. UNESCO's third-world members have been demanding that journalists use their skills and their outlets (print or broadcast) to improve and promote desirable social, economic, and political objectives as defined by governments which for the most part are dictatorships." Kent's approach "is a little more subtle but just as devastating to free expression of opinion as the restrictions advocated by UNESCO."

I believed then and do now that if it came to a court test, as it inevitably would, Kent's concepts would be struck down. My strongest invective, which included considerable sarcasm, was aimed at the lack of similar control over magazine content, what appeared between the covers of books, and, logically, what corporations wrote to other corporations and what individuals wrote to other individuals. If the words printed in a newspaper were to be controlled by government or by appointed or self-appointed committees of citizens, why omit exercising similar controls over magazines, books, and mail of all kinds? Try writing a love letter when Ottawa bureaucrats have the right to check on your letter's content or even on its validity after you've written and sent it. Ridiculous? No more so than the CRTC cancelling the licence of a Quebec radio station in 1984 for broadcasting music its listeners liked rather than what the CRTC ordered.

Kent would have set up in each city with a chain newspaper a committee composed of two publishers, two journalists, and three community representatives, appointed by the federal cabinet (then Grit, now Tory), to receive annual reports from editors, monitor the paper's performance, "and publish a review of that performance with any comment and advice to newspapers and government that it deems appropriate." Seriously.

In speeches, in talks with bureaucrats, members of Parliament, and cabinet ministers, as well as in print, I summarized my views in a sentence: "If the government brings in that kind of stupid and dangerous legislation I'll report to your goddam committee once a year: 'Dear Sirs: This year we did our best to publish a good newspaper. Sincerely,' and I'd sign it."

The nonsense about five-year contracts for editors was so ludicrous I largely ignored it but Bill Gold, then editor of the *Calgary Herald*, did not. At an International Press Institute meeting called in Toronto to discuss the Kent Report and the government's responses, Bill had a question for Spears, sitting at the speakers' table. If he refused to sign one of Spears's five-year contracts, he asked, what was his boss going to do, "fire me?" Spears replied there was no compulsion about the idea, which in itself was a modification of the original Kent proposals.

The greatest flaw in the Kent Report was the narrowness of its outlook on the flow of information in Canada. Its legislative program presupposed that newspapers were the only means of distributing information to the public and therefore introduced grossly irrational means of trying to diversify ownership. The reality of the last quarter of the twentieth century is that increasing numbers of newspaper readers have become television viewers. In London a quarter century ago, the *London Free Press* sold newspapers to 92 per cent of city households. In 1984 household penetration was about 62 per cent — and about 90 per cent of households (in a much larger city) had cable television. *Free Press* circulation increased, but not nearly as much as households.

Londoners have access to four American networks (ABC, NBC, CBS, PBS) and to four Canadian networks (CBC, CTV, Global, TVO). From early morning to late at night, and during the night for that matter, news programs are available. When Anwar Sadat was murdered, Canadians saw the actual shooting on television half a day before newspapers could report it. In addition to news, television networks carry an astonishing variety of other information — talk shows on international affairs, documentaries on everything from the mating habits of geese to how a nuclear power plant works, vigorously argumentative debates among politicians of widely varied convictions, and how-to-do-it programs on cooking, gardening, and carpentry.

Londoners who want a newspaper but dislike the *London Free Press* have access to both the *Toronto Star* and the *Globe and Mail*. On AM and FM radio twenty to thirty channels can be picked up, and three of those radio stations are local. One of the radio stations and the city's only local TV station are both owned, along with the

London Free Press, by the Blackburn Group, which bothered Kent but, on the basis of testimony before the CRTC on several occasions, doesn't seem to bother Londoners a bit. That's understandable — the newspaper and the combined radio and television stations are vigorously, sometimes viciously, competitive.

In the real world, the idea that newspapers have a monopoly of any kind is so far from actual practice it's hard to understand how a newspaper journalist (Spears), a businessman, bureaucrat, and university professor (Picard), and a journalist and bureaucrat (Kent) could be so divorced from that reality. The government which appointed the Kent Commission in time became leery of it and its recommendations. Perrin Beatty, then an opposition MP, now a cabinet minister in the Mulroney government, was given a copy of a report marked *Ministers' Eyes Only* and titled "Response to the Royal Commission on Newspapers." The bureaucrat who wrote it reflected the government's then current wisdom that something had to be done to control media — that is, newspaper — ownership, but concluded, "there are, nonetheless, real problems: constitutional — tax policy — appearance of government meddling in newsrooms." Then came the clincher: "The government's response must address both the problems identified *by* the commission and the problems identified *with* the commission." (The emphasis is in the original.)

In other words, so smoothly put only other bureaucrats and politicians were expected to understand it, the collective Ottawa opinion was rapidly turning to the view that the damn Kent Commission had been more trouble than it was worth. Long before the Liberals were tossed out of office in the fall of 1984, Jim Fleming, the minister who had drafted the legislation which would never fly, had been dropped from cabinet and the Kent Report and its recommendations had been shelved.

Only two significant results came from the Kent Report, one good, one not so good. Faced with the threat of government intervention, voluntary press councils were formed across Canada. In Ontario, a pioneer in the field, chairman J. Allyn Taylor was able to twist enough arms to bring every daily newspaper into the Ontario Press Council. About the same time, as a result of a suggestion by an Ottawa researcher, Alti Rodal, and my later motion from the floor of a conference in Quebec, Taylor took the initiative in forming a loose federation of press councils across the country.

The not-so-good result was a 1984 capital grant of $500,000 by the Liberal government, just before its demise, to fund research in journalism by the School of Journalism of the University of Western Ontario. This long-delayed and last-minute grant seemed to be an almost desperate attempt to find at least one result from the expenditure of more than $3 million of taxpayers money on a royal commission. There's no concern that the dean of the school, Peter Desbarats, sought the grant — more power to him and congratulations. The funds will be well spent. What's worrisome is having journalists accepting funds of any kind from government.

Aside from public debates through newspaper and magazine articles, several speeches, and being matched with Tom Kent on a Pierre Berton show (at the end of which a majority of the audience voted with Kent), there were other intriguing minor, but enlightening, incidents over the Kent Report.

One came during an interview with Judy Erola when she was minister of consumer and corporate affairs in the last Liberal government. Near the end of the government's efforts to put the Kent Report behind them, Erola was given the job of finding something useful which could be attributed to the money spent on the report. I was invited to Ottawa to review with her my vociferous objections to the entire concept.

During an hour or two's discussion, one of her staff asked a question with wide-ranging implications: "I've read several surveys, and a surprisingly high percentage of readers say they don't believe everything they read in the papers. Shouldn't we be doing something about that? Doesn't that bother you?" She was implying, of course, that newspapermen thought themselves above having to put their house in order. She was also implying that surely it was time government put things in order for them. Given such fiascos as the National Energy Program, that suggestion, coming from a bureaucrat in the last Liberal government, was hilarious.

"No, that doesn't bother me at all," I replied. "That's the way it should be."

She sat there, a frown on her face, not quite believing what she'd heard. I gave her a few moments to try to figure it out — aware that with her obviously bureaucratic mind, she could not.

"Most newspaper stories are a record of what someone else says — we report what Idi Amin says, what Richard Nixon says, what Ronald Reagan says, what Yuri Andropov says, what Pierre Trudeau says — most of the time much the way they say it. Readers are intelligent. They don't believe anything Amin says, are doubtful about what Nixon says, cast a jaundiced eye at what Reagan, Andropov and Trudeau say — *of course*," raising my voice, "*readers don't believe everything they read*. They'd be stupid damn fools if they did."

The essence of a working democracy is that people have the right to read anything they wish, and then to say to anyone, including their political servants, "I don't believe what you're saying." That sometimes results in those political servants being tossed out on their ear. Anything less is the greatest danger faced by any democracy. "And," I added, "that is why the idea of politicians, their appointees or their civil servants being allowed, directly or indirectly, to manipulate the free flow of information across the country — or around the world — is so desperately disturbing. . . . The day the public begin to believe everything they read, we're all in deep trouble."

She said no more, but watched me closely throughout the rest of the discussion, leaving the impression that as I'd dropped a verbal bomb, there was a danger a real one would follow.

That's the reason newspapers lack credibility — and, let us hope, will continue to do so indefinitely in a free society.

The very nature of a newspaper's role is to act as an open pipeline for society — a conduit along which information can flow freely. There are constraints, of course. Newspapers can't print the equivalent of shouting "fire" in a crowded theatre; there are standards of good taste which must be met to a greater or lesser degree (compare the *Globe* with *Hush*); and the laws of libel are operative to protect individuals from gross falsehoods.

Where the lack of credibility among the public arises is in the impossibility of finding a credible person to offset the bias of every bit of information distributed. If President Reagan says in a major speech that a larger deficit is good for the United States, that speech probably will be reported without amplification. Next day, his Democratic opponents in the Senate may refute the argument vigorously. Opponents of Reagan, on the first day, think newspapers lack credibility for publishing such an obvious falsehood. Republicans next day think the paper is equally lacking in credibility for publishing what Democratic senators think. Of course newspapers lack credibility. That's the way it should be.

Caller Angry about Content
of Newspaper He Doesn't Read

One of my rules on telephone conversations was refusing to talk to callers who would not give their name. They knew who I was because they had phoned me; not giving their name allowed them greater exuberance in expressing their view — whatever it was.

This time, however, the fellow on the other end launched so quickly and so vigorously into his tirade, and continued at such a noisy level, I wasn't able to get in my usual pitch about his identifying himself. He disliked intensely what was in the paper, the headlines were usually wrong, the stories were inaccurate, editorials were not based on fact and were grossly bigoted, and sports stories never told "the truth." In an editorial the previous week about the Middle East, he added, all the facts were completely wrong.

I put off the identification bit for a moment and asked what was wrong in the editorial; he replied he really didn't know too much about the Middle East, it was a very complicated subject, and he hadn't read too much about it.

"How," I asked mildly, "if you lack knowledge on the subject, did you know we were wrong?"

After a two-second pause, he hung up. Pity. I never did get his name.

There Are Fine People
and Famous People,
but They're Not Always Both

"God will provide." That was Mother Teresa's theme all afternoon as she answered questions in a tiny office and took us to the Home for the Dying she had founded in Calcutta's teeming streets. Thin as a rail and homely as a barn fence, she was suffused with a light from within which could only come from a faith beyond most mortal understanding. I spent an afternoon with her in Calcutta, along with David Jenkins, a tall, broad-shouldered Red Cross official from Vancouver. It was the first and probably the last time I'll ever meet a saint.

Her Home for the Dying is an L-shaped building with the entrance at the bend. A blackboard read "58" and "51," men on the left, women on the right. As we walked through the ward Indian nuns wiped sweat from men struggling to die. Mother Teresa stopped frequently, holding a hand here, patting a coughing shoulder there, sublimely aware of God's grace even in death — maybe the more so in death.

At an orphanage she'd founded for babies left to die on the street were long rows of cribs, babies with black eyes and black hair, gurgling, smiling, screaming for milk, and sound asleep. A nun picked up a grinning doll and passed her to me. Cradling the child in my arms I murmured, "She's sweet — I should take her home."

The nun's smile was as sweet as the baby's: "We could arrange that easily."

Startled, I handed back the baby while David roared with laughter.

Down in the courtyard Mother Teresa explained that God had told her to open an orphanage for street babies.

"How do you feed them all? Calcutta is poverty-stricken."

She'd opened the orphanage without knowing where to get milk. Within a day or so a phone call came from Chittacong, a port in what had been West Pakistan. An Australian three months before had sent an old tramp steamer loaded with powdered milk to Mother Teresa. "You see, God will provide. When God told me to open the orphanage He had already made sure we'd have milk."

David had already experienced God's intervention. The then new ruler of Bangladesh, Mujibur Rahman, phoned Mother Teresa and asked her to open a hospital for women raped and made pregnant by rampaging West Pakistani soldiers during the war which ended with Bangladesh's independence. They were dishonoured even though raped; their families simply turned them out on the street.

Mother Teresa said "Yes, of course," and called David. She needed planes to fly beds to Dacca. David explained all his aircraft were fully committed to delivering medicine, food, blankets, and other aid to Dacca. He said he'd see what he could do.

Next morning David's pilots came in to say they could make two morning flights, then they would have to wait for more supplies. David raised his eyes to heaven and said, "How many of those Indian flat rope beds could you fly over?"

"Several hundred. They're not heavy."

David phoned Mother Teresa. He knew the response. "God will provide."

Thinking to offer trucks to pick up the beds, he asked where they were, and how many. The tiny creature in her blue and white habit at the other end of the line said she didn't have the beds but they'd be there by noon.

All morning word circulated in the bazaars. All morning men and women carried rope beds down the long road to Dum Dum airport outside Calcutta. By evening they were in Dacca. When the last beds had been delivered, plentiful supplies of drugs, food, and clothing arrived and the regular ferry service began again.

From Canada I sent Mother Teresa a copy of an article about her. Three months later a postcard arrived, surface mail. A crabbed hand had written: "God love you for your beautiful story. Mother Teresa."

I'm not Roman Catholic but sometimes when I run my finger over that simple postcard I sense again the presence of God.

Allyn Taylor, sometime president and chairman of the board of Canada Trust, has been spark-plug for scores of worthwhile city, provincial and federal ventures to make life better for Canadians. Mind you, he's hardly a saint like Mother Teresa. He can be devastatingly frank when the occasion demands. He also is enormously effective in anything he tackles. Persuading him to undertake a venture can be tricky. The important thing is to ask, but don't push. Just ask and wait. He has his own sources of information, his own business and personal friends he trusts, his own assessments of community needs. When he's ready he'll say "yes," or "no" and explain why.

During a year as president of London Art Gallery Association my only contribution was to ask Allyn to raise $1.5 million as a start on construction of an art gallery in London. That was something he'd have to think about. He'd get back to me.

Three months passed. The art gallery board was getting restless. Had Mr. Taylor called? Why not? Would I call and check? No way. "Let him be. When he's ready, he'll call."

He called in July, a sharp note in his voice.

"Bill. You didn't call me."

"No."

"That's downright mean. If you'd called, I have several good reasons for not taking the job. I just don't have the nerve to call and say I won't. So I'll do it."

Several months passed. Again the board was restless; again I cautioned patience. About November the phone rang again.

"Bill, I've got a problem."

"Donors not coming across?"

"No." Long pause. "You said a million and a half, didn't you?"

"Well, that's what we were hoping for, but if it is a problem we can go back to the drawing board."

"Well, my problem is I'm at a million eight. What do I do now?"

When I got my breath back, I said, "Allyn, just keep going — just keep going."

He hit two million five before he finished.

All United States presidents are famous, at least in office. Lyndon Johnson's presidency will be written about for centuries — he was an astonishing man.

I met him when he entertained a convention of American editors at the White House. There were casual tours of the main floor rooms, bars in the east room, a Marine band playing in the entrance foyer where we danced, and a receiving line to meet the president.

I detest name tags. Mutton and pork are labelled; people shouldn't be. If one is pinned on me it soon disappears.

My wife and I reached the president: "Bill Heine, from London, Canada, Mr. President, and my wife Vivian."

Lyndon smiled but said accusingly, "You're not wearing a name tag."

"That's all right, Mr. President, you're not wearing one either."

His boisterous roar could be heard all over the state dining room. We had a nice long chat.

Lacey Winsor wasn't famous but he was a fine man and doctor. For fifty years he sewed up axe-cuts on legs, visited homes as many times a day as necessary, left the bodies of accident victims to be taken away in a hearse while he rushed a score or two-score miles to hospital with those still alive, brought thousands of babies into the world, and before he died was slapping the new-born bottoms of their grandchildren. He had broad shoulders, a stocky, sturdy body, a thick shock of hair which over the years went from dark brown to grey to white, a broad face with a smile which could even comfort the dying. Universally, he was known as "Doctor."

I'd driven him on the back roads of New Brunswick for a few years before going overseas. He was kept behind at Fredericton where he examined thousands of men entering the army or on their way overseas, as well as caring for the sick and injured. In the evening he'd drive an hour or more back to Norton where he'd tend those who needed him most. After a few hours' sleep, he'd drive back in the middle of the night in time for morning sick parade. Given the sleep he lost and the physical punishment he took, it's a miracle he lived into his eighties.

He even found time to write me overseas but, except for the date which was guessed at and the signature, I had to write back and say none of his letter had been translated into English.

When the village, and the countryside for miles around, marked his fortieth year there and it came his turn to speak, he was as usual modest and low key. He did make one boast, so warm it was without vanity — he said he could call every one of the hundreds of people in the room by their first name. And he did so all evening. When my turn came, as the local boy who'd gone away and become an editor, it seemed appropriate to mention that my family had had a tough time during the Depression and that in all those years he had never sent a bill. Our family wasn't the only one. In the postwar prosperity such recollections were not always well received.

He died universally loved. His wife marked his grave with a tall black granite obelisk which looks out over the valley and the rolling hills he loved so much and had driven by so often. Two words summed up a lifetime of devoted service: "Family Physician."

David Peterson, who has been sweeping like a fresh breeze through the musty rooms of Ontario's government, has a highly developed social conscience. For him and his brothers Jim and Tim it began at the family dinner table where social, economic, and political issues were debated at length.

When he was seventeen, his mother took him to a friend's house where I'd been asked to show what were then considered dramatic slides taken by astronauts in space. As an avid fan of the American space program I'd watched several launches, interviewed astronauts, and collected colour transparencies taken in space.

David wasn't too impressed by U.S. space ventures. He thought the money would have been better spent to improve the lot of those who lived in the inner cores of American cities. He sat politely, however, while I waxed enthusiastic.

When the lights went on, Marie Peterson turned to her son. "Well, David, now what do you think of the American space program?" David remained skeptical. "I think it's a lot of money to spend just to amuse Mr. Heine."

Pierre Elliott Trudeau is famous and God knows he has a brilliant mind, but though I had several long interviews with him I didn't know him well enough to judge whether he was as fine a man as he was famous. From personal experience, he could be brutally blunt and absolutely charming.

The bluntness appeared in a car driving to St. Thomas during an election campaign. His press people had arranged an interview in the car. As we pulled away, Harold Stafford, MP for Elgin, was on the left, Trudeau on the right, myself in the middle. Outside the city when there were no more knots of pedestrians waving, Trudeau turned to the interview.

After half a dozen questions, Stafford interrupted to tell Trudeau something about St. Thomas. Trudeau politely suggested it wait until the interview was over. A second interruption brought another polite reply, this time with an edge to it. Stafford didn't seem to understand. A third time he cut into the conversation.

Trudeau leaned forward across my knees and stared at Stafford: "I said shut up."

We finished the interview without further interruption.

He was equally devastating though not as rude at a gathering laid on by Marc Lalonde to explain the National Energy Program to publishers and editors. A dozen of us listened to civil servants and politicians all morning, were entertained at lunch by Jean Chrétien, who was then in the midst of constitutional debates in Canada and Britain, and ended the afternoon with an hour's talk with Trudeau.

All day Pat O'Callaghan, then publisher of the *Edmonton Journal*, had dominated the conversation, aggressively challenging each speaker. It was entertaining and we learned a lot from Pat's questions, but by mid-afternoon I for one had a stock of unanswered, indeed unasked, questions. When Trudeau arrived, Pat kept right on — hammering away, challenging the prime minister's statements, arguing about the NEP and its impact on Alberta.

Trudeau's face tightened. Was he going to give Pat the Stafford treatment? He looked down the table when Pat paused for breath. "Mr. O'Callaghan," the prime minister said coldly, "I don't intend to bargain with the province of Alberta through you."

I sent an article mentioning the incident to Pat, who mailed back a mimeograph of a speech he'd made in which he referred to the Ontario editor who wasn't in favour of newspapermen arguing with prime ministers.

It would have been delightful to argue with the prime minister; the point was I couldn't get a word in edgewise.

Trudeau's charm showed one night at Ottawa's Press Club when he stayed on to talk informally. I wandered over and asked if he had seen a Ting cartoon of Trudeau's visit to Stratford Festival's *Romeo and Juliet*. It showed Romeo at the foot of the balcony looking puzzled, while Juliet was down in the audience kissing Trudeau.

Yes, he'd been shown the cartoon. "Nice touch."

I collect some of Ting's cartoons and have them autographed.

"Prime minister, I have the original of that cartoon and I wondered..."

Trudeau's smile was brilliant. "Oh, thanks. I'd love to have it."

That was not what I had in mind and it must have shown in my face.

"You wanted it autographed! Of course. You send it. I'll be glad to sign it."

Now there's a pretty howdy-do. As the nation's leader his wishes took precedence but, damn-it-all, I wanted that cartoon. Thinking furiously, I made an offer he couldn't refuse.

"Prime Minister, when I get home I'll force Ting under threat of dismissal to do another original. I'll send both to you. You pick the one you want, then autograph the other and send it back to me. That fair?"

"To everyone but Ting."

Ting wasn't fired. The PM got his cartoon; and I got mine.

On the other side of the world I had a fascinating insight into the Asian mind. Mujibur Rahman was the leader of dissident Moslems in East Pakistan, now Bangladesh, who opposed rule from West Pakistan and fought for independence. He survived fifteen years in West Pakistani jails and several promises to hang him by rulers of Pakistan. When civil war resulted in Bangladesh independence, Rahman returned as father of his country to be its first president.

It took a day's trotting from one civil servant to another before I finally was given an 8:30 P.M. appointment at his residence. No one asked to see my pass; I walked boldly through grounds crowded with people, elbowed my way into the house, and found an English-speaking aide who looked at the pass and shook his head. "No good here. Only good at palace," and tried to shoo me out the door.

No damn way. He tried another tack.

"Tonight he is very busy. We have a Russian delegation. We have a French delegation. We have army officers' delegation. No. I can do nothing for you. But you wait. I will try."

An hour later after the Russians left I was hurriedly beckoned into a large room where about a third of the space was occupied by Rahman on a vast sofa with a dozen men standing in a semi-circle behind him. In the remaining space were about a hundred people on folding metal chairs watching their new president run the country. Fiercely admonished just to shake hands and go back to my seat,

"*JULIET, JULIET, WHEREFORE ART THOU, JULIE?*"

I was introduced as a "very important Canadian newspaper owner." We shook hands and I turned to go, but he pulled me forward and introduced me to his new cabinet. They were also spending the evening watching their new president govern the country.

Then Rahman launched into a vivid description of his country's plight. "They destroyed my bridges, they killed my people, they blew up my railways, they burned my homes." The list was long. He was "spared by God to save my people."

The West must help. I must tell the West that they must help. I assured him that would be done, we shook hands and I was led away by the aide, nervous because his instructions had been overruled. For an hour I watched delegations being received, including an old man who whispered in Rahman's ear and was told sternly not to bother the ruler of Bangladesh with such nonsense.

A fine man of great courage, but he had the mind of an Oriental potentate more interested in holding court than in solving problems. His cabinet, rather than standing around obsequiously, should have been trying to restore order out of chaos for the new nation's eighty million people — who now, more than a decade later, are still one of the world's economic basket cases.

As little was then known about the country's internal affairs and even less about Rahman, my articles on returning home were sent by Canada's External Affairs Department to embassies around the world. The article ended by predicting the father of his country couldn't survive indefinitely — the country needed a ruler to solve problems, not a mere father image.

Two years later President Mujibur Rahman was shot in a military coup.

Buyung Nasution also spent years in jail, not because he considered himself the father of his country or believed his destiny was to be president, but simply because he believed in liberty and said so. He has a deep and abiding faith in the rule of law, a Jeffersonian conviction of swearing "on the altar of God eternal hostility to any form of tyranny over the mind of man." He's not a communist nor is he at the other extreme of fascism. Elected to Indonesia's parliament, he spoke out vigorously against corruption and repression of either the left or right. At first out of his own pocket, then with money from friends and international corporations in Indonesia, Nasution founded a legal aid centre where, on a quiet street in a Jakarta suburb, a dozen lawyers handle hundreds of cases, taking on new ones daily.

Indonesia's right-wing dictatorship threw him in jail. He was not tortured but was moved from jail to jail to discourage his making friends with his guards, which he did anyway, and was denied both books and visits from his family. Two years later without explanation he was released.

"Before I went to jail," he said, "I knew in my head it was wrong to arrest people except under the rule of law. Now I know in my heart it is wrong — liberty is the most precious thing men enjoy. We must be free to speak the truth as we see it."

In Jakarta everyone knows Nasution. In government and among the consultants, percentage entrepreneurs, and the foreign corporations, reaction is mixed — admiration and distrust. An Indonesian consultant said, "He is a hero and I am a coward," then rationalized his own contribution. "Who does more, Nasution who gets people out of prison, or people like me who help build factories and open mines so our people have work to do?"

Nasution had an answer. "The rich get richer and the poor get poorer. There is too great a gap between those who rule and those who are ruled. Until corruption is brought under control, it will be difficult to maintain stability."

When it was time to go I asked how much "of what you have said is it safe for me to use?"

"All of it," he replied. "I am not afraid."

Nor was Maureen Brown famous like Rahman, except among tubercular Vietnamese around Quang Ngai, up the coast from Saigon, halfway to what was then the demilitarized zone. She ran a clinic which handled forty to fifty new tuberculosis cases a month. When the flow of patients fell off, she headed into the countryside by truck and helicopter with an aide and a bag of medicine, testing sputum for TB. She always found it.

Her work was funded by Canada. Originally, she had several Western nurses and technicians working with her; when I met her there was only an x-ray specialist and herself. In a war-torn land, hers was a lonely and potentially dangerous life. Whatever her fears, she kept them to herself.

She wasn't a Mother Teresa, she had no pretentions to that level of dedication. Though her commitment was relatively short-term, she was as dedicated as the saint of Calcutta.

Even in our few hours at Quang Ngai her warm, loving, wonderful personality left an indelible impression. As the plane taking us back to Saigon taxied away I felt a surge of emotion at leaving her there — and blew a kiss through the aircraft's window. Her face lit with a wonderful smile, she threw back her head and laughed gaily, then there was just enough time to blow one back before she was gone.

Harry Truman is being rated as among the best presidents the United States has had; he was also a fine person.

While he was still president I was on vacation in Washington and wangled an invitation to one of his press conferences. In those days visitors from other countries were invited to stay and meet the president. Harry was in fine fettle. He had nationalized the railways during a strike and the Supreme Court had ruled he had not had the authority to do so. Yet he told the press conference that if he were faced with the problem another time, he would take the same action. American newsmen were writing stories that in effect said the president was challenging the Supreme Court.

I thought differently. What Truman was saying was that he had supreme executive authority in the government of the United States. Under any circumstances he would act as he thought best to do what his inaugural oath required: to uphold and protect the constitution of the United States. He was not challenging the Supreme Court; he was merely stating that as president of the country he would act in what he considered to be its best interests. When we were introduced it was natural to try out that concept. His reply was brief. "Exactly."

"Mr. President, you were surprisingly relaxed at the press conference. There were 300 newspapermen out there, every one ready to pounce on any error you made. That didn't seem to bother you at all."

"Oh, no, they're on my side, most of them. It's their publishers back home who are against me."

Then he offered advice to Democratic politicians. "As long as newspaper publishers are opposing what I'm doing," he said, "I'm sure I'm on the right track." He grinned. "When they begin to agree with me, then I get worried."

Shrewd.

If you ever meet Clair Barnaby, be fast with a retort or you'll be left far behind in conversation.

Clair's a former nun who went over the wall and became, of all things, the manager of a settlement in the Northwest Territories and has now graduated to a slot in Ottawa, where she undoubtedly drives bureaucrats crazy. She has a vocabulary which, as Professor Higgins puts it in *My Fair Lady*, "would make a sailor blush." When Inuit at Repulse Bay went hunting, they wanted her along. She's a deadly shot.

When I met her, she was wearing an absolutely superb white parka decorated with magnificent seals, whales, sleigh dogs, igloos, and fish. When I admired it, she said, "Wanna buy it? Only $500." With a leer she added, "For another $500, I'll throw in me, too."

For once on the bit, I suggested she call me "when you're having a 2 for 1 sale."

She did by mail years later. She had testified at the Berger inquiry into the development of the Mackenzie River valley, loudly and firmly disputing most of the conventional wisdom about the North and, as it turned out, contradicting vigorously the thrust of the Berger Report. I also thought the Berger Report was a disaster. Canada has only one major river system in the entire Arctic, the Mackenzie. For oil, gas, minerals, whatever the North has to offer, there needs to be a corridor down the Mackenzie all the way to the delta and the Beaufort Sea with a road, oil and gas pipelines, and communications. It should have been developed years ago. I wrote Clair, then in Norman Wells, and told her so.

Back came a quick reply, pleased as punch someone agreed with her. She ended the letter with an invitation. If I was in the North, "come and see me. You can shack up with me anytime."

Trouble is, I'm unlikely ever to find out if that meant taking up my "2 for 1" offer. It was weeks before I dared take the letter home. Now my wife won't let me go north any more.

Arthur Rutherford Ford was a brilliant journalist, a fine editor, a delightful person to know, and a certified character — at least in his old age. I met him first when he was sixty-five years old in 1945 and had been editor of the *London Free Press* for twenty-five years. He was to stay on another seventeen years until he was eighty-two.

His previous career was distinguished. He happened to be in New York when word arrived of the sinking of the *Titanic* in 1912 and scooped Canada with news of the tragedy and of Canadians involved. His great interest in life was politics. He had been a member of the Ottawa Press Gallery for the *Winnipeg Telegram* before becoming editor of the *Free Press*.

Working summers while attending university I saw little of him, yet enough that when the managing editor waffled at hiring me on graduation I felt free to query Ford and found myself on the payroll next day. We had an affinity based on I know not what — certainly I didn't wholly share his dedicated support for the Conservative Party, nor was I happy with his willingness occasionally to suppress news which might offend his establishment cronies around town. His staying on almost two decades past normal retirement age was also irritating because that denied the job to his eventual successor John K. Elliott. Yet we liked each other, enjoyed each other's company, and would sit and talk, this long-time editor in his seventies and the young reporter in his thirties, like old cronies over the front-yard fence.

Even after I succeeded John I called the older man "Mr. Ford," though in time "Mr. Blackburn" became "Walter." (To Walter, his editor until he died was "Mr. Ford"; to Ford his publisher was "Walter.") Twice when I was considering offers from Toronto dailies Ford intervened with pay increases and I learned second-hand later he had told the publisher "young Heine" should be editor "some day." He knew he wasn't immortal but he preferred not to be called for a while yet.

He knew everyone in London and everyone knew him. He wrote extensively, travelled a good deal, was chancellor of the university, close friend of the town's movers and shakers, active as founder and president of Kiwanis, chairman of the library board, president of Canadian Press — name it and Ford was involved. When my turn came I wrote and travelled but kept my distance from local movers and shakers on the grounds many of them had no concept of the impropriety of trying to manipulate the content of a newspaper. As editor, I wouldn't even attend local political rallies, casually brushing off invitations on the grounds of dislike for chicken and green peas.

What endeared Ford to me was a combination of shrewd political judgement and an absent-minded unawareness of anything in which he was not interested. When typing an article or editorial he would sit with his hat on, both his hearing aids unplugged and sticking straight up and out from his collar, oblivious to anything going on around him. To get his attention, it was necessary to move partly around the desk and stand in front of the typewriter. He might then reluctantly stop pounding the keys, push in his ear plugs, and ask "Yes?"

Until he died at eighty-six, Ford and I compared notes on elections. He had a network of friends across the country, staunch Tories in every riding who would give him off-the-record assessments of each riding and who might or might not win in an upcoming election. From these detailed reports, by letter, telephone, and visits, he built up shrewd predictions of election outcomes. He followed American political life with equal effectiveness. In Harry Truman's 1948 election he predicted Thomas Dewey's defeat. Curious and somewhat disbelieving I pressed further.

"Why?"

"There's more Democrats."

Made sense. I risked the best part of a month's pay at odds as high as ten to one and soon sported a less-scabrous second-hand car.

He was a true-blue Tory. There's a story that when the *London Advertiser* folded in 1936, young Walter suggested to his editor-in-chief that from then on the *Free Press* should be an independent newspaper (it had been Tory and the *Advertiser* Grit for decades).

"All right, Walter, if you say so," Ford is reported to have said, "but those damn Grits aren't going to get any space in *my* newspaper."

Walter remembered that — years later he complained to me that Ford had been talking again about "my" newspaper. I turned it aside by saying I often referred to the *Free Press* as my newspaper, out of pride, not ownership. Small thing, maybe, but to Walter who owned the paper it was a mite touchy.

When I became editor and publicly tried predicting elections, I avoided riding-by-riding inputs and tried to assess public moods in the five regions of the country — the Maritimes, Quebec, Ontario, the Prairies, and British Columbia. For the first Trudeau/Stanfield election in 1968 I ran an article broken down by provinces predicting 151 seats for the Liberals. They won 155. In years following I didn't always do so well, predicting for example that Hubert Humphrey would defeat Richard Nixon.

Ford wrote a book about his years as editor, *As the World Wags On*, a delightful look at Canadian journalism and politics in the first half of this century. In this autobiography, Ford is brutal about a distant relative of mine, Sir George Foster, whom he knew well. "Probably no parliamentarian was ever the centre of more bitter controversies," he wrote. "Possessor of a sarcastic and vitriolic tongue, he never spared it on his political opponents; on the other hand, he was pursued with almost vindictive cruelty." He missed being prime minister, Ford notes, because he "had too many enemies" and quotes doggerel he remembers from a Press Gallery dinner:

> For as Rufe said slow, one night below,
>   When the boys were having a smile,
> 'Say George, ole man, you could run dis lan'
>   If you'd licker up once in a while.

Foster was of Loyalist farming stock; his grandfather was my great-

great-grandfather. Reading his autobiography and other reminiscences, Foster emerges as a tall, thin man who boot-strapped himself into a university education, for years lectured across Canada and the United States for the then vigorous temperance movement, entered politics, and in 1884, while in his thirties, ended up in the federal cabinet as minister of finance, where he balanced the budget for years, no little accomplishment then and seemingly impossible now. More than a bit of a stuffed shirt, he served in several Conservative governments and in Robert Borden's World War I Union government, was acting prime minister for a year or so while Borden tried to regain his strength from the strain of the war years, and died in the early 1930s. Having since read extensively about Foster's career, I wish I'd known more about him earlier and tapped Ford's vast memory for more than appeared in these political sources.

Open identification with one political party became Ford's Waterloo. This was bad enough when there were two papers in town, but far worse after the *Advertiser* folded. When Lester B. Pearson was making a bid for office, Walter decided he couldn't have his newspaper supporting any man who'd messed things up as thoroughly as John Diefenbaker. He insisted on an editorial endorsing the Liberals under Pearson and, doubly frustrating to Ford, that it run on page one. Ford called me into his office, hat perched on the back of his head as usual, and asked my advice. While it was flattering to have such confidence from the dean of Canadian journalism who had covered the political scene in Canada for half a century, it was also potentially awkward. Walter might not appreciate the advice I offered. No matter, the old gentleman deserved an answer.

Ford said that as a dedicated Conservative he couldn't remain editor of a paper that endorsed the Liberals. What he really meant was he didn't feel he could face his friends locally and across the country. I argued he need not take responsibility for the publisher's decision (with which, incidentally, I agreed fully). There was nothing dishonest or shameful in supporting another political party. It was a matter of who held the ultimate responsibility — and that was clearly the publisher. All Ford's friends would understand and accept that the decision was contrary to his views. It made no difference. He listened sorrowfully and within a few days resigned.

Anecdotes about Ford abound. His long-time secretary, Mary DeLuca, told delightful stories about his absent-mindedness. My favourite is his ushering a visitor to the outer door, then turning back and asking, "Mary, that chap Henderson who was just in here, what's his first name?"

Unsure herself, Mary paused a few seconds drumming her fingers on the desk, then replied brightly, "Oh! It's George, Mr. Ford."

"George who?"

He didn't have a car, fearing his sons would use it most of the time. He travelled around town by taxi, shedding hats, gloves, rubbers, canes, scarves, and other odds and ends everywhere he went. Mary would call the club, the university, hotels, and other places around town, then send a taxi to pick up the loot so he could lose them again the following week.

My best encounter with his absent-mindedness was at the news counter of the old Hotel London. While we talked he shoved his cigars in a coat pocket and his change in his right trousers pocket. As he walked away the coins clattered down to the tile floor and rolled in all directions. He was oblivious. A bellhop and I picked them up and at the entrance to the dining room handed over the coins. "You have a hole in your pocket, Mr. Ford. You lost these coins on the lobby floor."

"Oh, thank you, Bill. Thank you. Much obliged." Whereupon he shoved the coins back into the same pocket and disappeared into the dining room, coins rolling in all directions. Those watching laughed and left them for the cleaners.

He summered in Bayfield for many years and kept sending back long chatty columns about activities there, some of which worried his staff in London. One which caused consternation related the village's delight in a liaison between a minister and a choir leader, both clearly identified, in one of the churches. Several calls went to Bayfield trying to persuade the editor that such a column shouldn't run. To all protests he had an engaging answer: "It's no problem. No problem. Whole village is talking about it. Everyone up here knows about it. Run it." They did. A lot more people were soon talking, including the minister's superiors. He left soon after.

There was another column recounting a conversation with a hotel owner whose main building had burned. While it was being rebuilt, he put up half a dozen small temporary cabins. Mr. Ford found him sitting on the porch one day and asked how was business. "Just great, Mr. Ford, just great. You know, I rent some of them cabins three and four times a night." Also caused a bit of a stir in the village.

After he retired, whenever I was up that way I'd phone ahead to see if a visit was convenient. The second Mrs. Ford took unkindly to her husband having brandy at his age and he saw little of it, particularly as his legs began to give out on him. Well aware of the situation,

I'd chat with his wife, then be ushered into the garden where Ford was slumped cheerfully in a lawn chair. It wasn't long before the old gentleman would mutter, "You bring anything?" He wasn't talking about newspapers, either. We would empty the ginger ale on the lawn, tilt in two-ounce bottles of brandy and sip happily in the summer sun, talking about provincial and federal politics.

Beginning a friendship with John Plumtree required a little ingenuity. My wife and I were browsing in an antique shop north of London and saw a chair which had been beautifully restored. We needed someone who could do work like that but antique dealers are notoriously reluctant to say where they have work done. I asked, but the lady replied only that he lived "up north somewhere." When she wandered off to talk to another customer, I commented casually to her young assistant that the Goderich chap repairing furniture did superb work.

"Oh, no," she replied. "He lives in Clinton."

Next stop Clinton. At the main corner I nipped into a men's clothing store and bought half a dozen handkerchiefs, asking as the bill was made out if the storekeeper knew of anyone in town who restored antique furniture.

"That would be John Plumtree — just down the street past the dairy. His shop is on the lower level at the back."

Years before I'd written an article entitled "I'm a nut about wood" which, when we introduced ourselves, he remembered, particularly the old English song I'd found printed in a Scottish magazine:

> Beechwood fires are bright and clear
> If the logs are kept a year.
> Chestnut's only good, they say
> If for long its laid away.
> But ash wood new or ash wood old
> Is fit for a queen with a crown of gold.
>
> Birch and fir logs burn too fast,
> Blaze up bright and do not last.
> It is by the Irish said
> Hawthorn bakes the sweetest bread.
> Elmwood burns like churchyard mould
> E'en the very flames are cold;
> But ash wood green and ash wood brown
> Is fit for for a queen with a golden crown.

Poplar gives a bitter smoke
Fills your eyes and makes you choke
Applewood will scent your room
With an incense like perfume.
Oaken logs if dry and old
Keep away the winter cold.
But ash wood wet and ash wood dry
A king shall warm his slippers by."

John liked that. A self-taught woodworker, he spent much of his life as a barber. One day, he told me years later, he just decided he'd had "enough barbering." He closed the shop, sold the equipment, and began repairing antiques in his workshop in the basement of the building where he and his sister lived.

Much of the antique furniture in our house was rebuilt by John. A gentle, shy man who never married, he was uncomfortable in any setting other than his own shop and home. Though we were friends for more than twenty years only once was he persuaded to walk to the corner and have a morning coffee. Never were we able to persuade him to visit us at home to see how we were using the beautiful things he made and repaired for us.

I came to know him well enough to be able to tease him unmercifully about his habit of switching from wood turning to repairing antiques and back again. He'd weary of repairing chests of drawers which had been used to hold tools in a barn for a generation. Nothing would then persuade him to do anything other than turn out magnificent salad bowls, candlesticks, and wall brackets in pine, cherry and walnut. Six months later he'd not be turning anything; instead, he'd concentrate entirely on repair. It was a bit frustrating to have to wait six months for John to finish a woodturning cycle so a desk could be rebuilt, but then his walnut and cherry bowls were collector's items.

When I found him wearing a sporty shirt, selling his turnings at church and community bazaars in the months before Christmas, I'd goad him about the ladies who crowded around his booth — and even did so in an article on the *Free Press* editorial page. It didn't bother John. He just cocked his head a bit to one side and grinned sheepishly.

I'd phone on a Saturday morning to ask if I could drive up with a piece which needed work and he'd say he'd be there until noon, when he planned to go off into the country to take pictures. Came a Saturday when I drove up without notice and, finding him not home, left a chest of drawers outside his shop to be rebuilt. A few days later we left for a trip to the United States and, at a motel mid-week, remembered to phone back to make sure he'd found the chest. Yes, he said, he'd been working on it all day and it was just finished. That was a Wednesday. Next day he felt ill, was taken to hospital, and died there on Saturday.

Later I learned from his sister Catherine that his Saturday picture-taking was a consuming hobby. He wanted to capture on colour film every wild flower growing in southwestern Ontario. His camera work was superb; all slides were 2¼ by 2¼ inch, every one an absolute gem. Showing them to us, Catherine wondered if it would be right to give them to the local high school for the use of students. I assured her they deserved a wider and more specialized audience and suggested the Botany Department of the University of Western Ontario. I was back quickly with university staff, who took one look at the collection and were as excited as children. They had never seen, they told her, anything so technically and at the same time so beautifully perfect.

And that's where they are today, preserved for the use of future students who might spend a lifetime and not achieve the technical perfection of the sometime barber who became an antique restorer and who I was proud to call my friend.

Greg Marshall flew jets off USS *Hancock* in the Gulf of Tonkin during the Vietnam War. He was a quiet, sturdy fellow, on the go sixteen hours a day. To him I was an added chore, to be escorted around the American aircraft carrier, shown all I should see, not shown anything I shouldn't see, and prevented from coming to any harm that might embarrass the United States Navy. A veteran of World War II, *Hancock* helped sink three battleships and three cruisers off Okinawa and at Suriago Straits. She took a kamikaze aircraft on her deck, but survived to shoot down 700 Japanese planes and sink seventeen warships and thirty-two merchant ships.

Greg was a pilot with 212 attack squadron, bombing and strafing the Ho Chi Minh Trail while dodging anti-aircraft fire, SAM missiles, and MiG aircraft. About twenty minutes flying time from the coast, he'd spend half an hour over various targets and be back on board an hour after being catapulted off. Several times during my long weekend Greg excused himself, left me in the deck pit where launches were controlled, and was blasted off on another strike. His pals then served coffee and parked me in a steel cage overhanging the water near the stern by No. 2 wire, which would snag Greg's jet. On aircraft carriers jets don't land, it's a controlled crash.

One day I asked if it bothered Greg to be bombing and strafing helpless civilians on the Ho Chi Minh Trail. He grinned, knowing I knew the trail was a military target, but willing to provide a punch line for a visiting journalist. "There are no Sunday afternoon drivers on the Ho Chi Minh Trail." On a more serious note he added: "And they aren't helpless. We've lost pilots."

I liked Greg when we were introduced, and liked him even more on leaving a few days later, in part because he'd had a chat with his flight commander. I'd asked to be catapulted off the carrier. The captain said "No"; it took time to learn how to bail out of his jets and he wouldn't risk a pilot who would not bail out until his passenger was safe. Fair enough. Greg then suggested the Canadian editor might be catapulted off in the COD (carrier onboard delivery) which would take him back to South Vietnam. No problem. Goodbyes and thanks said, I was tightly strapped in and warned to brace my head tightly against the padding. Then — *slam* — we went from a standstill to more than 100 knots in less than 100 feet.

In Danang, scrounging transport south to Saigon, I scribbled a note to go back to Greg, thanking him for many courtesies, and asking him to ship my guts directly back to Canada.

The major mistake the Americans made in Vietnam was in not winning, which they could have done without nuclear weapons by blockading North Vietnamese harbours. If they had, Vietnam a decade later might have been as prosperous as defeated Germany and Japan became after World War II.

Then and now, though, I rated Greg as a gallant young gentleman.

During a tour of China with Prime Minister Pierre Trudeau in the early 1970s I met Chinese agricultural researchers who were keenly interested in Canadian farming. I was of no help to them whatever on farming techniques, but answered in general terms many questions about income and farming in Western Ontario.

Several spoke quite good English, but most listened carefully to an interpreter. When her colleagues were busy elsewhere, she had rapid-fire questions of her own. Was I married? Yes. Did I live in an apartment? No. You own your own house? Yes. How big is it? Seven rooms. Just the two of you? Yes. Is your farm large? No, I'm not a farmer. But you have land? Yes, about an acre. What crops do you grow? None, the land is all in trees and grass.

Her lovely eyes narrowed and her lips pursed.

"Ah," she said, "you are a rich capitalist landlord."

When her colleagues came back, she told what she'd learned, which led to more questions about my personal affairs, most of which I answered. Then professionalism took over, and we went back to discussing farming. By late afternoon, as I came to understand more of their attitudes, I passed around my business card, suggesting that if any of them came to Canada I'd see they had a day's tour around Western Ontario farms. A year or two later a phone call from the Chinese Embassy in Ottawa asked if the offer still stood.

It did, and three Chinese agriculturalists along with several Canadian farmers and one newspaper editor had a great day. A visit to a Holstein farm which exports cattle was followed by lunch, then a drive into Elgin County. Off the pavement, at the first crossroads, I stopped and asked the leader: "Which way, right, left or straight ahead?" He was puzzled but finally said "straight ahead."

Fifteen minutes later, after two rights, three lefts, and a straight ahead, I said, "OK, you pick any farm on this road you'd like to visit." The farmer was away, but his wife, momentarily taken back, rallied quickly and they all spent the afternoon in the barns, on pastures and corn fields. I stayed in the car.

On the way back they were profuse in their thanks. They also understood fully why the farm had been chosen as it was. "Everything else we've seen has been showcase," said their leader, "just the way we did for you in China. Today we have seen Canadian farming as it really is."

Made a fellow feel good.

The *Free Press* cartoonist, Merle Tingley, usually made a sketch of a cartoon idea. If the page's editor wasn't around, he'd bring it to me. Flapping a sheet of paper, he'd wander in saying, "I need an idiot check." I'd glance at it, usually agree, and he'd depart rejoicing.

What delighted him was the underlying joke that if I understood his cartoon idea, he'd feel any idiot in town would get the point.

People Do Love Their Honorifics

When the feminist concern about "Miss" and "Mrs." was at its height and "Ms." was popular, newsroom had a rough time. If every woman who was in the news was queried about how she wanted to be addressed, there'd be much time wasted, considerable room for error, and the certainty that some lady would not be available to tell us what she preferred. Added to that was the importance of keeping files on what every one of the roughly 300,000 women in London and Western Ontario wished for themselves. There was also the problem of a lady and gentleman who, in the delicate phrase of the Maritimes, "were married but not churched."

On the male side if we referred to Pierre Trudeau as "Mr. Trudeau," there were few complaints. But if we called Clifford Olsen "Mr. Olsen" during his trial and subsequent stories, there was strong criticism.

The whole thing got ridiculous.

In Britain they still use the honorific, with the result that in a story about Idi Amin, he's referred to as Mr. Amin, which is also the style for American murderers being executed — "Mr. Jones took three minutes to die."

We bit the bullet and adopted an increasingly common approach, identifying each person, on first mention, by their Christian name and surname. There would be no "Mr., Mrs., Ms., or Miss." If the person had a title (Sir Richard, Dr. Thomas, or whatever) it would be used, again on first mention. After that everyone was referred to by their surname.

Protests were vociferous, particularly from little old ladies who disliked Prime Minister Margaret Thatcher being referred to as Thatcher on second reference and a few stuffy Liberals who thought it improper to refer to Prime Minister Trudeau the second time in a story as Trudeau. To the little old ladies, who were usually strong Conservatives, I asked if they objected to just plain "Trudeau." No, but they didn't like "Thatcher." To the stuffy Liberals I asked if they objected to just plain "Reagan." No, they didn't, but they objected to "Trudeau."

In letters to the editor which still blast some of my columns my name is edited to read just plain "Heine." Suits me.

Even Minimal Exposure to UNESCO Enough to Turn Off Any Taxpayer

Standing outside UNESCO's Paris headquarters looking vainly for a taxi turned out to be educational. As a session broke up inside, delegates began leaving for their apartments and suites in and around Paris. In an hour, no fewer than twenty-seven limousines, Mercedes, Jaguars, Cadillacs, a few Rolls Royce, a couple of Audis, and a Lincoln or two left the building or stopped to pick up UNESCO officials. Those ushered into the back seats were delegates or senior officials; those who held doors and sat beside the driver were bodyguards; those who followed the first man into the back seat were aides. Of the twenty-seven delegates or senior officials, nineteen were clearly non-European.

An hour was long enough.

Back at the hotel, talking to others attending an executive meeting of the International Press Institute, I told about my hour's watch. Reaction varied. Americans and British reflected resigned indignation. Scandinavians, Dutch, and of course French tended to elaborate justifications of the great work done by UNESCO.

My reactions were rude and brutal. That hour along with two or three earlier visits to UNESCO headquarters merely validated the criticisms of UNESCO which were being heard in the Western world. Aside from the obvious authoritarianism of Amadar M'Bow, UNESCO's director general, and his extravagant lifestyle at UNESCO expense, including having the top floor of headquarters made over with entertainment facilities and living quarters for his family, the most devastating criticism of the organization was that 80 per cent of its budget was spent on salaries, expenses, and operating costs of the Paris headquarters.

UNESCO had been on my personal hit list for some time. The Paris visit merely confirmed second-hand reality. What caused my original concerns with UNESCO was its New World Information Order, the determined effort of communist and third-world nations "to control, directly if possible, indirectly if not, the most precious commodity in our complex world, information." To quote from a later article:

> The pattern is clear and evident at every turn. Argentina tried to prevent the rest of the world knowing about the thousands of its people who have disappeared under rightwing military dictatorships. Russia doesn't want news of its psychiatric prisons circulating in the Third World or anywhere else. South Africa tried

to prevent knowledge of the plight of its black majority from reaching anyone else ...

In less than a third of the 160 nations which occupy chairs at UNESCO ... are people free to say and write what they think about their governments ...

Western journalism isn't perfect, not by any means. But ... plural views are heard. Out of a multitude of opinions, free citizens of democracies can make up their own minds and vote policies reflecting their views. Anything less is a return to the dark ages ...

There's only one way ... to prevent the world's dictatorships from putting a United Nations stamp of approval on controlling the free flow of information around the globe. That's to cut off free-world funding.

A year later, the United States gave notice it would do just that if major reforms were not made; they weren't and it did. Later, Britain also left, and Singapore became the first third-world country to leave. Tiny Singapore's departure caused as much of a third-world stir as either the United States's or Britain's, which between them paid 30 per cent of UNESCO's costs. Singapore paid only a tenth of one per cent, but delegates from third-world countries began looking at each other and back towards the home capital trying to judge whether they'd be next to be called home.

Late in 1983, while the Liberals were still in power in Ottawa, another article reviewed the major reasons UNESCO funding by Western nations should end, concluding that while it "was most unlikely to happen, given current attitudes in Ottawa ... Ottawa should consider seriously following the American lead, at least until UNESCO gets back to its fundamental educational, scientific and cultural areas of concern." Given Prime Minister Pierre Trudeau's attitudes, that was most unlikely. Nothing out of Ottawa since Prime Minister Brian Mulroney took over suggests the Conservative government is any more likely to pull out. Pity.

Support for UNESCO surfaced in strange places, including the International Press Institute at its annual assembly in Amsterdam in the spring of 1983. IPI is an organization of free-world journalists. As a member of its executive committee I put a resolution to the closing session urging Western governments to cut off funding to UNESCO. The resolution was defeated, largely on the arguments of some very fine people, including Cushrow Irani, publisher of the *Calcutta Statesman*, a dedicated supporter of a free press. Their contention was that IPI should not suggest policy to governments. Fair enough.

IPI's chairman Max Sniders, then editor-in-chief of a Utrecht paper, had tried to prevent the resolution from being put, both in executive committee and in full assembly. He had ruled that the resolution was out of order because it had not been scrutinized by the resolutions committee. When I promised to challenge that ruling from the floor, he had let the resolution go to a vote. What was inexplicable was the prompt acceptance by the chair after my motion had been defeated of a motion expunging all reference to the resolution from the record. That's a characteristic tactic at international conferences where third-world and Soviet bloc delegates demonstrate the validity of Orwell's rewriting of history. At a conference of free-world journalists, such blatant rewriting of history was downright scary.

Later that year, Max turned up in the United States with plans to ask UNESCO to co-operate in a new international effort to be funded by UNESCO to protect journalists on dangerous assignments by issuing special press cards. This approach had been agreed at an informal meeting in Europe of several press organizations including one from Czechoslovakia. Max and his ideas met solid opposition in the United States. There was no way American publishers, editors, or reporters would have anything to do with identity cards under UNESCO or any other sponsorship. Canadian editors and publishers, who like me were not consulted, agreed fully with the Americans. Americans were blunt: "In some parts of the world, such a card would be sure to get you shot."

In a letter to Max I wrote that I'd "be delighted to talk to Mr. M'Bow, or even, with appropriate guarantees of safety, to Yuri Andropov or the Ayatollah Khomeini — but I would not trust funds to, or receive funds from any of them." I told Max the principle was the same I'd explained to a young lady working on implementation of the Kent Report who told me she could not understand why Canadian newspapers unanimously refused to accept government grants for Canadian overseas news bureaux.

"Miss, if I give you $1,000, for any reason, are there not going to be those who will consider you to be a lady of easy virtue?"

She smiled. "What you're saying is that it is the perception that counts in ethical as in sexual matters."

"Your discussions with UNESCO," the letter to Max continued, "exceeded your mandate from the executive committee — we've talked too long with UNESCO." At the next executive meeting in Rome a strong resolution put that kooky idea to rest.

About that time Lord McGregor of Durris, who headed the last royal commission on the press in Britain, had published a scathing indictment of UNESCO's efforts to control the flow of information around the world. He wrote that the lines have been drawn between states "which treat their media as instruments of government with a duty to justify and explain official policies, and a small minority of opposing states which sustain media as independent critics of government and all other concentrations of power."

Quoting Mac to Max (nice alliteration that), I used his concluding sentences. "These differences," he wrote, "are irreconcilable and beyond compromise. UNESCO may be approaching a tragic situation in which free countries can compromise no further. They may then be forced to weigh the advantages and disadvantages of membership."

Sadly, that's precisely what has had to happen.

The sooner other Western nations follow the American lead, UNESCO is reorganized, a new director general elected, the bureaucracy in Paris pruned and purged, and 80 per cent of UNESCO's budget is spent in the field rather than at headquarters, the sooner the Western world can begin giving UNESCO the financial support it needs and should have.

Of my decade's opposition to UNESCO on information gathered from the media, my own travels, and through the International Press Institute and the World Press Freedom Committee, I have no regrets. I do regret, however, not having accepted invitations to attend a conference organized by several journalists' groups as a direct result of UNESCO's efforts to control information. It was to meet at Talloires, France, in September 1983. I'd been overseas twice that year and was scheduled to go again in late November. Another overseas conference simply wasn't reasonable and I turned down invitations from IPI and from the U.S. group, WPFC, on whose executive committee I was also listed. When the Declaration of Talloires was released that fall, I'd have risked my hope of heaven (probably not worth much) to have had my name among the long list of those who signed that magnificent statement of what freedom of speech and freedom of speech in print means to free men and women.

In considerably less serious vein, I woke in a Paris hotel room the night after watching UNESCO delegates rolling away from the Paris headquarters. The refrain of a hymn of my youth, "What a Friend We Have in Jesus," repeated itself over and over. The parody was clear; I sat for an hour and scribbled these verses:

Hymn to M'Bow
(To be sung joyfully, allegro)

When M'Bow mutes all our voices
And we know our role in life

We shall balance all our ethics
and end our pluralistic strife.

We shall integrate our voices
to respond most joyfully
to the New World info order
and wear our harness cheerfully.

We shall never cause distortion,
we shall be his instrument.
His protection will be with us.
He will be our government.

When we are no longer problems
Plural views will not be heard.
We shall rest in M'Bow's bosom,
Stirring only at his word.

Glad to Move into Your Office — But...

What they are like on other newspapers I don't know, but around
the *London Free Press*, morning editorial conferences have great moments of humour.

One morning as the troops gathered to consider who we'd insult
in editorials on the morrow, there was good-natured teasing about
the supposed resentment of Rory Leishman's wife over his sharing
an office all day with Cheryl Hamilton, another editorial writer.
Cheryl not only has a mind like a steel trap, but also is perceptive,
articulate, and a most attractive young woman. She sat quietly while
the hazing continued, everybody saying they didn't want her in their
office — they'd also have spouse problems.

Ever the gallant ladies' man, even if bald and long in the tooth,
I charged in to the rescue. "Cheryl, don't you fuss about them. If
you've no place else to go you just move your desk right in here."

"But, Bill," she said without a second's hesitation, "where would
you go?"

Instrument of the Devil —
and Anti-Semitic, Too

Of all the attitudes newspapermen encounter, the most difficult to handle were the highly charged emotional concepts some people had towards the news. Reaction was strong enough towards many news stories. Writing editorials or signed opinion articles for the editorial page often brought explosive reactions. An editorial a few years ago on tension between Pakistan and India brought telephone calls the same morning from two professors at the University of Western Ontario. An Indian angrily charged that only a person paid by the Pakistani government could have written such a vicious and inaccurate article slandering India and Prime Minister Indira Gandhi. A Pakistani phoned an hour later. He wanted to know who was the Indian on our staff who had written such distorted garbage. One said he'd come down and shoot me. I said, "Fine, but don't complain if I break your skull with a two by four." He hung up.

This is known as equalizing the dissatisfaction.

A signed article suggesting that being a born-again Christian was a considerable handicap to President Carter brought phone calls describing me as a vicious instrument of the devil. Fundamentalists tend to think in black-and-white terms and to be unable to understand political and ethical subtleties.

It's normal for an article describing Russia's growing armaments on land, sea, and in the air to be followed by verbal and written abuse from Marxist-Leninist and other left-wing groups. Editorials urging stricter gun laws bring equally virulent responses from the extreme right.

It helped in dealing with phone calls to insist on obtaining the name of the caller. Repeating a person's name back to him sometimes tended to make him feel a little more responsible for what he said — though not always by any means. If a person refused to identify himself or herself, I said "You know who I am," and hung up. Anonymous mail went into the wastepaper basket without being read, though secretaries who opened the mail were sometimes subjected to obscene language to which they should not have had to be exposed.

Of all the subjects which have generated the strongest, sometimes downright vicious and obscene, responses, the Middle East was, and still is, by far the worst. Some of the more emotionally committed on both sides of that perennial conflict took the position that if a writer was not absolutely on their side, he was against them and they never missed an opportunity to say so. Because of a conviction that if a third world war ever starts, which God forbid, it is more likely to start in the Middle East than anywhere else, I travelled widely in Egypt, Cyprus, Lebanon, Israel, Jordan, Iran, and Syria, among others, eight or ten times in a dozen years, writing scores of articles on Palestinian refugee camps, civil war in Lebanon, fighting on the borders of Israel, the occupation of the Golan Heights and the Gaza Strip, and the wars along the Suez Canal. Doing so put me on the visiting list of Israelis and Arabs and of local Jews and Arabs.

On my desk was half of an anti-tank shell picked up in the Sinai desert on the east bank of the Suez Canal following the 1973 war. Weighing about five pounds, it sported viciously sharp edges. As it was the lower half of the business end of the shell, its flat base made it an excellent paperweight. Added character came from an enamelled badge worn by soldiers serving in the United Nations peacekeeping force.

When Arabs came to the office, whether they were Canadians or of Arab descent, journalists from Egypt or Syria, or diplomats from Ottawa embassies, invariably they noticed the broken shell with its U.N. badge. I told them that's "an Egyptian anti-tank shell I picked up beside a burned-out Israeli tank." Usually there were smug smiles. When Israeli diplomats and journalists and Canadian Jews came to the office, they too asked questions. They were told it was an Israeli anti-tank shell picked up along the Suez Canal beside a burned-out Egyptian tank. Their smiles were equally self-satisfied.

If these partisan visitors knew anything about such weapons, they would have known at a glance that shell had never been fired by anyone at anything. The band of relatively soft metal ringing the tough steel near the base did not have the ridges it would have acquired as it was spun by the rifling inside the barrel. Also, if it had been fired and hit a tank turret, it would have exploded into many small pieces after smashing through the tank turret. That particular shell had been stored as spare ammunition outside the tank where it was hit by an enemy shell. It simply blew up, leaving the rear third in a jagged but still recognizable piece. It was dishonest to bait visitors but I rationalized by telling myself one good lie deserves another.

Lies are epidemic in the Middle East. Arabs and Israelis both indulge. Israeli lies include their story about what happened to Kuneitra. Captured and occupied by triumphant Israeli forces in the 1967 war, it was occupied until after the 1973 war, when the area was turned back to the Syrians as part of a ceasefire on the Golan Heights arranged by the United Nations. Before that happened, however, I saw Kuneitra in 1971 while cruising the Golan Heights in a rented car. My wife and I drove and walked through the city for half a day. It had been picked over as thoroughly as a garbage dump after Calcutta street urchins were finished. Every house was empty not only of furniture but also of plumbing and electric fixtures, pipes and wires. Door and window frames had been ripped out. Fair enough. It was conquered territory and to the victor belong the spoils. But the buildings still stood. War damage was minimal. The structures were sound.

My second visit to Kuneitra was from the Syrian side on a quick tour of the Middle East with the then minister of national defence, James Richardson. He visited Damascus, arranging among other things for the resumption into Syria of Canadian and other United Nations supply flights. These had been discontinued after the Syrians shot down a Canadian aircraft, killing several aboard.

Journalists in the party were bussed to Kuneitra in a Syrian "show and tell" anti-Israel propaganda effort. It was all very emotional, with guides cranking out the current Syrian propaganda of the day. Their dramatic gestures and emotional appeals, however, couldn't obscure that they were telling the truth. Before the Israelis evacuated the city they blew it up.

In an article I reviewed the evidence which indicated clearly that Kuneitra was not bombed or shelled enough to destroy it. The houses had been carefully demolished by explosives placed at the four corners of each building. "In a war, the enemy's strong points are fair game ... militarily ... the destruction of Kuneitra was understandable, and it might even be justifiable. Israelis, however, piously say that they did not demolish it, that it was destroyed by shellfire. They then go on to protest that Syria is not carrying out its agreement to repopulate the city as evidence of good faith in the ceasefire. Considering the present state of the city, there's no way the Syrians can reoccupy the city, and the Israelis not only know it, but caused the situation about which they complain. What is puzzling about the Israeli demolition of Kuneitra is why they are lying about it."

There was a curious aftermath. The article was reprinted by Arab propaganda magazines which brought an invitation to testify before the United Nation's Special Committee on Human Rights which was investigating "Israeli practices affecting the human rights of the population of the occupied territories." I replied that everything "strongly suggests that your committee, while properly constituted and authorized by the United Nations Assembly, is part of a clearly evident effort on the part of a majority of Asian, African and Arab nations to discredit Israel."

> While I have been, and continue to be, a strong supporter of the United Nations, there has been a distressing tendency toward double standards ... not so much supporting Palestinian right to self-determination as ... attempting to deny it to Israelis ...
>
> I'm doubtful if it would serve any valid purpose to appear in Geneva to talk to your committee. Indeed, reading reports of some such committees suggests that if my view did not conform to the preconceived notions of the committee members, it would not appear in your reports. If your committee is prepared to give me control over the content of my remarks in your report, I would reconsider.

No more was heard from the United Nations Special Committee on Human Rights.

Yet protests about the Kuneitra article from Canadian Jews were vociferous. The stories varied, but endlessly they repeated the theme that Kuneitra had been destroyed in the fighting. Asked, "Were you there after the 1973 fighting?" they had to say no, because Israelis and North American Jews were not exactly welcome in Damascus and Kuneitra after it had been reoccupied by Syria. As my article noted, there was nothing wrong with blowing up Kuneitra. Conquering armies have destroyed cities since the beginning of time. But it made me angry when Israelis who knew better tried to argue that Kuneitra had been destroyed in the fighting. Years later I asked an Israeli in their foreign office why his government had lied about Kuneitra.

"I don't know," he replied. "We lost a lot of credibility on that one."

He was right. However, Israelis by and large come off well in comparison with Arab lies. I'd encountered Arab lies many times in the Middle East but never more sharply delineated than during a week's seminar on the media and the Arab world, sponsored by Arab money and organized by an American professor who seemed determined to spout every propaganda line generated by Arab states. At the closing session he was decorated by the president of Lebanon, who had just finished thoroughly insulting Western journalists. The president spoke in Arabic. When he finished we assumed he'd said something polite and gave him a rousing round of applause which allowed some local papers in Arabic to report that the Western journalists attending the seminar agreed vociferously with the president's criticism.

Another pro-Arab at the seminar was the late Dr. A. C. Forrest, editor and publisher of the *United Church Observer*. Early in the sessions Forrest made an impassioned speech in which he repeated most of the clichés of Palestinian attitudes towards Israel and endorsed all of them. He was an unequivocal supporter of the Palestinians, strongly critical of Israel and almost as strongly critical of the Western media.

I'd had frequent contact with Forrest when I was chairman of the Division of Communications of the United Church of Canada (in effect chairman of the board of Ryerson Press). As the board published the *Observer*, technically I was Forrest's boss for several years. I had always supported him in his handling of Middle East coverage because of his verbal assurances that he was not committed to the Arab cause. He argued he visited and talked to both sides and reported it as he saw it. Sometimes his reports strained credibility and I suggested that if he looked harder he might find something complimentary about Israel and Israelis. Basically, however, he had my support, though there were those on the board who questioned what they felt was his bias.

Beirut opened my eyes. When Forrest sat down I scribbled a note saying his problem was not that he supported the Arab cause but that he insisted he was an unbiased, impartial editor who was merely telling it as he saw it. His speech destroyed that façade completely. He should declare himself publicly on his return home as a dedicated supporter of the Palestinian cause. His readers would then assess his writing on that basis. Later I told him his posture was dishonest. Given his speech in Beirut, Toronto Jews were quite right to be concerned about his reporting and commentary. Nothing changed.

Another intriguing sidelight to that Beirut seminar was the anguished plea of many speakers for greater balance in Western coverage of Arab nations. When they weren't insulting about Western coverage, they were rude, and when they weren't rude they were grossly uninformed. After listening to the tirades for a few days, I blew my stack and took strong exception to the tone of the conference.

In any Arab country I'd visited it was often virtually impossible to go anywhere or see anyone. In Egypt, despite a week's trying, I was denied a visit to the Suez Canal. In Jordan I was not allowed to visit a Palestinian guerrilla camp, though I got to a refugee camp.

In Lebanon I was not allowed south of the Litani into the area where Palestinians were raiding into Israel. Censorship, rigid control of travel, and close-mouthed officials were universal. Arabs were irrational to ask for coverage by Western journalists who were not allowed to see or hear anything for themselves. The response was that Arab doors were always open to their friends, which was an outright lie — and they knew it.

The contrast in Israel was dramatic. To see the Golan Heights when Kuneitra was in Israeli hands, it was easy to rent a car and drive there. To see the Suez Canal from the Israeli side, a phone call to army public relations brought a car and a driver to the hotel door next morning. To talk to an Arab tribal leader in the Gaza Strip to whom I'd been introduced, another rented car got me there without hassle and a captain in the Israeli occupation force went out of his way to give directions.

Many Arabs are assiduous in attempting to flim-flam reporters. So are Israelis, but they're more sophisticated about it. They let you see for yourself and then try to persuade you to their point of view, which is fair ball.

The biggest lie of all was that so many Arabs, and Arab nations, indulged in the most extravagant rhetoric about their support for the Palestinian cause, while carefully refraining from any real commitment to help the Palestinians achieve their dream of a national homeland. Too many Arab nations want to retain the Palestinians as pawns in their game of shafting the Americans while milking both the Americans and the Russians of aid and arms.

I chuckled wryly during an earlier visit to Beirut over the vehement protestations of Palestinians in Lebanon that the Lebanese were solidly behind them in their war against Israel. The civil war that finally exploded in 1975 and 1976, in which at least 50,000 people died, gave the lie to that. Dedicated supporters of the Palestinians there were, but they were by no means in the majority. When the civil war broke out it was a fight between those who wanted to join the Palestinians in a holy war against Israel and those who wanted to continue trading, as Phoenicians have done for millennia, for profit. Christian Lebanese and many Moslem Lebanese merely wanted the Palestinians out of the country. When these divergent objectives eventually erupted into civil war, scores of thousands of Lebanese and Palestinians died. Lebanon has been a battlefield ever since.

Other Arab nations react to the Palestinians with deep suspicion. Egypt allows few into the country and then only under the most rigid police controls. After all, Egyptians really don't see themselves as Arabs; they are proudly Egyptian. Syria allows Palestinian units to exist, but they are as much under the control of senior Syrian military authorities as any Syrian army unit; they are prisoners in guarded camps. Kuwait and Saudi Arabia welcome them not as freedom fighters but as workers in the oil fields and in business, provided they support the anti-Israel rhetoric of the Arab world without doing anything specific about disrupting oil-rich countries' sales to Europe and the United States. Jordan fought a bloody war to break Palestinian power in the land, which was almost equal that of King Hussein. I found it easier to get through Jordanian checkpoints than Palestinian checkpoints — in Jordan.

Irrationality is also evident among Palestinians. On the first visit to Beirut I visited Palestinian refugee camps in and around Beirut. In one, a young man was assigned by camp authorities (PLO agents) as an escort through the camp. As we visited day-care centres for children, food distribution depots, talked to Palestinian youths who had trained in guerrilla camps and to sad-eyed mothers who knew their sons had virtually no hope of surviving the then frequent raids into Israel, my escort talked about himself. He was a teacher of history and English. "I teach my pupils to hate. I teach them to hate the Americans who give so much aid to the Jews. I teach them to hate the Jews who stole our land from us. I teach them to hate all our enemies who prevent us from returning to the land we love."

"Do you teach much history or English?"

His command of English was not quite good enough or he was too emotionally involved to understand the insult.

"Oh, yes," he replied, "I teach them history so they know why they must hate the Jews and I teach them English so they may tell the world why they hate the Jews."

He also made it clear during the afternoon's walk around the camp that he was committed unto death to the Palestinian cause. Nothing would ever divert him from fighting all his life for the cause, for that great day when he and his people would drive the hated Jew out of their promised land and return it to the sons and daughters of those who would fight and die so valiantly. The refugee camp guide spoiled his contribution to the Palestinian cause by drawing me aside as we headed for the gate where I'd get a taxi back to Beirut. Making quite sure we were not overheard, he urgently asked the question he'd been saving all afternoon.

"Do you know anyone at the Canadian embassy in Beirut?"

Sensing what was coming, I allowed I did. He pressed a grubby calling card, Arabic and English, into my hand. "Will you tell them how much I want to go to Canada, please? I have called there several times and they will not let me go."

"But what about your dedication to the Palestinian cause?"

"Ah," he replied triumphantly, "I can continue the fight for freedom in Canada. Canadians," he added ingratiatingly, "know how the Jews have treated Palestinians. That is why I want to go there."

"Would you continue to teach young people to hate Jews?"

"Of course." He was eager now. "Canadians need to understand how Palestinians can hate."

"Maybe that's why the embassy officials won't let you go as an immigrant."

He was honestly puzzled. I told him Canadians are strange people. They expected people who settled in Canada to become Canadians and not bring with them the hatreds they knew where they came from. He began a heated argument which wasn't worth pursuing, so I mollified him by taking his card and promising to speak to the embassy people next day. At the thought of getting away from the refugee camp his hatred and anger dissolved into supplication again. His attitudes were as illuminating as the squalor and agony of his people crowded into their refugee camp on Beirut's outskirts.

Several years later my wife and I visited another family in an apartment in Jerusalem where we met the teenage son of an Ontario doctor who was going to school in Israel. The couple were in their late fifties. She showed us the tattoo number of the German concentration camp she'd survived. The youth was arrogant and objectionable — Israelis were destined to rule the Middle East, Israel would conquer Lebanon, most of Syria to the Euphrates, all of Jordan "except the desert where the nomads could live," and build a new state out of the chaos of the Arab world. The older couple listened and said nothing.

The youth, warming to his topic, shouted other outrageous concepts. Jews in Israel needed Arabs who lived there, as "hewers of wood and drawers of water," while Israelis pursued more intellectual activities. To achieve its destiny Israel had to have second-class citizens like Arabs.

"Do your classmates agree with your views?"

"Of course."

"And your teachers?"

"Of course. It is the natural order of things."

The older couple appeared to be unaware of how similar was the thinking of the Canadian youth who visited their home each weekend to the warped ideas of the Nazis they so hated and feared in World War II. We had planned to stay and talk most of the evening. An hour was enough. Making excuses about a non-existent appointment, we left, sorrowing. Faced with such arrogance in an Ontario-born youth, I worry.

Locally, relations with the Jewish and Arabic communities went through several years of tension, followed by relative calm, even acceptance. In 1975 there was an editorial from the *London Free Press* reprinted in the *Canadian Jewish News*, a Toronto weekly. The editorial warned that Israel should be wary of Russian offers to guarantee Israel's security in return for Israel withdrawing from all occupied Arab territory. "If it weren't such a serious business," the editorial continued, "it would be hilarious — Russia of all nations, piously urging Israel to give up its occupied territories." That's a doubly valid comment now that Russia has occupied Afghanistan.

In the beginning, however, it was more difficult. On returning from my first visit to the Middle East in 1968 I was invited to speak one weekend at a synagogue and the next at a mosque. The speech delivered to both audiences was careful to make both sides equally unhappy; another instance of equalizing the dissatisfaction. "Israelis have fallen back on the old biblical injunction of an eye for an eye or a tooth for a tooth, only now they want a whole mouthful of teeth, while the Arabs are living in a dream world of their own making, seeking only revenge."

The essence of the talk was a conviction, reiterated often in the following decade and to this day, that there is no hope of a peaceful solution to the problems in the Middle East until the national aspirations of the Palestinians are met. On the same visit to the Middle East an article on the Palestinians noted that "the people who once lived in Palestine have a simple case to make. They just want to go back to their lands and homes."

Another article stressed that "as long as the Israeli scorns the Arab, and laughs at his impotence and frustration, the Arab will continue to react as he does, with implacable hatred ... The initiative lies in Israeli hands because they are the victors." The headline referred to the Palestinians in exile as "New Jews seeking their promised land." While Arabs in London and Toronto were quick to respond to critical comment about the Palestinians or other Arab nations, most of the local problems came from Canadian Jews. Canadians of Arab birth or descent were not nearly as vociferous as were Canadian Jews, possibly because there were relatively few of them and those not born in Canada had difficulty expressing themselves fluently in English. Some Jews made it clear that unless I demonstrated publicly and frequently 120 per cent support for the Israeli side of the Middle East conflict, I was on the side of the Arabs.

That was frustrating because my tilt, if there was one, was the other way. I made many good friends among Arabs of several nationalities and sympathized deeply with the dispossessed Palestinians, but in no Arab nation was there anything approaching democracy. An exception, until the mid-1970s, was Lebanon, where an uneasy balance between Christians and Moslems erupted into a bloody civil war and an Israeli invasion which is still destroying the country.

Israel is a democracy, for all its strengths and faults. The most serious fault is the requirement that full citizens be Jews. Technically that makes Israel a theocracy, not a democracy. Neither a Christian nor a Moslem can enjoy the full rights of Israeli citizenship, though both can live in the country as thousands of Christians and more than a million Palestinian Arabs attest. There are representatives of Israel's Arab population in the Knesset but they are not in proportion to the population and are relatively ineffective.

Saying so irritates North American Jews more than almost any other criticism. They are proud and rightly so of Israel's Jewishness, of Israel's democracy, of their determination to forge a Jewish enclave in the land of their fathers, and of their astonishing success in doing so. Yet if it is suggested that Israel is a theocracy many react vigorously, denying the obvious fact that citizenship is dependent on religious courts which determine whether a person is a Jew. Israelis are more honest and realistic. Israeli newspapers report the convoluted religious arguments associated with a person trying to prove they had a Jewish parent to qualify for citizenship. Other nations have such restrictions; the Ayatollah Khomeini is not granting citizenship to Christians. What's odd is that North American Jews know about the Israeli restriction but resent the fact being mentioned. It may have something to do with knowing that if Jews in Canada were restricted to the same citizenship status here that Christians have in Israel, the outcry would be understandably noisy.

In Israel restrictions turn up in other areas, some irritating, others merely amusing. A waiter at the Dan Hotel in Tel Aviv refused me cream with coffee after beef for dinner. Kosher meals don't mix meat and dairy products. The Dan is kosher. I politely explained I wasn't a Jew.

"No, sir, I'm sorry, but I can't serve it to you."

Looking at the menu for dessert, it listed ice cream. I ordered that, triumphantly spooned a large scoop of vanilla into coffee and caught the waiter's eye. He stayed one up.

"That ice cream is made from a vegetable base, sir."

Next meal included a small container of cream from a nearby delicatessen. The waiter shrugged. I was rude; normally, it's proper to respect the customs and laws of any country. The truculence of the Israeli in his native environment has to be experienced to be believed; it leads to reciprocal rudeness.

It's not only directed at Gentiles. I've heard Israelis being far more scornful and derogatory towards North American Jews than towards Christians. Many Israelis look on many North American Jews as "fat cows to be milked" and have used that phrase to me more than once.

Israeli aggressiveness, however, is what makes the country work. What impressed me most on my first visit, in a superficial but nevertheless meaningful way, was the contrast with Cairo where I'd been a week or ten days. In Tel Aviv and Jerusalem, telephones worked. Five minutes after checking into the Dan Hotel on Tel Aviv's waterfront, I was talking to my wife in Canada. A week of trying in Cairo yielded only disinterested shrugs from telephone operators. Cairo taxis were crumbling disaster areas. Tel Aviv taxis purred contentedly.

Underneath that superficial façade, however, Israelis live in a state of continuous tension. As the 1970s arrived, Israel's internal troubles, indications of which I'd seen and reported in the late 1960s, became more apparent. The country's economy was in chaos, with inflation reaching 400 per cent per year. Israelis are deeply divided on the best way to maintain national security. Many retain the truculent intransigence which had marked Israeli reaction to their Arab enemies for three decades and believe that only direct, hard-hitting, continuous, and aggressive military action will ensure Israel's survival. Surprisingly large numbers believe that Israel has to learn to live with its Arab neighbours, which requires concessions involving the territory captured in the 1967 war, particularly the West Bank. Few Israelis will even discuss the possibility of returning any part of Jerusalem to Jordanian rule; on that issue most of them would stake their lives. The moderates march two-score thousand at a time carrying signs, PEACE NOW. The militants march equally strong, carrying signs, NEVER AGAIN. The government often seems in disarray as the bewildering collection of parties which make up the Knesset struggle to maintain enough support from opposing factions to continue to govern. As in the early days of Israel, when government troops fired on Jewish militants importing arms for their own war, new militants were blowing up Arab mayors in the occupied territories and challenging the Israeli government to do anything about it.

Despite these and a great many other troubles, Israel is a lively, sophisticated, exciting place where irritation at the truculence evident on every side is more than balanced by what they have achieved in a tiny land under unbelievable handicaps. While I admire all the fine qualities of the Israelis, I can never forget Palestinian refugees in the camps and their more prosperous countrymen in a dozen Arab nations, who have a simple dream, common to all the millions who have been disposed in this century's wars.

My attempts to present a balance, however, failed to satisfy some Jews in London, Toronto, and elsewhere. There was abuse on the telephone and by mail from many who were so dedicated to the Israeli cause and were so deeply (and understandably) conscious of the obscene fate of their people at the hands of the Nazis that they could not tolerate the slightest criticism of any action by people whose slogan was "never again." Despite the rude, crude, and insulting mail and telephone calls, there were wiser and I like to think more appreciative Jews in London who could always be counted upon to give helpful advice. Among them were Burt Myron, then president of Kaiser-Roth, a local hosiery and lingerie manufacturing firm; Sydney Vaisler, a clothing retailer; and a personal friend, Larry Agranove. He took considerable abuse in the Jewish community over his friendship with the local editor who insisted on writing what he saw and heard in the Middle East. Sue Agranove once had a wall plaque made for her husband, with incidents and sayings associated with his life pressed into the clay by metal type. One line stemmed from his having to say constantly, "I am not responsible for the editorial opinions of William Heine."

Larry voiced strong, and hurt, opinions when a few months after becoming editor I was invited to join the London Club. He was incensed that I'd join the city's leading business and professional club which had no Jewish members and, indeed, years ago had black-balled former Londoner and Ontario Supreme Court judge Meyer Lerner. He had a point, of course, but I argued reform would come only from within. Larry wasn't impressed.

A few years later another Jew was proposed as member. The day voting was scheduled I dropped into the office of all *Free Press* managers who were London Club members and offered to drive them to the club to vote. There were no black balls this time. And a year or two later, when Sue wanted to give her husband a London Club membership as a birthday present, I was delighted to be one of his sponsors. To this day we lunch there regularly.

Incidentally, women are not members of London Club, nor are members allowed to bring women as guests, which is irrational and a bit ridiculous. To women who argue with me about it I have a flip retort, that I'll cheerfully open up the club the day I can join the Imperial Order of Daughters of the Empire. All that reply earns is a glare. Actually, I agree with them fully — not enough to resign on the issue, but enough that when membership for both sexes comes up, as it probably will soon, I'll just as enthusiastically drive supporters to the voting which will be needed to change the club's by-laws.

Larry wasn't consulted, however, when London suffered a period of vicious anti-Semitism sparked by a local apartment building owner, Martin Weiche. Self-styled leader of the Canadian National Socialist Party, Weiche was (and is as far as I know, since he has faded from public view) an unreconstructed Nazi who believed that Canada needed another purging of Jews and was prepared to take over as leader to do it. The crude swastikas which decorated his mimeographed hate sheets were appropriate symbols for the viciousness printed on them. He lived in a large home on the outskirts of London with a high fence, grounds patrolled by police dogs, searchlights at night, and other paraphernalia of his ilk.

He was not adverse to physical intimidation, either. I looked up from my desk after we'd published an editorial on his dangerous nonsense to find him stomping into my office in a long leather coat which reached to his ankles. Flanking him on either side were two stupid-looking goons also in long leather coats, one with a police dog on a leash. There's only one way to deal with a kook like that. I grabbed a paperweight, a heavy oil drill bit which had been 10,000 feet down in the Mackenzie delta, and started across the room at the obscene trio. The thought they might be physically dangerous never crossed my mind. Bullies usually don't think fast enough to deal with the unexpected.

"Don't you dare come into my office without an appointment," I shouted. "You get the hell out of here and stay out."

Weiche mumbled something about an editorial.

"You want to talk about an editorial, you phone and ask and you come here alone. Get out."

They backed to the door, past my secretaries and down the hall. I left them halfway to the front door and went back to the office, trembling, breathing hard and now they'd gone, scared. In six years of war I'd not seen a German, even a prisoner-of-war, but Nazi viciousness was vivid in my mind. To encounter the mindless evil of Nazi fascism face to face was nothing else than frightening. He never came back, alone or with his goons.

Our first major exposure to Weiche also created a conflict in the Jewish community. Weiche turned up downtown one morning and began handing out anti-Semitic leaflets. The newsroom soon had one, sent a reporter and photographer to interview him, and wondered what to do about coverage. Hundreds of people had been handed the leaflets; the story could not be ignored. Yet publishing anything at all about Weiche and his tainted concepts was exactly what he wanted. We kicked it around internally for an hour or two and finally concluded it was a page-one story with picture. We would follow that coverage with a strong editorial condemning hate-mongering of that or any other kind. Then we'd let him hand out literature as long as he wanted, without further coverage, unless he was arrested or there was some other disturbance.

Some Jews in London reacted with highly charged emotionalism. How dare we publish stories about hate literature? Were we Nazis at heart ourselves? Were Jews not safe in London, Ontario? Did we understand what that man meant to men and women who'd lost their parents, their husbands or wives, or their children in the Nazi gas chambers? Had we no decency? Were we interested only in sensationalism to sell newspapers? Some of the responses were so emotionally distressed they could hardly voice their horror or fear. Others were coldly and dangerously furious.

I reminded all of them that in a free society the only way to deal with such people was to expose them to the light. If nothing were written about such people as Martin Weiche, the evil they represented would fester and grow, in part because there would be no one to label it for what it was. An aroused community would deal with Nazi hate-mongers far more effectively if people knew what was going on. The six million Jews who went to the death camps began going there without the world knowing the truth; silence made the death camps possible. To Jewish callers there was no point in stressing the often forgotten fact that another six or seven million non-Jews also died in German concentration camps; what was horrifying about the treatment of Jews was that those who died represented such a large proportion of European Jewry. It was gratifying to have the support of London Jews who understood what was happening. Weiche faded from public consciousness largely because the people of London recognized him for what he was, a warped mind.

Yet that year there were reports that some in the Jewish community were saying, publicly and frequently, that I was anti-Semitic. Incensed, not only as a professional journalist but as a person who believes sincerely in the brotherhood of man, I wrote a three-page letter to Syd Vaisler, then president of London Jewish Community Council, rewrote it, put it aside for a week, heard the rumours again, rewrote it again, waited another few weeks to cool off, polished it again, and finally delivered it to Syd. Parts of it read: "Two or three times in recent months I have been told by friends about comments by some members of London's Jewish community who ... consider me anti-Semitic."

A long paragraph outlined my visits to Israel and Arab countries and access to influential Israelis who considered my reporting critical but fair, and mentioned a formal report by the Canada-Israel Committee which considered my articles to be "unusually well-informed and perceptive" about Middle East problems and other aspects of coverage of the problem there. I quoted John Donne's beautiful lines from the sixteenth century that "no man is an island ... any man's death diminishes me" and went on to note that "it is as intolerable for members of the minority group to discriminate against a person they think is part of a majority group, as it is for the reverse to occur." "I detect the beginnings of an attempt by some members of the Jewish community to discriminate against me ... (because) ... I am not a dedicated supporter of the most extreme elements of Zionism ... and ... allowed anti-Zionists, both Jewish and others, to express their sentiments in this newspaper ... Several years ago ... I wrote that when all else failed in efforts to persuade writers to support Zionism, the ultimate weapon was to charge anti-Semitism. Though I predicted it, I'm not going to sit quietly while it happens to me."

Reminding Syd that he had asked me to consult him on any serious question concerning the London Jewish Community, I wrote that if another charge of anti-Semitism came to my attention, "I will consider whether to begin a civil suit against the persons involved. I think it is time a precedent was established that it is as illegal for a Jew to incite hatred against a Gentile on invalid charges of anti-Semitism as it is for a Gentile to incite hatred against a Jew because he is a member of a minority religious group."

A couple of people to whom the letter was shown before sending it said it was an over-reaction. Maybe so, but the tag of racial discrimination was intolerable. The letter was delivered.

Two weeks later Syd replied most graciously. He had discussed the letter with the executive board of his organization and wrote that "all members of the Executive stated most emphatically that they did not consider you to be anti-Semitic in any way and further, that as far as they knew, this was the general feeling in the Community." If there were any, "these individuals represent a very small minority." While his organization was informal and could not be responsible for the opinion of individual members, he and his board would "do all we can to make clear ... our utter rejection of the imputation of anti-Semitism to you." I was grateful.

How or what they did I don't know and didn't ask, but there were no further rumours of anti-Semitism about the editor of the local newspaper.

Business as Usual
in the Wee Sma' Hours

The phone rang one morning at 3 A.M. Groggily answering it, I heard the voice of a local lawyer, very angry, demanding that a story about his client in the morning paper be killed for the afternoon paper and an apology published. At that hour, the press run was almost finished. There was no point in getting excited until business hours, so pretending to show some concern appeared indicated.

"Ah huh, OK, let me check it out — get back to you."

Next morning the story was double-checked. Perfectly valid. His client had been found guilty of impaired driving and fined $200. It was ordered into the afternoon paper, with an aside to my secretary to answer the phone for the afternoon and not pass on calls from the lawyer.

Going to bed that night, I set the alarm for 3 A.M., and phoned the lawyer at home. After a long time his wife answered.

"But he's asleep."

"This is important, wake him up."

Another long wait, then a muffled voice came on the line.

"Yes?"

"It's Bill Heine, from the *Free Press*."

"Goddam it, it's 3 o'clock in the morning."

"Yes, I know, I thought that was when you did all your business."

He hung up. For years, at various functions, he avoided me like the plague. Word got around, partly because I was not adverse to telling the tale, and in seventeen years there were only one or two other such calls.

Process Servers — Bah!
and Libel Suits — Ugh!

Most people who came to the office called ahead or asked from the lobby or at least put their head in to see if the bald-headed old bastard of an editor was busy. Not process servers. Manifestations of their ilk for a time marched into my office, growled "You the editor?" and slapped a wad of paper on the desk. That cheesed me off.

One day a nondescript nitwit barged in while I was talking to a visitor. That did it. I dressed him down in fine army style, like a spit-and-polish colonel blasting a private with mud on his boots. He trotted out meekly, waited in the hall, and tapped gently on the door after the visitor left. After that they were more courteous, even though there was a sudden rash of libel suits.

It started when a city detective, George Bruton, arrested a former candidate for mayor, self-styled "Airborne Fairborn." Fairborn's campaign tactics had included parachuting into the city to attend political rallies. During the arrest (long after the mayoralty campaign) Fairborn used language to Bruton which, when repeated in the *Free Press* by a reporter who was there, caused Bruton to sue the paper for libel.

I was quite prepared to let him take his libel suit to court and said so vociferously. Police and editors expect to hear nasty things said about them on occasion. The *Free Press* lawyer thought maybe there'd been a libel. The publisher, over my strong objection, settled out of court. That was a mistake.

In the next few years libel suits flowed through the door like the Mississippi in flood. Usually the suits were threats to try to persuade the newspaper not to report things people didn't want reported, even though the matter was clearly in the public domain. By then the publisher had come around to agreeing we should fight every one on the assumption our reporters usually reported facts we could prove were true, which is the ultimate defence against libel. Maybe the publisher wasn't fully convinced; he might merely have decided to let the editor have enough rope to hang himself. Anyway, with new lawyers for libel matters I was free to fight.

The Board of Directors, however, became understandably edgy one year when we (read the editor) had eighteen libel suits pending. Asked to comment to the board, I said all the writs were "attempts to pressure us not to report what is happening. None of them is likely to come to trail" — and went about my business with fingers crossed.

Once in a while we settled quickly out of court when it was obvious we'd goofed. Most of the time I checked with the legal eagles and left it to them to acknowledge receipt of the writ. Then we did nothing. Neither, usually, did those who issued writs. Soon even their lawyers gave up. A libel suit can be expensive.

Libel is about the only instance where it is up to the defendant to prove he's not guilty. Failure to do so gives the case to the plaintiff. Yet juries usually have a healthy respect for an open society and, unless they detect malice or sheer stupidity on the part of a newspaper, tend to be skeptical of pressure tactics by individuals unreasonably claiming libel damages.

As I recall, all eighteen of the batch of libel suits which rightly caused the board concern lapsed after the original writ was received. In a few instances where the matter was a public issue and we were very sure of our facts, I added insult to injury by approving the alleged libel being repeated after the writ was served.

Incidentally, for a quick definition of libel, try this: It is to offer publicly in some permanent form (a newspaper, book, radio or television broadcast) a slander (the verbal form) which diminishes the professional or personal reputation of a person (with emphasis on his or her professional means of earning a living) in the eyes of reasonable persons reading, seeing or hearing the material. For instance, you might get away with calling a doctor a shyster, a minister a quack, and a lawyer a hypocrite, but don't call a doctor a quack, a minister a hypocrite, and a lawyer a shyster. It isn't necessary to publish 130,000 newspapers. One letter which gets into the wrong hands translates slander (what you say) to libel (what you publish or broadcast).

Things get far more complicated than that, of course, but that's said to be reasonably sound law.

Example of a quick settlement: Our Stratford bureau reported that an alderman had said at a council meeting, in effect, that another alderman, who was a teacher, was there to ensure higher salaries for teachers. That very definitely damaged his professional and personal reputation both as a teacher and as an alderman. Seeing the comment in the morning paper, I didn't consult our lawyers. I made loud noises, the echoes of which were clearly heard by night editors as well as by our reporter in Stratford. I wrote a personal apology to the libelled teacher and ordered an apology published prominently in the next day's paper.

The original story, with a copy of the letter and the printed apology, went by hand to our solicitors with a covering note asking them to "make the best settlement you can if a writ comes in." It did and they did, but with minimal payment because of the prompt apology.

All of which illustrates that when you're in the hot seat you quickly learn a hell of a lot more libel law than most lawyers. It's called survival instinct.

Newspaper Men Ain't News

Jack Gore, sometime managing editor of the *London Free Press*, a cantankerous character who ran the newsroom with a firm hand, had a flat rule: "If it happens to a newsman, it ain't news."

He may have been right. Who's to judge when journalists become newsworthy? Thomas Barnes made *The Times* what it became to generations of British readers. When he died in 1841, his obituary was one line in the days when an obscure baronet rated a column of pious prose. Undoubtedly the paper's greatest editor, he disregarded society, had few friends, and lived only for *The Times*. His brief obituary he had himself insisted upon before he left this world to investigate life's last great story.

His successor, J. T. Delane, was also a great editor. He spent much time with royalty and prime ministers, knew everyone who was anyone, was privy to most of England's secrets, published many of them, and was duly honoured at great length in *The Times* as a public figure when he left to find out where Barnes had gone. Gore would have disapproved.

While most journalists seldom make news in their own field, they may find themselves making headlines in other areas. I had it happen more than once, most hilariously over a novel written in 1974 which is still going strong. *The Last Canadian* for some years has been on the list of books for use in Ontario high school English classes. It became the Case of the Confused Censors and brought page-one coverage in several newspapers.

A phone call from the *Owen Sound Sun-Times* started it. "Did you know," a young reporter asked, "that your book *The Last Canadian* has been banned in Grey County by the Board of Education?"

I replied it was flattering to be in such distinguished company as Margaret Laurence. To radio interviewers I said the novel had no four-letter words, not enough sex to titilate a Victorian virgin, and little violence, except the ultimate violence of most people on this continent being wiped out by germ warfare. It is the story of survivors in an almost empty continent.

In the Owen Sound story, Cathy McKay quoted me that "after the book came out, the University of Western Ontario *Gazette* reviewed it and ... panned it terribly because it had no sex in it." In a subsequent editorial, the *Sun-Times* wrote that "we're fed up with the puritanical attitude exhibited almost every year by some members of the Grey County Board of Education as they bring down their censor's hatchets on books recommended for use in the schools — for all the usual foolish reasons." Referring to *Viva Cicano* by Frank Bonham, *My Shadow Ran Fast* by Bill Sands, and *The Last Canadian*, the editorial said all three books "have significant messages in them and the authors and their books have been well received. Except in Grey County." The *Sun-Times* added that this "recent shameful example of book-control is no credit to those trustees who backed the form of banning."

The *London Free Press* did not comment editorially. Norman Ibsen, editorial-page editor, said it was happening so often in Grey County it was hardly worth writing about. If a *Free Press* editorial condemned the Grey board's decision, as we would if one were written, it would appear to be self-serving on the part of the editor. Not having that editorial was one of the hazards the publisher of the *Free Press* faced in having an editor who wrote novels as a hobby instead of golfing or curling like most normal people on staff.

The publisher of *The Last Canadian*, Jim Smallwood of Paper-Jacks, sent twenty promotional copies of the novel for members of the board. With each I included a note asking them to read the novel if they had not done so already and send back their reasons for wanting the book banned. None replied.

While the initial reaction was of "astonishment and amusement," I also told radio interviewers it should not be forgotten that the Board of Education had a responsibility to those who elected them to monitor the reading choices for schools in their county. Despite the quip about Confused Censors, the board was not censoring *The Last Canadian*. Censor means to edit prior to publication. The board had a right, indeed a duty, to decide, preferably in consultation with teaching staff, what books were to be used in high school teaching programs. In a free country, however, the board could neither deny publication of the book nor its sale. They could only exercise their responsibility to choose books for Grey County students. Both parents and students had the right to go out and buy the

92

book, read it, and decide for themselves what was wrong with it. Parents had the further right, if they thought the decision ridiculous, to vote next time to elect other people to be members of the board.

Word filtered back from Owen Sound (that's another wonderful thing about a democracy — it's almost impossible to keep the public's business behind closed doors) that some members of the board confessed they had not read the books before banning them, which was my reason for sending copies to each board member.

Things were relatively quiet for a couple of weeks, with an interlude from Joan Barfoot, a *London Free Press* reporter on a year's leave of absence to work on her second novel. Her first, *Abra*, had been critically acclaimed on publication, which was more than could be said for *The Last Canadian*. Roy MacSkimming, for example, writing in the *Toronto Star*, said the novel was "a candidate for the year's dumbest book ... the most scurrilous sort of anti-Communist propaganda ... the worst piece of junk I've read in a long time." As *The Last Canadian* passed the 50,000 to 100,000 sales mark it was a pleasure to send MacSkimming short bulletins keeping him informed how his review had helped the book's sales. There has been no reply.

Joan wrote to the *Sun-Times*:

Editor: Well, I am hurt.

I mean, some of us gave some of our best years to schools in Owen Sound, and now that we've grown up and made bad, where's the gratitude? If the Grey County board of education is going to have the indecency to ban books, why haven't they sought out local authors, giving all that publicity that just can't be bought to us? It's unfair that works by outsiders can capture, for whatever tacky reason, the front page of Canada's national newspaper, while the rest of us languish on the book review pages ...

Anyway, please, trustees, keep us in mind. This authoring business is a tough racket, and we need all the help we can get.

Besides, we deserve some compensation for the embarrassment of having to admit that we come from a place that bans books.

Later, *The Last Canadian* and the banning story were spread all over the bottom of page one of the *Globe and Mail*. There was even a photograph of the cover of the novel. It was characteristic of the *Globe*. Their attitude has always been that if it hasn't been printed in the *Globe* it didn't happen. Two weeks after Western Ontario newspapers carried the story of the banning of the three books, the

Globe caught up with the story and, though long out of date, on page one it went. The *Globe* did have one new fact (buried in paragraph eight) which confirmed rumours about who had read the book. Barbara Taylor, one of the board members who voted for the ban, said she "had just read two of the three books and now is 'not happy' with her decision. 'I think they're good books. I don't know what my next course of action is,' she said." The *Globe* story added that another board member, Helen Johnstone, also said she regretted voting against the books.

In a *Sun-Times* follow-up, Taylor said that "after reading ... Heine's response to the banning, she read his book, found that the language was good, and although there was a little bit of violence, it was not offensive. 'There's a moral in that story too.'"

These stories and Barfoot's letter smoked out one of the instigators of the book banning. Board member Peter Hillyer sent a letter to the *Sun-Times*.

Editor: In response to your editorials placing reading freedom ahead of parents' concerns about profanity, blasphemy, sex and violence in our high school textbooks, I write to inform the public that our disapproval of these proposed novels is well sustained upon reading them.

The book, *The Last Canadian*, contains 10 occurrences of the words "goddammit" and "bastard(s)" as well as the blasphemous "Jesus H. Christ." What amounts to an internal inspection and search of a nude female from the rear in a bent-over position is found on Pg. 172 along with an extremely gross whipping done by the hero of a man hanging by the neck wherein it is stated "the next swipe brought a scream of agony from the gasping figure because the knotted end of the rope (whip) curled around his hips and flicked viciously at his testicles." The book also contains five bedroom scenes in the nude including some unmarried couples along with a very constant theme of the brutality of life and some very explicit murder and rape scenes. This is not an exhaustive list ...

The sequel was not long in coming. At a later meeting of Grey County Board of Education there was another vote. All three banned books were restored to the high school reading list with only two dissenting votes, one of them obviously Hillyer.

Weird though it was, there wasn't much mystery. In every community in North America there are people who are so far over on the right-hand side of the political spectrum they think Richard Nixon is a communist and other people whose religious fundamentalism is so extreme they think Billy Graham is soft on sin. Grey County, like the American mid-west, just happens to have a few more than usual.

Obviously, at least one board member thought there were too many "goddams" in the book, and that though every male animal including man has testicles it's dirty to mention them. Obviously, too, he has no idea what are the procedures in any police station for a normal body search.

My reaction was vast amusement. At church soon after, a friend who was an usher sidled up and murmured, "What's a porn merchant like you doing in a holy place like this?" In London, in Toronto, and even at a conference in England where American and Canadian friends had seen the news stories I was looked at oddly by people who had not read the novel and with vast amusement by those who had. No matter. It put me on page one of Canada's most widely distributed newspaper, which is book advertising it is impossible to buy (it either happens or it doesn't). It left the more irrational members of Grey County's Board of Education with egg all over their faces and my friends doubled up with raucous mirth. I just laughed all the way to the bank while regretting that the book was off the banned list — sales fell off to normal.

How Editorials Were Written and Why Decisions Were Taken

In 1968 the new Liberal leader, Pierre Trudeau, was eyeball to eyeball in a federal election campaign with the new Conservative leader, Robert Stanfield. In London, the *Free Press* was considering which party it would support on the editorial page, as were newspapers across the country.

Recently appointed editor, I was suffering from a severe case of Trudeaumania. This exciting Quebec intellectual should have a chance to show what he could do. Prior to the Liberal convention which chose Trudeau over John Turner, Robert Winters, and others, I'd written that Trudeau "will hold a strong position [from the start] ... anyone who intends to beat him may have to catch him and pass him.

That turned out to be an understatement.

My boss didn't trust Trudeau. For that matter, there were few Quebec politicians he did trust. Walter Blackburn also felt Stanfield lacked the flair to win the election and run the country. Stanfield's record in Nova Scotia made little impression on Walter; it's a small province and he didn't think running it qualified anyone to run the country.

I wrote an editorial endorsing Trudeau and the Liberals, though with some reservations. The publisher preferred to endorse Stanfield and the Conservatives, though with quite different reservations.

There were two or three lengthy discussions. As editor I could theoretically have insisted on having my way, but it wasn't so simple. If it were an ethical matter, a question of principle, I'd have my way or resign. It wasn't; not supporting Trudeau might have been unwise but it wasn't dishonest. It was a judgement call and the publisher owned the paper.

Did the publisher, then, insist on calling the shot? No, he didn't, though many if not most publishers would. He wasn't about to get heavy-handed over an election — nor for that matter did he ever do so in seventeen years, a contrast to his approach with Arthur Ford.

Two weeks before the election we again talked it over. The publisher had a compromise to suggest. Two editorials side by side, one on Trudeau's strengths and weaknesses, the other on Stanfield's. I hesitated, unwilling to be editor of a paper which wouldn't take a stand, but soon realized what the publisher was making clear —

both of us had a say in the paper's editorial posture. In due course two columns ran side by side. Sure it was a cop-out, but it demonstrated both the editor's stubbornness and the publisher's integrity.

I know little about how other newspapers reach decisions on such issues but that's the way it was in London. Under by own byline, as a prediction which is different from a preference, I wrote that the Liberals would win.

It's highly doubtful if a newspaper's position in its editorials significantly affects voter decisions. There are so many other influences — what voters read in the news columns of newspapers, see on television, hear on radio, read in magazines, read in political advertising, experience in direct contact with candidates, and discuss with other people during a campaign, to say nothing of inherited or acquired bias on religious, commercial, social, or sexual bias, or just plain bigotry. Yet for many reasons, including historical, newspapers continue to take a position prior to an election.

During my tenure as editor there were several municipal and provincial elections in all of which there were illustrations why and how newspapers do what they do. At the municipal level, we didn't endorse individual candidates. In a one-paper town voters should be provided with full coverage and editorial comment on specific issues, but endorsing a candidate who won could result in the loser claiming the newspaper was trying to run the city. The "kiss of death" was also a factor; reading an endorsement for one candidate, the public might reflect resentment by voting for another candidate.

Nevertheless, we broke our rule once. In 1974 there were two candidates for mayor. Jane Bigelow, a card-carrying member of the New Democratic Party, had been appointed mayor when the elected mayor had to retire because of ill health. Her opponent was Frank Matthews, a controller and businessman.

The editorial board felt strongly that Bigelow was by far the better choice and that Matthews's election was not in the city's best interest. So did I. None of us even considered changing our long-standing rule about not endorsing local candidates — except a relative newcomer to writing editorials, D. B. Scott. Having flogged the *Undone Flea Press* unmercifully while editor of the university's student paper, he later joined our staff (and still later became a personal friend). When someone commented it was too bad we couldn't endorse Bigelow, Dave said, "Why not?" As I glanced around the room, all eyebrows were raised and there were Cheshire-cat grins on most faces. It had nothing to do with the candidates' political affiliation, just that we all felt strongly about the two candidates.

"All right. Let's think about it. It's your idea, Dave, you write it."

In the day or two before the editorial came up, honed, polished, and set in type, I concluded this was one instance we should stand up and be counted in a local election. Next stop, because we'd be violating basic policy, was the publisher's office. Briefly mentioning Dave's question, my personal views, and those of our colleagues, I gave Walter the editorial. He read it carefully, read it a second time making a few minor pencilled changes in emphasis, then handed it back. "Good. When are you running it?"

Nice thing about a good publisher, it doesn't take a meeting of the Board of Directors to change policy.

When the editorial ran, there were angry calls from Matthews to the publisher, to me, and several others on staff. From Bigelow, then and later, nothing. Bigelow won hands down.

At the provincial level our election editorials consistently supported John Robarts, Bill Davis, and the Conservatives, partly because they gave the province good government, partly because we saw no credible alternative. Between elections our editorial page lambasted their more glaring mistakes, which became increasingly frequent.

One editorial included strong words for Darcy McKeough in 1974 when he was provincial treasurer. While minister of municipal affairs more than two years earlier, Darcy approved a land development plan in Chatham in which his family had a financial interest. The *Toronto Star* broke the story. The subdivision plans were in order. Darcy had no direct involvement and had signed on the routine recommendations of his staff. Yet he had violated the public's perception of the principle of ministerial responsibility. Our editorial argued he should resign his cabinet post.

When the story broke, Walter was at his cottage. I decided the editorial needed to be checked with him. That involved a phone call to a store, a boat trip by messenger to his cottage, his cruising over to call me and then going back to the island. Walter was in full agreement with the editorial. I also suggested a second editorial should soon suggest that, as the principle of ministerial responsibility had been met, Darcy's undoubted merit and integrity should be recognized by a new cabinet post (which soon came to him). There too Walter agreed.

What gave me considerable reassurance as editor was Walter's final comment. "Bill, it really isn't necessary to call me on something like this. You just do what you think best." Sure was a nice way to be editing the paper.

By the spring of 1984 I was writing it was long past time to kick the Grits out of Ottawa and the Tories out of Toronto; both had been too long in office. Walter had died a few months before. I felt certain that if he had lived he'd have agreed fully, in both provincial and federal fields. If I had stayed on a year or so as editor, I'd have pushed hard for strong support for David Peterson and the Liberals on the "time for a change" theme alone (though there were many other good reasons). As it was, the paper, somewhat oddly in my view, chose to endorse the Conservatives again. No matter, locally the Liberals took all three ridings and David broke a forty-two-year Tory stranglehold on Queen's Park.

In federal politics my initial assessment of Trudeau in 1968 had been that he'd bring common sense, determination, and intellectual integrity to the federal government. It didn't turn out that way. Out of indifference, or because he felt it was the only effective way to retain control of the party and the government, he soon, and continually throughout his terms, allowed a long list of political porkers to feed at the government trough. Our editorials didn't hesitate to call a spade a dirty shovel.

The 1968 federal election, which had seen a compromise on which leader and party to support, was to be the only time Walter and I failed to see alike on such major issues, though there were often significant and sometimes acrimonious differences in approach and emphasis. By the 1972 election I shared the publisher's concerns about Trudeau. We supported Stanfield, who ended up with 107 seats to the Liberal 109 (my published forecast was for a tie). If two seats had shifted, Stanfield would have formed a minority government. If his record in Nova Scotia was any indication, he'd still be in office.

At one Ottawa interview (for years I spent a few days there every month or two) one of Trudeau's cabinet ministers gave me a devastating appraisal of his leader. He said Trudeau had a "great intellect but a small mind."

The great intellect was reflected in the subtlety (and during the FLQ crisis and at other times in the ruthlessness) with which he manipulated events in Canada and Quebec. In my opinion he was probably the one person in Canada who could have so effectively prevented the separation of Quebec. Only a Québécois could have acted and reacted as he did. For that he deserves the country's grateful thanks.

So too with his determination to provide Canada with a constitution. Bringing together nine premiers (Quebec's René Lévesque, of course, opted out) and the federal government on a constitutional agreement was a major achievement for which he also deserves great credit.

Where he failed miserably was in fiscal affairs. He gave people like Marc Lalonde their heads and let them launch such absurdities as the National Energy Program, run a grossly inefficient post office, spend hundreds of millions of unnecessary dollars on the Northwest Territories, prevent the opening up of the only river outlet from the rest of Canada to the Artic (the Mackenzie River), vastly expand the civil service, and run up enormous national deficits.

The small mind was reflected in such trivialities as shouting obscenities at striking workers marching on Parliament Hill. Also, after asking cabinet minister Judd Buchanan, a London MP, to check the mood of the West and receiving a report the party was unlikely to win a seat west of Ontario, he dropped his messenger from the cabinet after the election.

When John Turner resigned as minister of finance, I concluded from previous interviews that he could no longer stomach the financial policies of Trudeau and Lalonde. The day he resigned I wrote an editorial saying so. Unable to reach Turner, I placed a call to Judd Buchanan, who got back to me late that evening. Outlining my assumptions, I asked for confirmation of a cabinet split, which Judd was prompt to deny. He knew of no argument in cabinet between Turner and Trudeau on fiscal policies. Cabinet and the prime minister had agreed with Turner's proposals.

I trusted Judd. He'd been a confidant on an off-the-record basis for years. Near press time I rushed back to the office and pulled the editorial. It was the first time the paper went to press with white space for a lead editorial. By the time the second edition was ready to roll, a substitute was ready.

Weeks later in Ottawa I had a glass of sherry with John Turner and told him the story.

"You were right the first time."

I raised an eyebrow.

Judd was like a lot of people in Ottawa, John said. They didn't understand that fiscal policy is hammered out with the prime minister long before it is presented by the minister of finance. Acrimonious debate on spending and priorities between Turner and Lalonde took place through the prime minister. Time and again Trudeau sided with Lalonde's spending policies, ignoring Turner's pleas for restraint. Turner quit, as I had thought, on principle over federal financing.

Pity. A good editorial was spoiled; no fault of Judd's. Pity, too, that a voice for sensible government spending was lost at a crucial time.

In 1974 the Liberals regained a majority, but in 1979 the public was disillusioned with Liberal spending and gave Joe Clark enough seats to form a minority government. Joe made several mistakes. He wanted to avoid the error of Mike Pearson who tried to do everything in the "100 days" of decision and spent years correcting resulting errors. Clark waited too long to call Parliament, accepting the then current wisdom (I was one of those taken in) that Trudeau would resign as he had announced. The delay gave the Liberals time to regroup and helped Trudeau decide to withdraw his planned departure. Clark also assumed the country had elected him to function as though he had a majority and introduced unpalatable gasoline tax increases.

Clark's policy mistake was in not finding ways to force out of his party the far-right elements who exercised unreasonable leverage. The place for them was a party of their own, matching on the right the New Democratic Party to the left of the Liberals. More than once in interviews I asked why he didn't get rid of them. Each time his response was the same. Conservative Party membership was open to any Canadian who cared to join. He stood on principle when he should have been using his boots.

His strategic mistake was in refusing to accept a two-thirds vote at Winnipeg as a leadership endorsement. Elmer MacKay, a Nova Scotia MP who later resigned his seat to give Brian Mulroney an entry into the House of Commons, insisted Clark needed 70–80 per cent to remain as leader. Listening to that nonsense, Clark was marching to the wrong drummer. Trudeau won the 1968 Liberal convention on the fourth ballot with a fifteen-vote margin out of 2365 votes cast — and ruled both the party and the country with an iron hand for sixteen years.

In 1980 the *Free Press* editorial reflected considerable disillusionment with Clark's performance but concluded Trudeau and the Liberals would be an even greater disaster, so half-heartedly supported the Conservatives. In retrospect I should have taken a much stronger position, not that it would have altered the result. It's a measure of the effectiveness of newspaper editorials that despite Clark being endorsed by a majority of Canadian newspapers, voters gave the Liberals a clear majority. So much for blood, sweat, and tears over editorial policy.

Retiring early meant missing the 1984 election, but it was no fun anyway. I wrote articles predicting and supporting a Conservative victory; the Grits had messed up too much too long. That didn't diminish my admiration for John Turner, but the party he inherited was a millstone around his neck. If he'd won the 1984 election he'd have had to work with a long list of discredited Liberals. Turner is in an increasingly stronger position now that Prime Minister Mulroney has failed to bite the deficit bullet in his first two years in office. It's probably too late now to begin to do all the unpopular things necessary to put Canada's fiscal house in order, among which should be getting rid of universality by taxing back family allowance and old-age security from those who don't need it. Even if he starts doing now what he should have done in his first year he may not be re-elected next time around.

Which leads to the first law of politics — the first duty of a politician is to get re-elected. The other ninety-nine laws of politics don't matter.

Pity the Poor Editor? Well, No, Not Really

A newspaper editor is a strange creature. He's supposed to be responsible, and is in law, for the news and comment in his paper. Actually he's more like President John Kennedy who, two years into his term, was asked how he liked the job. He said he liked it fine but it bothered him that when he gave orders nothing happened.

It's astonishing that editors, faced with the demands of partisan groups at both ends of every political, economic, religious, and other spectrum which exists, manage to get it all together daily. The publisher wants nothing less than the best newspaper in the country. The production manager wants as much copy as possible before the news event happens and the rest immediately. The advertising manager wants all the best display pages for his ads. Editorial staff want to cover every local, provincial, national, and international event, whatever the cost. The public, among whom are politicians, publicity flacks, and the poor, want their names in the paper when they think it should be there and kept out when others think it should be there.

If the editor listens to bleeding hearts he's soft; if he doesn't he's arrogant.

If he edits copy he's an autocrat; if he doesn't he's letting staff run things.

If he works eighteen hours a day in Brussels trying to understand how the European Economic Community will affect world trade, he's living it up on an expense account and pretending to be an instant expert on his return; if he stays home obviously he's uninformed about significant world events.

If he imposes his editorial policies on the newspaper he's trying to be a one-man band; if he listens to other people's ideas he hasn't got a mind of his own.

If he changes his mind on an editorial position he vacillates; if he doesn't change his mind he's a bigot.

If he publishes what happens in court to other people he's a bulwark of democracy; if he publishes what happens in court to people he knows he's vindictive, hardhearted, and has no compassion.

If he writes articles about current events he's publishing his own stuff instead of letting better writers use the space; if he doesn't write articles he's uninformed and probably a crummy writer.

If he gets drunk with staff he's trying to curry favour; if he doesn't he's a snob.

If he knows the local establishment he's part of it; if he doesn't know them he doesn't know what's going on.

If he knows labour leaders around town he's anti-establishment; if he doesn't he's divorced from reality.

If he goes to a political meeting he's marked as one of the party faithful. If he doesn't go he thinks he's too good for party politics. If he goes to the meetings of all political parties he's crazy.

If he interviews national leaders he's currying favour with the famous. If he doesn't he carries no clout up there where it counts.

If he argues with the newspaper's critics at a cocktail party he's unreasonably defensive; if he doesn't the critics are right.

If he supports medicare he's communist; if he writes medicare poses problems he's fascist; if he sees some good and some bad he's sitting on the fence on a crucial public issue.

If he visits Jerusalem he has no understanding of the wrong done to the Palestinians nor of their national aspirations and he's anti-Arab. If he visits Damascus he probably served Hitler in the concentration camps and is rabidly anti-Semitic.

If as a Canadian he writes an editorial suggesting it would be good for the Western world if President Ronald Reagan served a second term, he's a right-wing kook; if he writes that a Reagan second term would be a disaster for the world he's interfering in the affairs of another country. If he offers the opinion that it would be good for Canada if Walter Mondale won, he's out of his tree.

If he's right he thinks he's too damn smart; if he's wrong his stupidity was obvious from the beginning.

Why did I earn my daily bread as editor-in-chief of the *London Free Press* all those years? Because it was by far the most exciting, stimulating, varied, demanding, dramatic, and satisfying job I could imagine.

"The Complaint Is Upheld" — and Arguments Thereon

The Ontario Press Council was originally suggested by Beland Honderich, publisher of the *Toronto Star*. Almost single-handedly, he arm-twisted another half dozen Ontario publishers, mostly Southam papers, into an agreement to fund an Ontario council. Walter Blackburn was initially uncertain about the merits of a press council but I was enthusiastic from the beginning. I'd read Lord Devlin's book on the British Press Council, had some concept of how it worked, and was impressed by what it had done in establishing, by precedents in its adjudications, a working body of ethics which have become an informal body of journalistic law in much the way the decisions of centuries of British jurisprudence became the common law.

My views of press councils and how they worked, or should work, were reflected in an article the American Society of Newspaper Editors asked me to write for their monthly *Bulletin*. It read, in part:

> North America's print media are unwise to continue indefinitely as the only major element of democratic society from whose decisions there is no appeal.
>
> A president can be impeached.
>
> A prime minister can be defeated in Parliament.
>
> Parliament and Congress can be reconstituted by the electorate.
>
> Lawyers can be disbarred.
>
> Doctors can be denied the right to practice.
>
> Labour union leaders can be voted out by members and controlled by law.
>
> Corporate officers can be removed by boards of directors.
>
> Corporations can be reconstituted by law, specifically by trust law.
>
> The list is endless, and includes broadcast outlets, which can lose their license by decisions of regulatory boards in both Canada and United States.
>
> The print media, however, by common law, tradition and precedent in Canada, and by the First Amendment to the Constitution of the United States, are answerable to no one — and certainly not to any legislative body, for unethical or improper conduct. It can be argued that the reader, by his impact on circulation, is the ultimate control over the print media. That argu-

ment is invalidated by the reality that most North American cities have one newspaper, which is almost incapable of going out of business and most unlikely to be driven out of business.

North American readers of daily newspapers are increasingly sophisticated political, economic and cultural creatures. Spiro Agnew and his ilk had only a peripheral impact on public attitudes toward the media. His position smelled so strongly of incipient dictatorship that it was only the politically insensitive who seriously accepted his concepts of the media. That was little comfort to the print media, however, because many millions of people in the United States, as in Canada, had developed a fundamental suspicion of the print media long before Agnew appeared on the scene. Nor did his fall improve matters.

Too many readers believe the media are monolithic, establishment, powerful organs with the capacity (for selfish, personal or profit reasons) to make or destroy individuals, corporations and organizations of all kinds, and indeed to put political parties into or out of office. The readers are wrong, of course, because the media's power is limited and effective only where it is publishing fact and expressing fair opinion about those facts.

Where readers are right in their attitudes toward the media is in feeling they have no recourse from the often arbitrary decisions of media people.

Short of libel, the irate reader or news source has no recourse at all.

That in itself is a good enough reason for press councils ...

Newspapers which piously point their finger at the deceits of others, and at the same time refuse even to consider participating in a press council, are irrational. It is as if they considered themselves to be above error, infallible creatures without whom democracy would flounder and disappear. Nonsense. Newspapers are as prone to error as any organization — no more, no less. The reader is entitled to relief from those errors, if not from the newspaper involved, then from an independent body.

Canadian and American newspapers which now refuse to participate in press councils should not complain if, in the future, machinery to redress the worst mistakes of the media is set up by governments, in the United States notwithstanding the First Amendment ...

It is our firm conviction that newspapers which cannot see the need for self-discipline and self-examination in these critical areas of professional and ethical conduct thereby make themselves terribly vulnerable to the extremists of both the left and the right who would invade freedom of the press for their own selfish purposes.

Though the *Free Press* publisher was hesitant at first, he came to feel the Ontario Press Council was worthwhile, especially after it was endorsed by his good friend St. Clair Balfour of Southam newspapers. K. A. (Sandy) Baird, publisher of the *Kitchener-Waterloo Record*, the late Borden Spears of the *Toronto Star* and the unlamented Kent Commission, and I were asked to draft a constitution and by-laws. Honderich suggested funding on a circulation basis, which meant the *Toronto Star* paid about half the costs. Dr. Davidson Dunton, sometime journalist and former president of Carleton University in Ottawa, became chairman, and Fraser MacDougall, former bureau chief of Canadian Press in Ottawa, executive secretary.

It was set up with ten professional members, among them reporters, editors, publishers, advertising and circulation managers, and ten non-professional members, including housewives, doctors, and farmers. I fought during the selection process to keep out lawyers, fearing they'd turn the council into a miniature courtroom with elaborate rules of procedure and cross-examination of witnesses. A press council should be an informal body to hear complaints and bring down a common-sense, not a legal, adjudication. I served two three-year terms.

During the quarterly OPC meetings I was vociferous in adjudication hearings, arguing strenuously for the right of newspapers to exercise considerable discretion in deciding what material was to be published. For example, a Toronto gay magazine complained to the council that the *Toronto Star* had refused to run an advertisement for a magazine called *Body Beautiful*. Council decided it was a denial of the rights of the publishers of the magazine to be refused publication. I argued it was the right of the *Star* to refuse to publish material it considered offensive to its readers. The *Star* published the adjudication but refused to alter its policy.

That's a major complaint against the press council concept. It has no power other than to require newspapers who are members to publish adjudications of the council. For newspapermen, however, more conscious of public attitudes than most people, that alone is a powerful pressure. Anything more, fines or other penalties, would inhibit free speech, which is guaranteed in the Canadian Constitution. No press council should have any more powerful weapon than the pressure of public opinion as represented by press council decisions. Any other penalty in a democracy should be enforced only by the courts under libel laws and by civil suits.

During my six years on OPC, it became a joke among other members that there were no complaints about the *Free Press* which were not resolved prior to adjudication. I had no sooner left the council than there were a series of major adjudications in some of which the *Free Press* was roundly criticized.

The most devastating, and deserved, criticism from the Press Council came from what the newsroom referred to as "the Harry Smith caper." If caper means having fun it was the wrong word. A reporter, concerned that few voters knew much about the twenty-three candidates who were running for twelve seats on the Board of Education, wondered what would happen if a candidate went through the qualification procedures and allowed his name to stand but did not appear in the media, attend election meetings, or campaign in any other way. How many people would vote for a candidate about whom they could not possibly know anything? The idea went to the assignment desk and from there to the city editor, James M. O'Neail. It reached Jim at a time when the managing editor was out of the country on vacation and he decided unilaterally to go ahead.

The Board of Education reporter, Emilie Smith, persuaded her husband to allow himself to be nominated and to qualify. His name duly appeared on the list of candidates.

I caught up with the scheme when the editorial-page editor, Norman Ibsen, heard newsroom rumours about it. I was absolutely appalled. It was obvious we would be accused of interfering with the electoral process, surely one of the most inviolate aspects of a democracy. The fact that we were doing so for no selfish reason, merely to demonstrate the ridiculous aspects of electing members to the Board of Education on a city-wide basis, was no excuse. We were fiddling an election.

Yet those involved had acted in good faith. The *Free Press* had published editorials condemning the city-wide vote for members of the Board of Education and urged a ward system, which was later adopted. If the result was what the originators of the idea expected and enough people voted for at least the name about whom they could not possibly know anything, that in itself might be a contribution to democracy. The objective was laudable; I had serious reservations about the means.

Moving slowly and carefully, I voiced concern at a meeting in my office but kept it low key for two reasons. If any situation needed a cool head this was one; recriminations could wait. What was needed was answers. There were none. If we went public immediately, saying we'd acted in good faith but had since concluded it was not a plan we should carry to its conclusion, we were very likely, as a result of the publicity which would immediately follow in our and other newspapers and on radio and television stations, to cause Harry Smith to be elected. As he entered into the venture quite certain he would not be elected and would not serve if he were elected, that would be an even worse manipulation of the electoral system than what was being proposed. It was not possible, a week before the election, to have Harry Smith's name removed from the ballot.

Against those realities was the certainty that the opposition media would jump on the story like a ton of bricks if they got wind of it. That included not only opposition newspapers like the *Globe* and the *Star* but also local radio stations CKSL and CJBK, as well as the *Free Press*-owned radio and television stations CFPL and CFPL-TV (which functioned very competitively indeed against the newspaper and would claw us badly if they had the opportunity).

Our only course was to sit tight and trust that opposition papers and stations would learn nothing. We could then break the story ourselves, and explain what we had attempted to do. No matter how it broke we were in for a rough ride. It was important to brief the publisher on what had happened but he wasn't available, so I went over the ground with the president, Peter White, who agreed with my decision to sit tight. The story almost broke the night before the election when CFPL-TV mentioned that a candidate who had not campaigned was running for an ulterior purpose, but it was not pursued by them or by any other competitors.

When the election votes were counted, Harry Smith had finished twentieth in a field of twenty-three, but he had gathered 8310 votes in the process. The point of the exercise was well made but, as expected, the roof fell in. Some of the candidates who had lost said that the votes diverted to Harry Smith might have elected them. There were threats of appeals under the election act, demands for a new election (at *London Free Press* expense of course), and vociferous demands for the hides of those responsible (me).

We broke our own story the morning after the election and explained what it was intended to demonstrate, but that was merely more gasoline on an already flaming pyre. The publisher caught up with the story a day or so later and was as appalled as I had been. His most devastating comment really hurt: "I'm ashamed to be publisher of a paper that would do such a thing." I could only agree and twice offered to resign. Walter declined both times but he was hurt and angry. So was I, but recognized to a greater degree than he did that those who had launched the scheme had no intentions other than to demonstrate the need for reform of the city's electoral system.

There was the fullest possible exposure on page one of all the criticism voiced by candidates and we ran all letters to the editor on the subject. I was interviewed half a dozen times by telephone from home where I was ill. (It wasn't a fake illness; later it required surgery.) I was relatively non-committal, saying only we had demonstrated what we set out to demonstrate. Privately, I was furious and desperately upset.

Predictably the issue went to the Ontario Press Council. At the enquiry committee hearing I said little in defence of the newspaper's initiative and granted virtually every point the complainants made to council. Predictably, also, the council adjudication was strongly critical of the newspaper. The adjudication ran on page one.

> The Council believes that the London Free Press committed a breach of journalistic ethics, meddled in the electoral process and may have altered the results by arranging to have the husband of an employee stand as a candidate in the London Board of Education elections ...
>
> The newspaper's action, aimed at demonstrating it would be better to elect candidates by wards than at large, was all the more mischievous since that same election day electors were voting on a proposal to adopt the ward system ...
>
> The complaints were upheld.

I agreed.

Another adjudication against us brought mixed reaction. We decided on a major examination of the drug scene in city schools, which meant city high schools primarily, though there were known to be some drugs in public schools. Our round-up was as comprehensive as we could make it, including interviews and comment from police, clergy, drug addiction people, judges, school principals, teachers, students, parents — you name them and we talked to them. The consensus was that drugs in high schools were a problem. Further, and this came from many of the most knowledgeable people directly or indirectly involved in the drug scene, including police, one school in particular was where "it was at": H. B. Beal Secondary School. There were drugs in all high schools but Beal was the most open of all in the drug trade. Derik Hodgson did a fine bit of research and wrote an excellent basic story. When all was ready to publish, newsroom decided local colour was also needed. Because Derik was past posing as a high school student, one of our summer students, Terry Brodie, was given the assignment of wandering around the school, the billiard parlour and stores of the neighbourhood to see what she could find. She wrote an excellent colour story to go with the main research, which made it clear she could have bought several drugs. We devoted a full page to the stories.

The overline on Terry's Beal story read "Dope City." All hell broke loose. The principal of Beal, Donald Prowse, said "we're all hopping mad this morning and I think we have reason to be mad — I'd like to see a retraction." Student Council president Margo Pfaff said the *Free Press* has "no right to smear our reputation," though she admitted the school had problems. The chairman of the Board of Education, Dr. Donald Reid, said the newspaper resorted to smear tactics and disgraceful journalism in the articles about drug use in city schools.

Douglas McVie, then director of education, with whom the *Free Press* had tangled on more than one occasion, wrote a letter to all high school parents condemning the stories. He asked them "to join with me in condemning" the *Free Press* for a "completely unreasonable" article on drug use at Beal. His letter said the news stories contributed "nothing of a positive nature to the question and provided no new information. It merely re-opened an old wound and poured in some salt." He regreted the impression that the use of drugs is widespread at Beal, "a charge that students deny." (He didn't deny it himself.) He added the point at issue was not whether some students are using drugs but whether "The *Free Press* article did anything worth while" to help solve the problem.

McVie particularly disliked an article I'd written, one in a series of "Letters from the Editor." It mentioned that another director of education, Kenneth Regan, of the London and Middlesex Separate School Board, had initiated the articles by phoning to complain about a short item in a Saturday magazine supplement mentioning leg purses which could be used to store money or a "pinch of hash." The *Free Press*, Regan charged when he telephoned, was "soft on drugs." I got downright snarly at that; over the years we had carried dozens of stories and articles on drugs and their abuse. One series was reprinted and made available to drug addiction organizations and to schools. If he was so upset about drugs in schools, it was time the *Free Press* had another look at the extent of the problem. So we did. Derik's and Terry's stories were the result.

To McVie's criticisms I replied, when questioned by *Free Press* reporters, that McVie seemed to be more concerned with the image of London schools "than with what we consider to be the point made by our stories, that there are significant amounts of drugs in the city's secondary schools ... there are enough drugs in Beal and in other ... schools ... to warrant the very serious concern of the entire school system." Regan and McVie should have got together to sort out which was the greater worry, Regan's new awareness of drugs in the schools or McVie's touching concern about Beal's image.

Of all the words generated, both in the original stories and in all the subsequent stories, letters, and other comment, by far the most delightful reaction came from a Beal grade nine student, Sherry Collins. Commenting on the inital news stories, she was quoted in a follow-up story as saying somewhat plaintively: "I like my school — I don't think even half the people smoke dope."

Though none of those who protested the most tried to suggest there were no drugs at Beal or other secondary schools, teachers at Beal brooded over the deemed insult. It took several months for the idea to occur to them, but two of them finally got around to complaining to the Press Council. (They may have been encouraged by the clobbering we took over the Harry Smith venture). In any event, they certified to the council they were not satisfied with our having published all their denials and all their letters. They wanted an apology from the *London Free Press*. On that, whatever the adjudication, no way. We stood by our stories.

At the Press Council hearing there was much emotional hand-wringing about dear old H. B. Beal but no one effectively refuted the essential thrust of the stories that Beal was where the drug scene was in London. Nevertheless, the council upheld the complaint, in part in these terms:

The complainants did not object to the main story, a general description of the situation that *Free Press* reporters had discovered. They objected strongly to a companion story, purporting to describe the situation at H. B. Beal secondary school ... They termed the Dope City story shoddy and irresponsible journalism that created, by implication and distortion, a harmful view of the school. The *Free Press* said it simply reported what it learned.

The Council agrees fully with a principle enunciated by the *Free Press* in the discussion — that full disclosure is beneficial in an open society like Canada's, that publishing the truth helps rather than harms.

It believes that the *Free Press* aimed at performing a useful public service by alerting the people of London to the extent of drug traffic in secondary schools.

The *Free Press*, however, did not have sufficient substantiated evidence to justify publishing the Dope City story and to do so was irresponsible.... The *Free Press* said ... each fact was verified by at least two other students ... Council does not believe that three students constitute a cross-section of a student body of 2,200.

The Council would also like to note that, to ensure accurate and complete reporting, newspapers ought to use extreme care in using impersonation to gather information especially when dealing with juveniles.

The complaint is upheld.

I was furious with the irrationality of the Press Council not being able to read past the headline "Dope City." Particularly galling was the reference to impersonation. Try gathering information about drugs starting with "Hi. I'm a *Free Press* reporter. Tell me about the drugs you're selling."

The entire adjudication was a contradiction in terms. "Full disclosure is beneficial" but don't use words that upset starry-eyed teachers who turned out to be emotional about their wonderful students. Most of them are wonderful, but a significant percentage of students at Beal were and still are using drugs and many are selling them.

While the Press Council was mulling over the "irresponsible" stories of the *Free Press*, there were other interesting developments. Among the protests were a few from parents of high school students. Many knew what their children were doing or knew of neighbours' children who were involved in drugs. While they didn't turn out to rally around the local newspaper, they did ignore McVie's clarion call to condemn the newspaper and, more important, they talked to Board of Education members and city aldermen and, along with others, they began to see some results.

By February a grade twelve Beal student was fined $1000 or jailed for six months for trafficking in LSD. Another student was charged and a special federal prosecutor told the court that drug offences involving LSD were increasing. Drug convictions seemed to be more frequent and, as usual, were reported.

By March about forty parents met with Beal students and staff to discuss drug abuse. Student Council was asked to consider a program to bring experts on drug abuse to the school to talk to students in small groups. Staff spoke of "the pressures a student is under." Prowse said students caught smoking pot or taking drugs were suspended. He added that since a *Free Press* story about drug abuse in the school had appeared, only seven students had been discovered using pot. Four were suspended and "since have become model citizens." (That's what he said.) Both staff and parents expressed opposition to a pinball arcade near the school. There is no campus at Beal; "their campus is the street," said a vice-principal.

By June a drug and alcohol abuse committee of the Board of Education was holding its first meeting. That raised two questions. If there was no serious drug problem in the schools, as McVie insisted, why was the drug and alcohol abuse committee formed? And if there was a problem why did it wait until June, more than half a year after the "Dope City" story appeared? The chairman, John Ferris, said the committee was set up earlier in the year after *Free Press* stories prompted the board to look into the problem. Reid, the board chairman, having apparently reconsidered and concluded there might be a problem, was on hand.

By June, also, parents had reached enough aldermen for them to pass a by-law on a 12–4 vote restricting pinball parlour operations. No new pinball parlour would be allowed to open within 750 metres of a school, though existing places could continue. Pinball parlours would be off-limits for school-age children before 4 P.M. on school days, would have to close by 11 P.M. Monday to Saturday, and not be open on Sundays and holidays. The penalties were stiff — $1000 or a maximum of twenty-one days in jail. Owners of pinball parlours took the by-law to the Ontario Supreme Court where it was quashed on the grounds that municipalities do not have the power to discriminate between people or "businesses of the same class." Late in the year the city passed another by-law, this time making no references to the age of patrons but restricting the hours of operation from 9 A.M. to 11 P.M., Mondays to Saturdays, and severely restricting areas of the city where any new places of amusement could be established.

I fumed for weeks about that adjudication, saying nothing publicly but using up a fine collection of four-letter words privately. When able to talk about it calmly, I took a senior RCMP officer out to lunch and asked if he'd protect one of our reporters from arrest if we undertook to do another story on the drug scene, this time telling the reporter to buy soft and hard drugs. We'd take pictures of the purchases and turn over the drugs immediately to the RCMP. He said he'd consider it but we never got around to doing it, which was a pity. In retirement I thought I'd sniff around Beal and write a wallbanger myself, but concluded my posing as a teenage drug user involved a few problems in credibility.

We had an equally poor, indeed ridiculous, adjudication on another school story a year later. Chris Dennett was following Prime Minister Joe Clark on the campaign trail in February 1980 and attended a rally for the Tory leader at John Diefenbaker High School in Hanover. Clark spoke to an auditorium full of students, with local residents crowded at the back. Among his subjects were income tax spousal allowances for capital gains purposes. If that weren't enough to turn off a few hundred kids, he switched to French — in Grey County, for heaven's sake. The students booed him roundly.

Chris's story said the prime minister bombed in Hanover, as did the stories of at least six other reporters for other newspapers, each of whom mentioned the booing. CBC broadcast a tape of the booing. That didn't matter to the supporters of Diefenbaker High School. They flooded the newspaper with letters of protest, and took their case to the Press Council. Chris and I turned up and listened for three hours to housewives, teachers, several elderly parties, and half a dozen students recite in turn the sins of the story. Yes, Clark had been booed, but only a teeny little bit, and they'd have us know that it was as well-behaved a crowd as any right-thinking Tory in Grey County would expect in Diefenbaker High School.

The approach seemed to be that the *London Free Press* should not have published, certainly not on page one where everyone could see it, a story that students in Hanover had booed a prime minister — and a Tory prime minister at that — because he spoke French. It was an insult to dear old Diefenbaker High School (but not to Dief the Chief; he'd probably have booed too if he'd been in the audience). When they finished telling what a fine school Diefenbaker High School was, they reiterated three "glaring" errors in the story: that there weren't 400 people there as Chris reported but close to 800; that he had referred to people in the area as Anglo-Saxons when in fact many of them were of German origin; and that he had put Hanover in Bruce County instead of Grey County.

Well, Hanover is on the border of Grey-Bruce; people in Grey County sure as hell aren't French, which was the point of the story and of the booing; the Saxon of Anglo-Saxon *is* German; and the crowd was estimated by other reporters to be in the 600 range, which made the delegation from Grey County as wrong as they claimed Chris to be. Nevertheless, the adjudication was critical.

The story was interpretative, in effect an impression of one part of Joe Clark's activity in the election campaign on Jan. 30, and by its very nature contained conclusions bordering on opinion. The council recognizes that this is an acceptable form of newspaper writing.

However, the council concludes from the evidence it heard that the story contained at least three inaccuracies and also tended by implication to give a misleading impression of student involvement in the incidents at the Hanover event.

It reported that a "400-strong student crowd" attended the meeting, although the evidence clearly points to more than twice that number of people, of whom about one-third were not students. It described Hanover as "this largely rural and very Anglo-Saxon part of Bruce County," although racial background in the area is strongly German and the county is Grey. The council recognizes that the story erred in the name of the county only in the *Free Press* morning edition Jan. 31. The evening edition named the county correctly.

The story implied that all the students and only the students were involved in talking, in booing and in rushing for the door after the Clark speech, by using such phrases as "the assembled school body" and the students.

As a result of the errors, the story presented a distorted picture of the event.

The complaint is upheld.

The adjudication missed the essence of the complaint entirely, which was that the *Free Press* should not have reported the distressing fact that Hanover and Grey County students booed a Tory prime minister of Canada in Diefenbaker High School. We published the adjudication on page one. Chris swears he will never appear at another Press Council adjudication. I don't blame him. I'm still committed to the concept of a press council, so I continued to turn up when we were the subject of a complaint.

Prior to those traumas, we'd had a major incident which brought a more favourable adjudication. A thirteen-year-old boy, Robert Schroeyens, stole a car which was recognized by police who gave chase. The boy hit speeds close to 100 mph, crashed into a feed mill and was killed. When a *London Free Press* photographer got there, the boy's body was lying under a tarpaulin, with an Ontario Provincial Police constable standing guard. It was an unpleasant photograph to put on the breakfast tables of London and Western Ontario readers but night news desk was aware there'd recently been two or three major accidents in which more than half a dozen people were killed as a result of high-speed police chases.

All weekend, newsroom tried to get a local coroner to say he was going to call an inquest in this death, but no answers were forthcoming. We decided to draw the whole question of high-speed chases to public attention. We published the photograph on page one. Next day an inquest was ordered. Police were very unhappy about the photo; they felt it made them look like hunters standing over fallen prey. There was so much argument about the photograph and about the high-speed chase that I wrote an article, one of a series of "Letters from the Editor," mentioning the reasons we had run the photograph. Among them were the age of the boy, that other deaths had been caused by high-speed chases, and that for two days there was no indication an inquest would be held. "Most of all," I added, "there was a strong feeling that publication of the photo might cause other teen-agers who saw it to think twice about the potential dangers of driving too fast or of attempting to run away from police. If only one young person, some night, remembered that picture, it was properly published."

At the inquest the boy's mother was sharply critical of the newspaper's coverage of the death: "My son is gone and will never be back but I hope that if any good comes of this, the *Free Press* will perform differently and there will be no more chasing." The jury exonerated police involved, properly so, noting that policy and procedure "on pursuit driving is adequate and was followed." The jury also recommended that "journalists use more discretion in their selection of pictures of deceased persons."

Dr. H. B. Cotram, Ontario chief coroner, wrote to the Ontario Press Council enclosing a copy of the jury's recommendation about journalists. Several months later, after consulting other newspapers in the province, the Press Council replied in part:

> Before framing its comment, the Council asked its member newspapers to provide information on their practices regarding publication of pictures of deceased persons and to comment on publication of the *Free Press* of the picture concerned in the case. Copies of the replies are attached.
>
> The Council fully appreciates the jury's concern about publication of the picture. Such a picture can only increase the burden of a bereaved family by adding to the poignancy of grief.
>
> Yet the Council also recognizes that there may be a distinct benefit to society in publishing pictures of that kind.
>
> In deciding whether to publish any picture that he knows may cause pain or sorrow to some, a newspaper editor has a responsibility in each case to consider whether the public good outweighs private grief. Exercise of that responsibility demands the utmost discretion.
>
> Although the Council is not able to make an adjudication it appears from a study of all the material published in the case that the *Free Press* exercised adequate discretion, particularly in view of the interest aroused at the time by a number of similar accidents in Ontario.

Given the Press Council response to the complaints about the drug story on Beal and about the Hanover booing, I was surprised they didn't suggest that newspapers should avoid reporting that a thirteen-year-old boy had been killed in a high-speed chase on the grounds that it might offend the police and the parents. If that leaves the impression of being more than a little cheesed off with the organization, good. I was.

That's not sour grapes at being clobbered by the Press Council. We deserved criticism over the Harry Smith episode. In both the Beal and Hanover complaints, however, Press Council's enquiry committee was far too prone to be sympathetic to the emotional outpourings of people who didn't want next spring's school yearbook to be spoiled either by boos or drugs.

In my last year as editor one more confrontation developed between the *London Free Press* and the Ontario Press Council. A lawyer was unhappy about a story we published concerning a client's appearance before a juvenile court. The boy had taken a shot at his step-father who he thought had molested his sister. The court, in a lengthy discussion with our reporter, Helen Connell, agreed to our covering the case. The court directed us not to refer to "incest." We didn't. After internal discussion and consulting our solicitors we did, however, refer to the boy's sister having been "molested," which can have connotations other than sexual.

The lawyer, Christopher Campbell of Tillsonburg, wrote to the Press Council asking for an anonymous adjudication, on grounds that a normal adjudication would further distress his juvenile client. Press Council, through its secretary Fraser MacDougall, agreed.

I reacted vigorously. Of all voluntary organizations in the country, a press council had to function openly. The *Free Press* would not be bound by the Press Council decision to issue an anonymous adjudication and considered it grossly improper. Press Council's constitution provided that member newspapers were required to publish adjudications involving that newspaper. With Walter Blackburn's agreement, I suggested the *Free Press* might have to consider withdrawing from Press Council if anonymous adjudications continued. Given the furore over the Kent Report and the danger of a federally funded national press council being formed to monitor the print media the way the Canadian Radio-Television and Telecommunications Commission tells the broadcast media how much of what kind of music written by whom to broadcast, that was a serious threat. Even a hint of the beginning of a break-up of Ontario Press Council would trigger government action to form a national press advisory council, with grievous consequences to Canadian journalism.

Allyn Taylor, who had become council chairman, saw the problem clearly. He quietly asked Peter Mason, a retired Kitchener business executive and chairman of Press Council's enquiry committee, to sound me out on a solution to the impasse. I suggested we might agree to participate in an anonymous adjudication in this instance, to take Press Council off the hook, providing it was understood there would be no future such adjudications. Mason quickly agreed. When I tested that against the publisher's views, he demurred. It would be unhealthy for any newspaper to dictate terms to the Press Council. He was right. I sent a letter saying we'd accept this anonymous adjudication, provided Press Council would consider the wisdom of future such decisions.

Enquiry committee eventually heard our views and the lawyer's, then sent along their anonymous adjudication. Since then I've heard not a whisper in local legal circles of the adjudication's content. Simply because there's been no leak, lawyers around London courts, being as cynical as journalists, assume the adjudication was not critical of the newspaper. I had insisted that if we heard the adjudication's terms from a third party — that is, on the province's legal circuit — we would feel free to publish it. Frankly, I rather hoped it would leak, either way.

When it came to the council meeting at which the adjudication issue was to be discussed, the chairman of the committee involved stole virtually all my thunder. Donald MacDonald, sometime leader of Ontario's New Democratic Party, said his committee had leaned over so far backward to protect the rights of the complainant, "they'd fallen flat on their faces," which was most generous of him. I'd have been content to leave it at that, but Allyn was determined the issue be aired. Canadian Press moved this story on the discussion, in part, with these paragraphs:

PRESS COUNCIL WON'T KEEP RULINGS SECRET
The Ontario Press Council ... will no longer keep some of its rulings secret ...

William Heine, editor-in-chief of *The London Free Press*, convinced members of the independent watchdog organization at a meeting yesterday that readers who complain about newspaper coverage should be prepared to hear a public ruling on their cases ...

"Any issue before ... [council] ... should have the light of day shone on it," Mr. Heine said. "A free press is an open press and the press council should be as open as the media and the public it serves ..."

Later I offered another bone on which council could chew. Twice in the previous year the *Free Press* had had to answer to complaints made by lawyers who said they were not acting on behalf of clients but who frequently referred to "my client." Council was reminded that their constitution provided that complainants could not be represented by counsel. If we were again required to appear on a complaint and a lawyer turned up and referred to "my client," we would insist on having a lawyer to represent us, in which case council would be well advised to get a lawyer of its own. No lawyers have appeared since.

Despite all these hassles, however, the press council concept is sound and deserves the full, if sometimes argumentative, support of Ontario newspapers. As my article quoted at the beginning notes, there needs to be a place where complaints against the media can be heard. Anything less is unwarranted media arrogance.

The council's effectiveness has been bolstered immensely in recent years by Allyn Taylor. Highly principled, an astute judge of people and their motivations, and endowed with bulldog determination blended with superb verbal arm-twisting, he worked over those opposed to the press council concept and one by one brought them in. All Ontario daily newspapers, and weekly newspapers as a group, now are members. He was helped, of course, by publisher awareness that if newspapers did not monitor their own performance, government might try to do it for them.

Beland Honderich's far-seeing initiative led to the Ontario Press Council being in place when needed to forestall government intervention in the printed word. This threat was the most dangerous element of the rapidly discredited Kent Report.

Good cartoonists exaggerate personal characteristics. In this drawing Ting included ears (still there), cigar (long since snuffed out), writing (still at it), and travel (now somewhat inhibited; no expense accounts).

An afternoon in a punt at Oxford was relaxing in 1940, but flying Harvards in the RCAF, 1942–45, was far more exciting.

Walter J. Blackburn, publisher of the *London Free Press*, 1936–83, built a loyal staff and a profitable, expanding media corporation. The trio at right were editors of the newspaper for sixty-four years: the late Arthur R. Ford, centre, 1920–62; the late John K. Elliott, right, 1962–67; and the author, 1967–84.

On the Egyptian side of the Suez Canal, a soldier told by his captain to let a visiting editor heft his automatic rifle was so upset he almost wept, though he smiled again when he got it back with a warm handshake and a few packs of cigarettes.

Captain James Sorfleet, then with the RCAF aerobatic team, the Snowbirds, took an eager editor up for some tight formation flying, then off over Lake Huron to let the old coot try his hand, after thirty years, with a few four-point rolls.

In an Amsterdam restaurant, during an International Press Institute conference, with Cushrow Irani, from the *Calcutta Statesman*. Both vocal spokesmen for freedom of speech and the media, we seem impressed with the speaker.

126

On a visit to the *London Free Press* for an interview, Prime Minister Pierre Trudeau, along with the paper's editor, was obviously puzzled by something, though later no one could remember what.

In our

... WHENEVER WE WANTED
TO GET YOUR EAR, IT WAS ALWAYS AVAILABLE!

Here's wishing you a happy retirement, Bill –

Wes   Cheryl   Rory   Jill   Marjorie   Ting   au' revoir!

The Editorial page gang, Sept 7, 1984

Ting's version of my ears turned up again in the most heart-warming tribute the editorial-page staff could have offered their retiring editor-in-chief.

Ultimate Truth Is Elusive
Even for Chiropractors

There is an old saw among newspapermen that the world is made up of two kinds of people, those who are fighting to get their names in the paper (politicians, salesmen, and do-gooders) and those who are fighting to keep their names out of the paper (drunk drivers, bankrupts, and politicians suffering from foot-in-the-mouth disease).

What few people realize is that most of the time it isn't important whether the news is good or bad; the worst thing that can happen to people in the public eye is to be ignored. A story is told in England about Henri, the barber of King George v. If you could get an appointment with Henri you were somebody in England. There you could learn more than in some cabinet meetings. One pompous new cabinet minister finally wangled an appointment, settled in the chair and asked, "Well, Henri, what do they say about me in the country now?" The answer reduced him to silence. "They never mention your name, sir."

A classic example of the problems faced by a profession "trying to create a good image" involved the columnist Ann Landers, who had some rather blunt, even unkind comments to make about chiropractors. She suggested they gave a good massage and little else. We ran her views without editing and without comment.

Soon afterwards I was confronted by immensely irate London chiropractors. Their questions were:

(a) What right had Ann Landers to write such lies?
(b) Why didn't the *Free Press* do what the *Toronto Star* did, provide a Canadian version of Ann Landers's comments?
(c) With all the wonderful publicity provided about their work by Ontario chiropractors to Ontario newspapers, why didn't we publish the truth about chiropractors?

It took time and occasional blunt talk on both sides, but I convinced them the *Free Press* had no axe to grind about chiropractors nor any other profession.

I answered them in this vein (taking their points in reverse order):

(c) About 2000 years ago men learned what came to be known as the ultimate truth about God. It was a divine message, Christians believed. For two millennia Christians have been slaughtering non-Christians and more frequently each other in an effort to impose their version of truth on everyone else. The newspaper is not capable of providing the ultimate truth on any subject. We report what happens as accurately as we can, including what Liberals say about Conservatives, what Americans say about Russians, what revolutionaries say about the establishment, what pilots say about airlines, what Anglicans say about Catholics, and what Ann Landers says about chiropractors — and the reverse in each instance.

That's by no means an ideal situation. Far from it. Yet until we become omnipotent (and we'd be dangerous fools if we thought we were) we had to publish not the ultimate truth, but various versions of it. From such exposure to the views of many, intelligent and reasonable men may be able to evolve answers which would serve most people well in their time. Even so, answers change. As an old hymn put it, "Time makes ancient good uncouth ... they must upward still and onward who would keep abreast of truth."

The truth the chiropractors sought was an elusive thing. It might be their view of themselves, though I doubted it greatly. It might be Ann Landers's view, though I doubted that too.

(b) The *Toronto Star* version of Ann Landers's reply to the letter asking her about chiropractors was entirely different from her original reply. The *Star* version was less abrupt in tone, and correctly pointed out that chiropractic treatment was eligible under Ontario's medical care plan (the original Ann Landers version indicated chiropractors were not eligible under any American government medical plan). What the *Free Press* might have done was to have noted the reference to government medical plans and added an explanation that in Ontario chiropractic treatments were covered. We would not have changed the column without consulting the author.

(a) Ann Landers had an absolute right in both American and Canadian democracies to write as she liked about any subject she wished, subject to the laws of libel. The *London Free Press* had an equal right not to publish what she wrote (though we could have seriously eroded our credibility if we had done so for selfish reasons).

I pointed out to the irate chiropractors, who seemed to feel that they were being singled out for special criticism, that they weren't the only ones by any means. Politicians, labour leaders, and many

130

other people have been highly critical of the medical profession in recent years over OHIP participation, and the *London Free Press* has published that criticism. This newspaper has also published the response of the medical profession to that criticism.

That's the name of the game.

If chiropractors in London wished to reply to Ann Landers, we were delighted to carry their views as a letter to the editor. In fact, if they took time to tell their tale to a reporter, their indignation might well make a news story in itself.

When I last saw my visitors they were talking to a reporter. As I left, one said something to the effect that he'd come in pretty mad but he thought maybe he'd changed his mind a bit since. That was good to hear, because we didn't try to make enemies.

At the same time, we insisted on telling it as we saw and heard it — and we had no intention of suppressing one man's view because another man didn't like it. Despite our best efforts, that position sometimes created enemies. In time most people were like the chiropractors, they came to realize newspapers report what happens, not necessarily what people want to hear.

Oh To Be Saved — For Sure

Waiting at Nicosia airport for a flight to Israel, I heard strange sounds in the terminal — Baptist hymns sung with great gusto. Homing in I found thirty or more Americans shouting out the glory of the Lord. "When the Roll is Called Up Yonder" was followed by "Roll, Jordan, Roll" and "Will There Be Any Stars in My Crown?"

Fine people, but a good group to stay away from. Evangelicals on their first trip to the Holy Land, they'd be full of theories about biblical admonitions to Jews and Christians and determined to prove their views by endless quotations.

I took a seat at the back of the ancient DC-3 and opened a paperback hoping to be left alone. It was not to be. A huge fellow, broad shoulders, lean hips, wavy grey hair, and big white teeth plomped himself down and immediately identified himself as the pastor of an Illinois church. Mother taught me not to be rude, so I murmured, "Heine, from Canada," and went back to reading.

He went straight to the point.

"Have you," he asked in a low, sincere, ponderous voice, "been saved?"

"By the time I know for sure, sir, it will be too late to send word back to you."

It took a second or two for that to sink in, then he smiled bravely, let his head rest against the seat back, and closed his eyes in prayer. Or so it seemed; his lips moved slightly.

Maybe the Lord reassured him; the rest of the flight was peaceful.

It's a Long Time Ago But I'm Still Annoyed

Tangling with senators publicly isn't recommended as a way to win friends and influence people — even when the senator is Canadian and, compared to his American counterparts, a toothless tiger. Yet Senator C. R. McElman from New Brunswick made me so damn mad I consulted no one, simply asked the chairman for time. The chairman was Senator Keith Davey, who in 1970 set up a preliminary run at what later emerged as the Kent Commission. Davey's was called the Special Senate Committee on Mass Media. Its only apparent purpose was to generate ink for Davey — any political enquiry into the media was bound to be covered fully.

Walter Blackburn, *Free Press* publisher, took the whole thing seriously, which undoubtedly was wise. When the ludicrous hearings were over, Walter and the *London Free Press* came in for considerable praise. For me the whole thing was farcical. My approach would have been to suggest that if they'd like to talk, drop by London anytime, they'd be as welcome as any reader who wanted to discuss newspapers.

I had the same reaction to the Kent Commission, and to the hearings in Hull our company was subjected to when the radio station licence was to be renewed for a five-year term. At all hearings I attended, the arrogance of politicians, bureaucrats, and their part-time hired guns was hard to take. The Canadian Radio-Television and Telecommunications Commission hearings in Hull really turned me off — and by this time, third time around (broadcasters had to go through the nonsense regularly), my chippiness was showing. Peter White, president of what is now the Blackburn Group, in a hotel room briefing the night before the hearing made a special point of hoping "Bill can keep his cool."

My reply to their inane questions would have been a simple letter:

Dear Sirs:

We run a good radio station as you, the community and our competitors know. We assume, therefore, you will renew our licence. If you don't we'll go to court.

Go to a CRTC hearing and see for yourself. Huge room; TV screens all around; a raised dais for milords the commissioners who filed in self-consciously and took their places; the prisoners at the bar (us) not facing the judges but looking across the room at the prosecuting attorney who was ensconced between stacks of paper at a huge desk. From there back were the common herd, the taxpayers who were paying for it all. The CRTC's attorney didn't even have the radio station's call letters right.

CRTC headquarters in Hull seemed to have as much space, and looked as crowded, as Madison Square Gardens on a night when it was closed down. The millions of dollars spent in Hull to keep the CRTC counting minutes of time spent on Canadian and "other" programs for the hundreds of radio stations across Canada boggles the mind.

Well, that's another story.

To get back to McElman. As an afternoon session during the Davey Committee hearings broke up he referred to the "raw, naked, unadulterated power" of newspapers. He also was critical of newspapers for not commenting more on their editorial pages about the committee's hearings, which was when I bypassed my colleagues and asked for evening time.

An edited version of the transcript follows:

HEINE: ... we rather look on this as ... an investigation ... a trial ... [and] ... as *sub judice* ... When you make your report, gentlemen ... [then] we will pull no punches in saying what we think ...

That out of the way, came next point:

HEINE: ... the phrase "raw, naked and unadulterated power" ... of the media. This is a very common [view] ... I am surprised to find it among people with the experience of senators and members of parliament ... The media do not exercise raw, naked unadulterated power ...

We are adulterated — if you use it that way — in our power by the impact of other media ... other newspapers, magazines, radio, television, billboards, handouts, government information bureaus ... the public will not be picked up by the scruff of their neck and turned around 180 degrees in their opinion simply because an editorial writer says something on the editorial page.

I pointed out that 75 per cent of the 1700 newspapers in the United States are avowed Republican in their editorial-page approach, but in the last thirty-eight years (this in 1970) there have been only eight years of Republican government, and similar results were seen in Canada.

Senator Prowse cut in: "It could be the public has good common sense."

HEINE: Yes ... that's the point I'm heading for. The public has far more common sense than a great many politicians and a great many newspapermen give them credit for and is quite capable of surviving the manipulation of the so-called capitalist or establishment press ... .

People seem to think that newspapers in Canada ... get together ... on the phone every morning and decide what the Canadian people are going to think in the next 24 hours ... it simply is not so.

Davey interrupted to say he agreed with my view why newspapers had not so far commented editorially. McElman was asked to comment. He retreated to talking about "the potential" for manipulation rather than actual manipulation.

Davey then cited the American record, where "newspapers ... have enormous political leverage which they are prone to use on occasion," adding that he did not consider "newspapers have nearly as much capacity to manipulate public opinion as many people seem to think they have." There was discussion on the fact that publishers tend to be on the conservative side, reporters somewhat more liberal, at which point I subscribed "very strongly to the school that argues that it is neither the direction of the publisher or the editor ... nor the manipulative capacity of the media [which prevails] as the basic common sense of educated people in a democracy, which is the way we all survive in a democracy."

A little later counsel for the committee got into the act, which brought about this exchange.

FORTIER: Mr. Heine, I think you have made your point and I am not sure I do not agree with you with respect to the inability of newspapers to really manipulate public opinion, but isn't there another aspect to the issue though; that in your selection of news you, in fact, very much influence the issues on which people will think about?

HEINE: Yes and it is a grave responsibility which Mr. Williams and his staff and all of us, including Mr. Carradine and Mr. Blackburn, take very seriously.

FORTIER: Then in this respect would you not agree that this power to influence those events to which people in your community will apply their minds, is raw, naked and unadulterated power?

HEINE: We are back to that again, No, if the basic ...

FORTIER: The power is there, Mr. Heine.

HEINE: No.

FORTIER: The power is not there?

HEINE: No.

FORTIER: The power is not there?

HEINE: ... an educated and politically sophisticated electorate can tell you when you are manipulating the news for your selfish advantage and they will do something about it in the long run. They will probably find something else to read.

FORTIER: What will they do in a one-newspaper town?

HEINE: They tend to ignore the manipulative elements ... and I made the point concerning politics on an American and Canadian basis in order to illustrate the point.

FORTIER: There is no suggestion on my part this is being done by the *London Free Press*.

HEINE: No. We are arguing an academic situation, I realize that.

Fortier then switched emphasis a bit and suggested that journalists who "do not have the integrity you do have, then that power [of manipulation] could be exercised and public opinion moulded in a way which would not be to the advantage of the community."

HEINE: ... there are some rags of sex publications knocking about in the big cities. There are all sorts of things but are they widely accepted? No, because we have an educated people in this country who know integrity when they see it.

Near the end of the proceedings, Walter mentioned that "in the past five years three bomb threats [were made against] the *London Free Press*" and added that the newspaper had offered a reward of $1000 (later backed by $10,000 from City Council) for the arrest of the person responsible for the murder of "five young women in recent years."

135

I added the comment that "there are two people, one associated with the intense hatreds of the Middle East and another associated with the strong views on the right-hand side of the political spectrum, who come to my office regularly and I say in all seriousness that I am very careful to keep myself between them and the door ... crank calls are common to all of us."

DAVEY: It sounds like public life.
HEINE: It is ...

Senator Prowse commented that he was "going to say we have lost a couple of presidents but I have not heard of us losing a city editor yet."

HEINE: They used to horsewhip them.

Ah, well, that's a long time ago, but my opinions about Senate committees, royal commissions, and the CRTC haven't altered in the slightest.

More than ever, in a democracy, people gather information through so many media forms — newspapers, radio, television, magazines, books, lectures, conversations, and a great proliferation of each of them — so that no single person, no newspaper conglomerate, no group of people can possibly manipulate public opinion significantly for any length of time, however hard they try.

The Monarchy, It Seems, Stands on Sacred Ground

In the fall of 1984, a few months after retiring, I wrote two articles on the monarchy, reviewing a battle going on in Britain over the Commonwealth role of Queen Elizabeth II. I suggested the queen might be well advised to have her status changed from being queen of Canada, to being in Canada as head of the Commonwealth.

That kind of nonsense doesn't sit too well in some places.

An enormously irate lady phoned the house to protest bitterly any diminution of that "lovely lady's" role in Canada. She wasn't the least bit interested in the possibility of making Her Majesty more acceptable to French-speaking citizens of Quebec. She was just mad, mad clean through.

Having vented her rage, she ended with the ultimate pronouncement.

"Well, let me tell you, sir, that if it were Queen Elizabeth I, *your head would roll.*"

That kept me light-hearted all fall.

Advice Is Worth What You Pay for It — and This Is Costing You Nothing

As we age many of us develop an unfortunate tendency to give advice — sometimes asked, more often unsought. It's one thing to offer freely expressed and even vigorous opinion on the broad issues of the day as part of a general discussion; it's another matter entirely to presume to give advice to individuals on how they should live their lives. Making that distinction is crucial to continued friendship — indeed, essential to making friends in the first place.

It was particularly stimulating, therefore, when young people turned up with an introduction from a friend or even just a phone call to ask advice about journalism as profession. Bald-headed old editors don't get many such opportunities to give personal advice to anyone. Invariably the visitors were young, eager, intelligent, good-looking and oh, wonder of wonders — they listened (if they weren't going to do that they wouldn't have bothered to drop by in the first place).

137

They usually had two questions: What routes were there to becoming a journalist, and what courses should they take at university? Frequently they were naïve enough to ask which English courses they should take. That gave an opening for a favourite line that it is possible to succeed in journalism despite the handicap of having taken English at university. English courses are superb vehicles for teaching appreciation of the language, an understanding of the glory of its past and the flexibility of its present. Any even marginally literate person graduating from university needs at least one basic course in English literature.

But journalism is another world and people who take their degree in English often have great difficulty adjusting to journalistic language formats. What then to study? Economics, political science, and history.

Economics because, with spectacular advances in communication — written, verbal, and visual — the global village is becoming a reality. Asian countries on the Pacific Rim are growing industrially at two, three, or more times the rate in North America and Europe. A high percentage of stories in newspapers and on television screens involves corporate mergers, mortgage interest rates, automobile financing, tax shelters, plant closings, unemployment — and it is impossible to write intelligently about these events and much else without a basic knowledge of the laws of supply and demand, unit costs and volume production, and an understanding why bad money drives out good.

During the Trudeau years it became increasingly apparent that uncontrolled government spending, along with the irrationality of such policies as the National Energy Program, would drive down the value of the dollar and push up interest rates. It was not possible to write effectively about such issues from 1967 on without an elementary understanding of economics.

Political Science because there is intense public interest in government, both our own and those of other nations. A journalist who does not understand the differences between the British parliamentary system and the checks and balances in the United States government is doomed to mediocrity. It's essential to understand that a constitution by itself is merely a scrap of paper, which for practical purposes it is in Russia and in dictatorships of the left and right around the world.

If you doubt the fragility of constitutions, remember that in Canada during World War II thousands of Canadian citizens born in this country, who happened to be descended from Japanese immigrants, were taken from their homes, which along with their possessions and businesses were sold, and isolated on the prairies in internment camps. That was a terrible injustice which led many to argue "we must have a constitution." That finally happened, presumably protecting similar victims in future.

Yet the United States has a constitution, every word of which is revered and protected by the presidency, Congress, the Supreme Court, and most of its citizens. Despite that constitution many thousands of American-born citizens had the same rights taken away from them as did those in Canada. Neither the presidency nor Congress nor the Supreme Court nor the constitution of which Americans are so proud protected those American-born citizens.

What provides meaning, permanence, and power in a constitution and makes it work in emotional situations lies in the minds of the people who live by it and who believe it to be the ultimate test against which government "of the people, by the people and for the people" can be measured. Without knowledge of the form and function of governments it is hardly possible even to read and understand much of the current news of the day. Without a solid educational background it is virtually impossible to write the news of the day intelligently.

History because, if you don't know where you've come from, how do you know where you're going? The origin of democracy in Athens, the long agony of the Dark Ages, the Renaissance, the Age of Reason, the dramatically sudden emerging of the American constitution which has governed the country for two centuries, nineteenth-century colonial imperialism and its consequences, the devastating wars of the twentieth century, and the new horizons opening up to mankind with global communication, a vast volume of transcontinental flight in mere hours, along with the exploration of space: all this and more journalists must understand to cover events of the day even adequately. And now men and women have an entirely new tool, the computer.

In ages long gone man's ancestors learned to use an extension of their arms. It was called a club; millennia passed and we learned to make better clubs and tools of stone, metal, and iron. Then we found an extension of our feet. It was called the wheel and the world became a different place to millions who grew food and transported it. In the Middle Ages, men discovered that two pieces of glass ground just so would magnify the written word; they called them spectacles. That may well have sparked the Renaissance because, until then, most scholars could only work and study effectively until they were in their mid-forties, when they could still see but found it impossible to read. Glasses were an extension of man's eyes, and scholars who lived into their sixties literally doubled their working lives. Thus mankind developed sophisticated tools to extend his hands, feet and eyes. Now, thousands of years after recorded history began, hundreds of thousands of years after evidences of man's first chipped flints, we have evolved something entirely new — man's first extension of his brain. The consequences, even in the years before the twenty-first century dawns, are almost beyond comprehension. Lack of understanding of that historical evolution is a great handicap to anyone who wants to write about the world as it is today and will be tomorrow.

So I tell the young women and men to study economics, political science, and history. The fastest and most efficient way to do that is at university, using summers to try to find jobs in journalism (the *Free Press* usually hired fourteen to eighteen each summer) and, after graduation, decide whether to take a one-year postgraduate course in journalism.

The other alternative is to find a job, usually for peanuts, on a weekly paper or small daily and gain enough experience to move to a daily in a small city, then to a major paper, all the while reading voraciously to make up for the lack of university courses. That can take anywhere from five years to a lifetime and is not recommended, though some fine journalists have taken just that route.

Not suprisingly, because the best of them are considerably smarter than my generation, sometimes they take my advice, which is a delight to this bald-headed old retired editor. What has been even more satisfying has been to have these young people phone or write or drop by, a year, five years, or a decade later, to voice appreciation. I'm an old softie, really, and that just breaks me up.

Newspapers Call It
the Way People Say It

London's postmaster once wrote that he didn't like our using "junk mail" to describe what the post office classifies as printed matter (printed mail addressed to an individual) and householder mail (addressed to householders in general).

There was no way he was going to change things, despite what he called the "numerous directives" his office issued. Junk mail did indeed come from the press and public, but in the reverse order; householders, irritated by the flow of printed home mail, were sometimes deceived by it and called it by the name they thought fit best — junk mail.

One of the things newspapermen learn quickly is to use simple words which everyone uses in ordinary conversation. Regularly, letters also came in complaining about our use of words which someone didn't like applied to their product. If a person quoted in the paper asked for a coke, and the drink in his hand is Wishing Well ginger ale, sure as the sun will rise tomorrow there'd be a carefully phrased letter from some public relations office of Coca-Cola, reminding us that the word "Coke" is the registered trade mark of his firm and not to be used in connection with any other product. There were letters insisting we spell the word with capital "c" and not with a lower-case "c." One firm insisted we spell "thermos" with a capital "T" because it was their registered trade mark. They pay people good salaries to check papers and write such letters.

My response was an equally polite letter noting that in the popular language of the day, people often ask, "Would you like a coke?" and get the response, "Sure, I'll have ginger ale." The word coke has come to mean any kind of bubbly, sweetened drink sold in bottles. Coca-Cola can't sue over every casual conversation in a local variety store.

A manufacturer telephoned from out of town and came in to see me the next morning to make a strong case for two kinds of vehicles which could be towed behind cars and trucks. He was most unhappy that we constantly used trailer to describe his product. We should, he urged, use "mobile home" to describe housing units which could be moved by special truck to a site for more or less permanent housing. We should use "recreational vehicle" to describe what people pull behind a car in which to live on a vacation.

He was just a little irritated when I explained we wouldn't call trailers recreational vehicles — it wasn't the term used by most people and we'd just look silly. We had a cup of coffee over an interesting discussion about the problems of small manufacturing businesses.

Then there was a registered letter from a man who manufactures suitcases. His trade name is "The Traveller." He'd read in the paper about a motel in London called the National Traveller, which this newspaper called the National Traveller on the first mention, then used the short form, the Traveller, from then on.

Obviously, whether the suitcase manufacturer liked it or not, that's what the general public was going to call the motel. He demanded that this newspaper always refer to the motel as the National Traveller. I said I felt he'd have a rough time trying to persuade the 250,000 people in London to say the National Traveller every time they mentioned that motel.

It wasn't that we were trying to be deliberately sticky about these matters. We live in a changing world, where new words are entering the language at a fantastic rate, thousands of them to describe new products, new systems, new ideas, new life styles, new ways of saying things as old as man himself. New words which are used by our readers are no problem — we just use them too. What poses a significant problem, however, are people who insist we use their manufactured words.

Governments are the worst offenders and the provincial government once had a plan to take drunks (officially described as "inebriated individuals with a high level of alcohol content in their blood") out of jail ("a detention place for convicted criminals") and send them instead to what will almost certainly be known as a place to dry out (but which is officially designated as a "detoxification centre").

Detoxification centre, indeed. It's a drunk tank.

Hoist, Regrettably, on Our Own Petard

Contrary to usual public understanding, newspapers do not ignore the human factor in covering events of interest to the public. At the *London Free Press* we did not report the name of the victim in a rape case. Any citizen who attended a rape trial could learn the name of the victim and tell others. We didn't. Nor did we seek to publish the names of juveniles charged with crimes. Doing so was against the law but some jurisdictions in other countries and some newspapers considered it proper to do so.

The most agonizing situation to surface in my entire tenure developed out of a simple burglary. For reasons which will be obvious, the locale and names are not used.

Two men broke into the home of a factory manager and at gunpoint forced him to accompany one of them to the plant, where he was obliged to open a vault containing valuables and money. His companion was left with the manager's wife and small child as hostages. The story of the hostage-taking and the escape of the two criminals was quite properly reported extensively, including the names and addresses of the couple and their business.

Some time later two men were arrested and charged on several counts. At the trial it came out that the man who stayed with the wife and son had forced her to perform oral sex. Our reporter included that fact as part of his coverage. It did not occur to him or to the editors who handled his story in the newsroom that evening that the victim had already been identified by earlier stories about the hostage-taking and robbery at the time it happened. Everyone who knew the family immediately knew not only who the victim was but also what had happened to her.

I wrote an abject apology to the family involved, who understandably protested our coverage and demanded redress. The trouble was that though I was quite prepared to publish an apology as abject as the letter, doing so would again draw attention to the original insult. Legally, we had done no wrong. We properly reported names of victims originally, equally properly reported the crimes as outlined in court during the trial. Yet in doing so we violated our own rule not to publish the names of rape victims — and that incident certainly was rape.

Relatives of the family came to London more than once. I repeated willingness to apologize publicly in any way they wished but felt obliged to point out the consequences of doing so. Eventually, they accepted the facts — there simply wasn't anything to be done about it which wouldn't make the situation worse.

Meanwhile, desperate to do something, I gave newsroom a memo ordering that oral sex not be referred to in news stories under any circumstances. That wasn't very bright. Someone sent a copy of the memo to *Content*, a media magazine published at Humber College in Toronto; they published a facsimile. Completely frustrated by this time, I sent a scathing note to *Content* asking if any of their staff could suggest a better answer. None did.

In time I recinded the memo on the reasonable grounds that it was too broad a directive altogether. Medical columnists, social and sexual studies frequently mentioned oral sex, but the *Free Press* was prohibited from publishing such material. As well, the memory of the injustice we'd done to the wife in the hostage story had faded — but not so much that we ever again published evidence in a criminal trial which identified the victim of rape.

Years later the American Society of Newspaper Editors put out a slim volume, *Drawing the Line*, in which thirty-one editors described how they solved "their toughest ethical dilemmas." Asked to contribute, I told this story, which they captioned "Damned if we did, damned if we didn't." A brief outline ended on the note that we could "neither defend the newspaper's right to publish information the public was entitled to know, nor publish our apologies for what the victim would always see as a grievous error on our part."

There Are More Experts Around Than Most of Us Realize

In the mid-1970s, when few westerners had been to the People's Republic of China, I spent a couple of weeks there tagging along after Prime Minister Pierre Trudeau. Back in Canada, I was in demand as a speaker, and able as well to return some of the hospitality the Chinese had shown by taking a group of Chinese agriculturalists around Western Ontario.

At lunch we were guests of a Delhi service club, at which I was to be speaker. I've always been leery of appearing to be an expert, partly because I'm not, partly out of becoming modesty.

In this instance, damn good thing, too.

I said I'd only been in China a couple of weeks; then some sixth sense led me to ask how many of the thirty guests had been to China. Eleven had. They'd been to China to sell Ontario tobacco. Turned out some had been there several times and for fairly lengthy visits.

That helped a great deal a year or two later when I was asked to show slides on China to senior citizens at McCormick Home. As the lights went down I suggested residents who had been to China might stay after and talk about their trip. Trip? Five little old ladies came to have a wonderful chat; one had lived in China as a missionary for forty years.

Earlier lesson confirmed; always assume there's someone in the audience who knows more than you do.

What Does a Newspaper Do when One of Its Own Staff Dies?

Some newspapers publish an obituary on their news pages for every person who dies in the paper's circulation area. Obviously, only relatively small newspapers can find the space.

Other newspapers publish obituaries for one or two persons daily, arbitrarily picking deceased persons from among the classified notices. The *Toronto Star* does this and usually publishes an obit for any member of their staff.

Still other newspapers publish obituaries on news pages for deceased persons who, in the opinion of the editors, are widely known in the community. That's the policy I adopted for the *London Free Press*, almost from the beginning. Only once or twice a year was my opinion asked on an obit; staff knew the rules and the newsroom was sufficiently aware who met the definition of being widely known to make each decision reasonably straightforward.

That awareness, however, didn't extend to decisions on staff deaths. There was a strong tendency for staff to argue for obits on their colleagues whom they knew, despite maybe knowing they were stretching things somewhat.

Policy was clear, and unequivocal. All over London and Western Ontario, every day of the year, there were anywhere from a dozen to a score or two deaths. Every one of those families believed in their hearts that their dear father, mother, sister, brother, husband, wife, son, daughter, or even dear old auntie was well known and deserved a news-page obituary — as distinct from the formal classified notice. If the newspaper unreasonably published news-page obits on its own staff, people would remember our two standards and our credibility would be significantly diminished. When it came to death, people remembered.

It took a long time to get that policy established. Circulation people, working in specific city blocks and in small Western Ontario towns, argued strenuously for a more generous obit policy, best of all about four inches of type for everyone. Most days that would take a page of type. Everyone who was really close to the deceased already knew of the death; those who didn't found out in classified notices. For our other 129,850 subscribers that page was wasted. In time my approach prevailed.

Newsroom staff weren't as easy to convince.

There was no question about coverage when one of our best reporters, Joe McClelland, was killed in a plane crash in northern Ontario while covering a story about his Indian friends.

When Bill Webster, who wrote our movie-page reviews, died, however, a column about him was written by a colleague and features department wanted to run it next day. That posed several problems; the piece was too emotional — measured against other marginally well-known people who died the same day Bill might warrant an obit but not an emotional column — and staff pressure had developed strongly enough to have become an effort to change policy. The answer: no. It took a long luncheon discussion a week later to mollify the hurt feelings of those who wrote the column. They never quite agreed but at least they listened.

That was more than staff did when Mel Howey died. Mel was a newsroom favourite, everyone's friend, a musician who led a popular church choir which had made records, a character who went about summer and winter in a suit coat — no overcoat, no scarf, no hat, no gloves — and a fine editor.

He happened to die the Sunday night following the Friday night on which the publisher of the *London Free Press* died. As Walter Blackburn was very well known indeed in the community, having been publisher for forty-eight years and active in a host of community projects, there was a page-one story, his photograph, an editorial I'd written (a year before which he never saw), and my by-lined column about his personality and integrity as publisher. That seemed fairly comprehensive.

When Mel died, someone wrote an obit which the then assistant managing editor, Bill Morley, now editor-in-chief, showed to me with a recommendation it not be used. Well-known as he was to our staff (and liked by all of us) and to the small church where he was so active, Mel was no different from a dozen other persons who died that weekend in terms of being widely known.

Newsroom reacted violently. Scathing criticisms of the decision appeared on bulletin boards, dour looks were common, vocal protests were heard on all sides. There was no criticism of our coverage of the publisher's death — indeed, blended with the criticism of lack of coverage of Mel's death was resentment that neither a Ting cartoon nor a lengthy column by Del Bell about the publisher was used. Several paragraphs from the CP wire on the death of a former Southam president caused resentment, too.

I stayed loose — after all, we were running a daily newspaper. I'd taken advice, made a decision, and that was that. Then matters took another turn; staff were taking up a collection to buy advertising space to publish their own obituary of Mel. Fine idea, that. Anyone is free to do so. But when I complimented the organizer and fished out a $50 bill as my contribution, there were agonized protests. Sometimes a fellow can't win. The obit ad duly ran. Later I arranged to have the account for it cancelled and the funds went into the office flowers pool.

The disturbing aspect was that none of the protestors took their case to any editor along the line to argue a reversal. If they had, we might have reversed ourselves and run an obit; there was a case to be made, weak but possibly a case. Failing to do that put another connotation on the issue — establishing editorial policy by bulletin board pressure. No way.

It was the only time in almost two decades that I was really angry as an administrator. Drafting a two-page memo to those behind the newsroom reaction, I rewrote it more than once and checked it against the views of several senior editors before having blunt discussions, one to one, with several people.

The basic reaction was "Oh, I didn't know that."

To which the reply was "No, and you didn't ask, either."

Thus endeth that lesson.

Good News Syndrome Grossly Irrational

Nothing irritated me more than having to listen to people ask "Why don't you print more good news?" There are many reasons why newspapers "don't publish more good news." Oddly, those who complain the most are responsible. They simply don't read good news. For all practical purposes, people just aren't interested.

I illustrate that aspect of newspapers by noting that the Colborne Street crossing of CNR's main line runs beside the *Free Press* plant. If we ran a story every day saying, "hooray, hooray, 4739 cars and trucks crossed the tracks yesterday without an accident," readers would soon stop buying the paper. But if a fast freight from Toronto hits a car with five passengers and smears it for a mile down the track past the CNR station, believe me, everybody in town wants to know all the details.

When unusually aggressive callers became emotional and accused the newspaper of being sensational in order to sell papers, I'd get nasty.

"You say, sir, that you want nothing but good news in the paper?"

"That's right, there's too much bad news all the time."

"OK, if you want nothing but good news, have you ever thought of turning to your Bible?"

That usually terminated the conversation.

Interestingly, in my experience, people don't remember the good news when it happens to others (though everyone remembers such good news as themselves winning a million-dollar lottery). Who remembers, except their families, the safe return of thousands of U.S. Marines from Lebanon? But few of us have forgotten the tragic deaths of 271 Marines in a suicide attack on Marine headquarters in Beirut.

I was once asked the good news/bad news question after a service club talk in London. Fishing under my chair, I said, "Well, let's have a look at page one today," and held up the paper. The audience laughed with glee. The headline read "Price of Butter Increases 5 Cents." When the laughter died down I threw the hooker. "That's good news for most of our readers." A few smiled in understanding but most were merely puzzled. "Well, we sell a great many papers outside London. And in the rural areas, an increase in butter prices is good news."

Readers tend not to look at news objectively. A drop in the Canadian dollar against the U.S. dollar is bad for snowbirds heading south for a winter in Florida; it is good news for Canadian exporters by making their products more competitive. It was bad news to most United Church members that Toronto headquarters considered ordaining homosexuals; it was good news to the gay population.

News is neither good nor bad. News is information people need or want to live more satisfying and productive lives. People need to have all the information available about the risk of nuclear, or any other war so they can, through government, protect themselves either by eliminating nuclear weapons or by having enough to deter others from using them. People need information on the economy, how many are unemployed, what are loan rates for mortgages, what they can earn as interest on savings, where to shop for a new coat, what municipal, provincial, and federal governments are doing and why, and what effect there will be on taxes, how to bake a cheese cake, who's doing what to whom, where and when, and if possible to determine, for what reason. Depending on whether people are borrowing or lending, high and low interest rates are neither good nor bad; they exist.

Whether news is good or bad varies about as much as do individuals.

If Politicians Can't Stand the Heat, Better They Get Out of the Kitchen

Aside from the Kent Report which was in a class by itself, one of the most irrational attempts to prevent people from having information about the political system in Canada turned up in 1972. It was never clear who originated the idea, but the cabinet sheepdog on the venture was Allan MacEachen. He came up with amendments to the Election Act which would deny anyone the right to publish articles, editorials, advertisements or any announcement "of a partisan political character" on election day and the day immediately preceding election day.

I was vigorously and adamantly opposed. In a draft of a letter addressed to Prime Minister Pierre Trudeau which he tested on his good friend, St. Clair Balfour, then chairman of Southam Press and a *London Free Press* director, Walter Blackburn tried to be fair and suggested that if politicians, political parties, and the public are banned from campaigning on election day and the day preceding, "I do not think that the media would have any grounds for objecting to a similar ban on editorial content."

In his covering letter to Balfour he noted that "Bill Heine is opposed to [this] alternative" and feels strongly there should be no restrictions on the rights of anyone to speak about or advertise matters of "a partisan political character" right up to and including election day. "He feels that freedom of speech (including freedom of candidates to campaign) and freedom of the press are inseparable and that the latter is an extension of the former. I do not disagree."

Balfour replied that he agreed with Heine's "reluctance to volunteer any restraint on editorial comment ... we either have freedom of speech or we don't." He did argue, however, that lest newspapers be considered interested only in the advertising dollar, "we should forego advertising for a 48-hour period before election day."

I saw no difference whatever between our right to say what we wished on news and editorial pages and what we or others might say in an advertisement. It was essential to fight the issue on an absolute basis.

Next day an editorial ran which noted that

> any politician ... any citizen ... can hire a hall to express "partisan political" views, stand on a soap box and declaim his opinions, or invite the public to a corn roast and tell them who he thinks they should elect ... but [under the proposed Election Act

amendments] the country's newspapers would not be able to report what was said.

That would make second-class citizens of all those who couldn't get to the hall, who didn't pass the soap box, or who didn't attend the corn roast ... an outrageous invasion of an essential ingredient of democracy, the freedom of any citizen to describe and comment on political events before, during or after an election ...

If Prime Minister Trudeau is so all-fired determined to restrict election coverage ... let him tell Liberal candidates to stop campaigning at sundown two days prior to the forthcoming election ... if [they] say nothing, there will be nothing to report, at least about them ... and the prime minister, with two nights sleep and a quiet day, can face the electorate with a politically serene countenance on election day ... (if) Trudeau can't hack it to election day, that's his problem.

A few weeks later in an interview with MacEachen I reiterated the points in the editorial. I followed this talk with a letter, ending on the note that his party could do as it wished but that the "opposition of the day must remain free to exercise its right to be critical right up to the last vote being cast."

As chairman of the Canadian section of the International Press Institute, I also promised MacEachen that the matter would be raised on the floor of that year's IPI assembly. He seemed uninterested while I made the initial pitch but began listening intently at mention of his party's definition of free speech being raised at a meeting of free-world journalists.

When he pointed out that broadcasters, under Canadian Radio-Television and Telecommunications Commission regulations, were prohibited from "partisan election activity" on election day and the day before, I showed him an editorial which said in part that Canadian newspapers "owe an apology to their broadcasting colleagues. For years they've been under the same restrictions now proposed for newspapers ... [and that] Canadian newspapers largely ignored the [restrictions] ... newspapers should oppose not only the proposed restrictions but also existing regulations on broadcasting."

By June the government had second thoughts; a Canadian Press story reported that the government had withdrawn a plan which would have restricted newspaper coverage of an election campaign. In the "interests of equality" the report proposed amendments that would lift the same restrictions in force since 1936 for radio and television, while retaining time restrictions on election advertising.

Equally ludicrous legislation which would prohibit third-party election advertising found all-party support in 1983. It forbid election campaign advertising by third-party or special interest groups either for or against a party or candidate unless the group registered as a party and nominated candidates in at least fifty ridings. That meant, in effect, that individuals and groups could hire a hall and speak about election campaigns, and of course that newspapers, broadcast outlets, and magazines could report what was said, but that people who were not candidates could not advertise their views of the campaign — the intent being further to restrict campaign spending by candidates and parties.

Colin Brown's National Citizens Coalition took the issue to the Alberta Court of Queen's Bench, which found the law to be unconstitutional under Canada's Charter of Rights.

What was frightening was the all-party support for a law which denied citizens the right to print or broadcast their views in an election. Even opposition MPs seemed to assume that government, not the people, knew best. In a democracy, democracy has a tough time.

Inputting an Umbrage

It's a quiet morning and the lead editorial for next day is almost finished.

The phone rings.

"Heine here."

"Sir, I have an umbrage I want to input to you."

Easy now, take a little time with that one.

"Ah, yes. Fine. Does that mean you are angry?"

"Yes, and I want to input it to you now."

"Very well, I'm plugged in under 'u' for umbrage — begin input."

I made notes on umbrage but have no idea what the fellow took umbrage about.

Walter J. Blackburn, Publisher: People Liberal, Fiscal Conservative

For the almost half century he was publisher of the *London Free Press*, Walter's unswerving objective was to maintain the newspaper, which to him was a public trust, as an independent voice in Canada.

I worked with him closely for thirty of those years, first as an adviser on unions when pressmen were certified as a bargaining unit, then as we built and equipped a new plant and put it in operation, and, most satisfying of all, as editor of the paper. I came to know him well and in some degree to understand his complex personality. We never became friends in the sense of being golf partners (I've never held a golf club in my hands) but we understood each other — and probably worked together more effectively because we weren't palsy-walsy golf partners.

His grandfather had bought the *London Free Press* in 1853, a weekly then four years old, and converted it to a daily. A second generation, brothers Arthur and Walter, inherited the paper and passed it on to Walter (Arthur's son) in 1936. Walter was in his final year at university. He had his troubles but soon gained working control as well as ownership. He also had considerable foresight; believing that World War II was imminent he invested in a new press and laid in stocks of newsprint. Even then his management policies were people-oriented. When the *London Advertiser*, owned by the *Toronto Star*, folded and was sold to the *Free Press*, Walter hired most of the 'Tiser's staff. That was no small matter in the late 1930s. People may not have been well paid but they had jobs. At war's end pay improvements came rapidly, along with sick-pay policies, a forty-hour week, and a pension plan. Recently, the Blackburn Group was listed as one of Canada's best 100 employers.

From early in the twentieth century the Southam chain had owned 25 per cent of the *London Free Press*, security for a loan. It was one of Walter's greatest prides to have been able in the 1970s to buy back that quarter share of the newspaper — at a cost of $11.25 million (the original loan was said to have been $25,000).

For all his fine qualities, Walter wasn't always the easiest person in the world to work with. He could also leave the impression of being a stuffed shirt, which he wasn't. He thought there were proper ways of doing things and had a habit of saying so without too much regard for the views of others — a characteristic of inherited wealth. Ulcers I acquired eventually but Walter didn't cause them, though some managers were terrified of him. I didn't have that problem, partly because I liked and trusted him, partly because I had a sufficiently high (some would say overblown) opinion of myself. While avoiding confrontation in front of our colleagues, one to one we'd argue point for point, nose to nose, usually not backing off until one had convinced the other.

In all our working years I never knew him to do a selfish or dishonourable thing. He wanted a newspaper of integrity and, as long as he believed my motives were as honourable as his, that I had no axe to grind, we quickly found common ground for any decision which faced us about the editorial content of the newspaper.

One of the most revealing insights into our relationship came from an old friend and antagonist, Chuck Fenn, former advertising director. At a reception before a dinner marking my retirement, Chuck, also retired, reminded me how often we ended up in the publisher's office in my early days as editor when I was fighting daily to get rid of all kinds of readers (advertising blurbs disguised as news content) which catered to Chuck's advertisers.

"You never backed down," said Chuck.

"No, I guess not."

"You know why I backed off?" Chuck asked.

I tried a quip but that didn't deter him.

"The publisher called me in and told me he couldn't afford to lose you."

We looked at each other solemnly for a moment while I registered that revelation.

Chuck grinned. "He was telling me it was my job on the line, not yours."

That told me something about what Walter had really wanted even in the days when readers were used. It said a lot too about an aggressive and effective salesman named Chuck who was also honest.

Walter's integrity had to be experienced to be believed. When his only son Walter committed suicide in Toronto we were sick at heart for him. Next morning he called, listened to my condolences, thanked me, then asked a simple question.

"Bill, what is our policy on suicides?"

It was a measure of the man that he didn't ask to have his personal tragedy kept out of the paper. How many other publishers in the free world would have approached that story as he did I have no way of knowing, but I'll bet there are few. Out of personal regard for him it was with relief I replied that unless suicide was a public act or of a widely known public figure, our policy was not to report suicides as such.

Like all of us, he had his egotistical aspects. Throughout Arthur Ford's long tenure, as in John Elliott's shorter time and for a few years in mine, Walter would participate daily in the editorial-page conference and frequently do a thorough hatchet job on an editorial prepared for his scrutiny. For most of my tenure he was both getting older and had many other issues and concerns. He seldom appeared at editorial conferences. I doubt if he even commented on more than a few editorials a year. Seeking another opinion, I'd sometimes take an editorial to his office and "run it up the flagpole to see if he'd salute it." He would usually fiddle with the wording but the thrust he seldom disputed. Yet he would assure visitors and colleagues at annual media conferences that he kept a close personal eye on the editorial conference and often dropped in to discuss the issues of the day. He did turn up election nights, for federal budgets and major constitutional issues.

When an editorial was written on those nights by an editorial-page writer, the editorial-page editor, or by me, or segments by three people, we'd polish and hone the result then send it back to the computer to have it set in type for the publisher to see. Invariably he'd make a minor change or two, murmur "very good" and go back to a general discussion of the evening's events.

Reports were a different matter. His capacity to bore in on detail was devastating. He could take home a 600-page package and return next morning with the third footnote on page 503 marked with a pencilled "x," which indicated he'd found a flaw which as often as not invalidated the entire report — in his view. No lawyer could be more meticulous in reading a contract — and woe to the manager who signed a sloppy contract. He read thick documents of direct personal interest in great detail, chewed his careful way through them, then couldn't understand why his editor, who read three newspapers daily, a dozen magazines a week, and a score or more other magazines and books a month — to say nothing of great volumes of mail and miles of raw copy — hadn't read the documents he had.

He also had a tricky habit of asking a question about a subject he'd studied purposely, then measure a person's ability by the accuracy of the response. I had that happen one day with a casual question about Shi'ites and Sunni, the two principal elements of the Muslim faith. Having written articles explaining the origins of the two sects, having written about a few hundred other subjects since then, and having no recollection which sects were descended from which line from the Prophet, I just said I'd bring in the book from my home library which explained the complexities of the Muslim religion. Walter was not pleased.

Yet he also had a great capacity to delegate sweeping authority. The day he asked me to become editor of the newspaper I asked what policies he wished carried out. "You have a free hand," was his reply. An hour later, he put his head in the door and with a quiet grin said, "About that free hand — I'd like to be consulted before we endorse a political party in a provincial or federal election."

No editor could have asked for greater freedom in establishing news coverage and editorial-page opinion. He was the antithesis of Rupert Murdock, the Australian publisher who had thirteen editors in fifteen years on one of his Australian papers. My predecessors were Arthur Ford, editor from 1920 to 1962 (1936–62 working with Blackburn), and John Elliott, 1962–67. My term was 1967 to 1984; in sixty-two years the paper had three editors. Not all the newspaper's business, marketing, and production managers (by whatever title they were known) survived as long. He had a great capacity for leaving his editors to edit — and write, speak, travel, or whatever — but tended to delve deeply into the detail of other aspects of the newspaper's operations.

He had a disconcerting habit of wandering around the plant, talking for an hour to junior staff, then turning up in a manager's office with questions about which the poor fellow knew nothing at all. Some managers turned into jellied flesh, which cost them his respect. Others became defensive and argumentive, which merely made him bore in harder. The wise ones assured the publisher they'd take care of the matter immediately and did so by verbally beating the tar out of the talkative staff member in private.

He had other personal idiosyncrasies. He had a dozen briefcases at last count. Some contained unopened mail; when his long-suffering secretaries could derail one of them, mail would be sorted, filed, and sometimes even answered. One secretary told me with great glee she'd found an unopened letter in one briefcase dated 1947. He used briefcases as a kind of private filing system. It almost reached the point where he had to file the briefcases.

Walter's habit of equating rank or position with intelligence was an assumption which led more than once to disappointment. He'd grumble and grouse that the man had this position or that responsibility — how could he be so uninformed? He really believed that if people just took time to dot every "i" and cross every "t," and if preliminary work were done perfectly, then the outcome would also be perfect — that is, what one wished it to be. And he was always taken back when it didn't come out as planned. It came out as planned often enough to make him expect that it would every time — but he failed to accept the fact that people could mess up the works, for reasons which could never be predicted in advance, indeed, if there was a reason. He never learned the military lesson deeply engrained in every senior officer that there's always some bastard down the line who "doesn't get the word."

Oddly, also, he never understood the investigative capacity of a good reporter. He came down to my office one day to tell me in the strictest confidence about a major property deal underway in the city. It had not yet jelled but would be announced next day. I didn't say so to him but, by God, if there was a big deal underway and our street staff hadn't heard about it I'd have been surprised — and annoyed. Wagging an admonitory finger to keep it quiet, he went back upstairs. I headed for the newsroom and asked casually of the city editors, "Well, what big story is brewing this morning?" They offered a proof of a story with all the details about which the publisher had just sworn me to secrecy. Murmuring "Well done," I wandered into Walter's office and laid the proof on his desk. "Newsroom already had the story," I told him. "It's running in the afternoon paper." He wasn't upset. In fact, he was delighted. He just wasn't able to understand how staff sources were as good as his.

Walter also had a great capacity to see a conspiracy. I remember a strong pitch to do stories on a communist takeover in Quebec during the FLQ crisis; an equally strong conviction that Quebec would shut down the St. Lawrence when it became independent, cutting off the rest of Canada from the Maritime provinces; and a plot by oil pipeline workers to blow up all the pumping stations feeding oil from Alberta to Ontario and Quebec. The first I argued was illogical, though only partially convincing him; the second I discounted because the Canadian army wouldn't have to reopen the Seaway — the U.S. Marines would do that and indirectly thereby restore the south bank of the St. Lawrence to Canada as an east-west corridor, a thought which intrigued him; the third I went along with outwardly but in fact simply failed to assign a reporter to go out and try to pin down.

He assumed that any intelligent person should be able to understand mechanical and electrical drawings as well as he did. When our new plant was almost finished in 1965 he had me escort a group around the building, including St. Clair Balfour of the Southam newspaper chain and a director on the *London Free Press* board. In a vast room full of pipes and other gear, Walter asked me to explain what each set of pipes was for. I looked at him in astonishment, then described myself as an "expeditor, not a mechanical engineer." He hid his annoyance and we moved on to other rooms, but he really couldn't understand how I could have managed the construction project without knowing every detail.

Yet he also returned several years ago from a lengthy trip to Asia with a response to a question which said much about his honesty with himself and others. "What," I asked, "impressed you most about the Far East?" He looked out the window for some minutes before replying thoughtfully, "I learned there are a lot of people with dark skins in other parts of the world who are smarter than I am." He wasn't being condescending; simply reacting to exposure he hadn't had before. From a man who should have been an eighteenth-century English knight (Sir Walter would have been appropriate for his tall, distinguished figure), that answer said much about his concepts of twentieth-century democracy as well as his integrity.

His approach to democracy included unequivocal support for the constitutional monarchy. In his enthusiasm he could trap himself. When Pauline McGibbon was named lieutenant-governor of Ontario I wrote a highly complimentary editorial on the appointment. In casual conversation a few days later Walter demurred, saying the position required dignity and poise, that a man should have been appointed. I waited until he unburdened himself and, knowing his deep admiration for Elizabeth II, asked gently, "You feel a woman can't represent a queen?" He froze for five seconds, then exploded into laughter. A year later he was saying McGibbon was the best lieutenant-governor Ontario ever had.

He had little liking for politicians, fearing, rightly as it turned out, the collective instinct of politicians of all parties to spend tax dollars both to keep themselves in power and to try to control the free expression of information and opinion in Canada. Politically he was conservative but not a blind party Conservative. I teased him he was what in the nineteenth century was termed "of a conservative persuasion." More accurately he was a people liberal and a fiscal conservative. He believed strongly, as I did, that no one in Canada should go to bed hungry, cold or needing medical attention. After that, we both felt that the state had fulfilled most of its obligation to all citizens. Yet he believed also that the country could and should exercise fiscal responsibility, balancing its budget as must corporations, partnerships, and householders.

In his forty-eight years as president the newspaper supported anything which added to the quality of life in London. The list is long and impressive. The city has an unlimited water supply from Lake

Huron instead of rapidly diminishing wells; a flood control system on the Thames; parks and open land through almost the entire city; a superb university hospital; a new municipal hospital under construction; sharply reduced river pollution; a major annexation which permitted control of development and avoiding ribbon development; strong support for retaining a vigorous downtown area (which could have been self-serving but wasn't); development of The Pinery as a provincial park. We also ran strong campaigns on issues of the day; in-depth articles on local drug problems; investigation of a degree mill at church-related Philathea College; breaking the story on mercury poisoning in the St. Clair River and Lake St. Clair, following up with extensive coverage of similar poisoning in the French River system and sending staff to Japan to report on the effects of Minimata disease; first-hand reporting of women at a home for the aged being kept nude in a room while waiting for morning bathing; editorial opinion pressing for open county councils; and, always, determined efforts to ensure the right of taxpayers to know how their affairs were conducted at the municipal, provincial, and federal levels.

In the process we won a Michener award, along with two runners-up; several national press awards, and over the years scores of first and runners-up awards at the annual Western Ontario Newspaper Awards. Once when we'd won seven firsts and six runners-up in the Western Ontario awards (out of thirteen categories), I showed him a list of the award winners. He grinned. "When do you plan to make it thirteen winners?" I said we were working on it. Despite the teasing he made a point of sending a personal note to those who had won. His notes to me on several awards I won were heart-warming.

He was an unusual mixture of nineteenth-century paternalism and twentieth-century technological vision.

He died of cancer in December 1983. Several months later, for a number of personal reasons, I arranged to retire early. One reason, which I didn't really acknowledge to myself at the time, was that it wasn't fun any more without Walter around. I once told him, while declining an invitation to do something or go somewhere with him, that I was looking forward to retirement, when we might get to know each other better as individuals. He frowned for a moment, then grinned. He understood. His death eliminated any opportunity there might have been to build on our editorial relationship. Looking back, the mistake was mine. Given our ages (mine early sixties, his late sixties), I should have made a greater effort.

One of the finest tributes ever paid him he didn't know about and the person who offered it never met him. Some years ago the editor of a weekly publication in Toronto, Sol Littman, would come to London or telephone to ask advice on editorial problems, particularly his relationship with his publishers (as I recall he had three, which was an impossible situation in itself). When he understood the relationship Walter had with his editors, reporters, and other staff, and learned the Blackburn family had been more than a century in journalism, Sol said thoughtfully, "You know, sometimes I think it must take three generations to make a good publisher."

He had a point.

London Times *Creed Worth an Editor's Remembering*

It hung on a pillar in the front lobby of *The Times*. Whether it is still there with Rupert Murdock as publisher I haven't queried.

THIS IS A PRINTING OFFICE
CROSSROADS OF CIVILIZATION
REFUGE OF ALL THE ARTS
Against the ravages of time
ARMOURY OF FEARLESS TRUTH
Against whispering rumour
INCESSANT TRUMPET OF TRADE
From this place WORDS may fly abroad
Not to perish on waves of sound
Not to vary with the writer's hand
BUT FIXED IN TIME HAVING BEEN VERIFIED IN PROOF
FRIEND YOU STAND ON SACRED GROUND
THIS IS A PRINTING OFFICE

Years in Britain Generated Love/Hate Relationship

Three years in England during the war were prelude to a love affair with Britain which has grown during dozens of visits since. Physically, it's a beautiful country, its cities and countryside endlessly changing in lovely vistas. Culturally, the people of England, Scotland, and Ireland are the source of literature which inspires millions around the world. Politically, Britain developed a parliamentary system of government which had no equal until the United States developed its congressional/presidential/supreme court system. I still argue the parliamentary system is superior.

And the people are wonderful, gracious folk for the most part, whether farm hands or titled. A family in Eastbourne became second parents; a knight who lived in his gardener's cottage while Canadians clomped through his manor house taught me much about men and manners; girls from the cliffs of Dover to the Moray Firth taught me even more; and the ladies who ran a wide range of special services for restless Canadians helped me gain some appreciation of art, music, and the theatre.

All this and much more about Britain I learned during the war. The country's charms have remained never-ending on vacation trips beginning in 1959, on writing trips after becoming editor of the *London Free Press* in 1967, and to this day.

What sometimes soured the love affair was angry frustration with an arrogant minority who seemed to believe the empire of the eighteenth and nineteenth centuries still existed. During the war I began saying of Britain's officer class, and have had reason to repeat it since, that one in four Englishmen were the salt of the earth, men I'd cheerfully follow or lead to hell and back; two of four were solid citizens; and the remaining one in four were grade A number 1 unadulterated bastards. At times that last group can be so arrogantly, piously, and irritatingly superior, it's hard for "colonials" to remain civil.

In my war years I dated a lovely young London lady whose family skimped on their rations to feed a visiting Canadian. One night, spending a month's pay, I took her to the Trocadero for what in wartime Britain passed for a fine dinner. The line-up was long, but we were early and soon next in line for a table. A British lieutenant-colonel charged down the line and demanded the head waiter give him the next table — insisting that as a colonel he should be given a table ahead of a corporal. I refused flatly. When the head waiter stood by my rights, bless him, the colonel demanded to see my leave pass, made loud noises about laying charges, and refused to return the pass. Without it I was liable to detention by any military police- man who happened to stop me, or who might have been told to do so by an irate colonel.

We didn't let the stupid fellow spoil things. We ate and danced through a lovely evening, took the tube to Swiss Cottage station and walked home hand-in-hand.

Back with my unit, I was mad as hell and briefed our colonel. Sure enough, the English colonel laid charges. For once my colonel was on my side (he wasn't often, usually for good reason). He wrote back that Cpl. Heine had laid charges against the colonel for retain- ing his leave pass, which was strictly against regulations. Would the English colonel, wrote the Canadian colonel, confirm that he still wished to go ahead with his charges.

No reply. No charges.

The memory of my seething anger over that incident came to mind several times on trips to England when, in the early 1980s, Canada sent a resolution to the British House of Commons which gave Canada a constitution and cut the last token colonial link be- tween the two countries. Scores of British members of Parliament took the resolution seriously and debated at great length, in and out of the House of Commons, what should be Britain's response. Canada's Prime Minister Pierre Trudeau had an answer; he told them just to hold their noses and swallow it. I agreed completely and added that if they didn't, Canada should find a way to force-feed them.

During interviews with several British members of Parliament and peers I came close to losing my temper, which was hardly the best approach for a supposedly unbiased journalist. I wasn't there as a reporter gathering factual information (there were lots of those); my interest was in writing opinion columns and that gave me legitimate reason not only to probe for information but also to argue personal convictions. After listening to their ludicrous views that they felt a deep sense of responsibility to the Canadian people, I had a rude question: "Who among the Canadian people elected you?"

That sometimes concentrated their attention wonderfully but as often didn't register at all. Their responses were at times astonishing. When I asked Jonathan Aitken what led to his forming a discussion group of MPs on whether the British House of Commons should pass the resolution, he replied, "Oh, my great-uncle was a Canadian, you know." His great-uncle was Lord Beaverbrook. Having a Canadian great-uncle gave him as much authority over Canada's constitution as my having a great-great-great-grandfather who fought with the British against the Americans in the 1770s gave me to tell British generals how to run the war in the Falkland Islands.

Some members of Parliament recognized the validity of the question about who elected them, but argued the constitution was "a matter between governments." To that I predicted what Trudeau would do if Westminster rejected the Canadian resolution. He immediately would have called a general election in which his campaign would be built around one question: "Who is governing Canada, the British House of Commons in Westminister or the Canadian House of Commons in Ottawa?" Trudeau would have been elected with the kind of majorities John Diefenbaker and Brian Mulroney received.

There were more subtle but devastating dangers from the British point of view. Queen Elizabeth II would have been put in the impossible position of having to choose between the advice of her first minister in Canada (to approve a resolution of her Parliament in Canada) and the advice of her first minister in Britain (not to approve a resolution which had been rejected by her Parliament in Britain).

If she refused the advice of her British prime minister not to sign the resolution, she would have precipitated a major crisis of British precedent. If she refused the advice of her Canadian prime minister to sign the resolution, she would have destroyed the monarchy in Canada. Trudeau, having won an election on the "Who is governing Canada?" theme, would have had the constitution passed by Canada's House of Commons and signed into law by a newly appointed head of state (president, governor general — call it what you will) who would obey the decisions of the Canadian House of Commons and the advice of the prime minister. Once by-passed on such a crucial issue, the monarch would never again be asked to sign a bill passed by the Canadian House of Commons. That would have been the end of the monarchy in Canada.

That might not have been entirely bad. As I wrote in articles a year or so later, there is a good case to be made for Queen Elizabeth II relinquishing her status as queen of Canada for the same reason her father relinquished his title as emperor of India. That came about when India was achieving her independence after the Second World War. Determined to become a republic, with its own president, India appeared about to leave the Commonwealth as well. Wise heads prevailed; Indians agreed to accept George VI, not as king of Britain but as head of the Commonwealth. Theoretically, the next head of the Commonwealth need not be Charles III; any Commonwealth citizen could be named to the position.

Why bother following that precedent in Canada? Because in Quebec today the queen would not be welcomed by a majority of French-speaking Canadians. To them she represents all the arrogance of Englishmen who ruled Canada after the Conquest, and of Anglophones in Canadian governments which ruled, with equal arrogance in French-Canadian eyes, after Confederation in 1867. As head of the Commonwealth, however, she might be as welcome in Quebec in the future as she was in India during the recent Commonwealth conference there.

Her Majesty is reported to be a very wise lady. She has seen a good many governments come and go in Britain, scores more do so around the world. Her advice is often sought. Sometimes she offers advice before she is asked. On the Canadian constitution resolution Queen Elizabeth fully understood the issues and made certain her views were known. The Canadian resolution passed the British House of Commons with only thirty-odd dissenting votes, and unanimously in the House of Lords. That was a fraction of those originally interviewing Canadian Indians, delving into precedents, and generally making themselves obnoxious on what they claimed was an issue for which they had responsibility.

A year after the resolution had passed, a senior member of Prime Minister Margaret Thatcher's government told me the queen herself had intervened in the matter. I opened my mouth to protest that the monarch wasn't supposed to intervene in House of Commons affairs. He held up a restraining hand — "just a moment."

The queen had not intervened personally, never would. But she let it be known directly to Prime Minister Margaret Thatcher and indirectly through trusted aides to members of all parties in the House of Commons that she did not wish to be put in the impossible position of having to choose between conflicting advice from her first ministers in Canada and in Britain. Faced with that reality, most of those at Westminster who thought they had a "responsibility to the Canadian people" quickly grasped the reality that Canada was, and had been for more than a century, an independent nation. Out of courtesy, Canada was asking the British House of Commons for a formality the government of Prime Minister Mackenzie King had not had the courage to accept when the Statute of Westminster, at their request, provided constitutions to Australia, New Zealand, and South Africa. Like it or not, they would be well-advised to follow Trudeau's advice and "swallow it."

Throughout the debate I had sent back articles and editorials on the issues involved to those from whom I'd gathered information and opinion, on or off the record. When common sense finally prevailed at Westminster I modestly admitted to myself that possibly those exquisitely written articles had registered with some of the more intransigent British MPs. That bit of egotistical nonsense disappeared on being told about the queen's intervention. Yet, as we are all to some degree egotistical, I confess to considerable residual satisfaction at apparently having shared so closely Her Majesty's views.

Straight Autobiographical Stuff

In his brilliant autobiography, *Left Hand, Right Hand*, Sir Osbert Sitwell recalls details of conversations when he was less than five years old. Whether people actually remember or just think they remember, who knows? My own early memories are vague, not only conversations but also visual images.

My first clear memory is of Uncle Will and his open four-door Ford charging at 20 mph down the steep hill from Hampton, N.B., towards the bridge crossing the Kennebecasis River. I clung to the dashboard, terrified at the clatter of loose floor planks.

At Norton, out of the profits of years of hard work farming and selling fertilizer by the carload, Uncle Will built a great frame house on high ground with a verandah across the front facing the road. The woodshed and outbuildings were at the back facing a magnificent view up the Kennebecasis towards Sussex. It was important in that village in those days to see and be seen.

On that verandah Uncle Will would bounce me on his knee, singing innumerable verses of "Billy Boy" and delivering homilies. I remember vividly his pointing to a photo in the Saint John *Telegraph-Journal* of a man with a cigarette in his hand. "Coffin nails, Billy, coffin nails." I grew up to ignore his advice for years, then read the first lung cancer stories and quit, three decades after he was in his grave. He'd been right all along.

His house is now a nursing home and there is no one with the Heine name living in the valley. They were there for more than two centuries after John Haney arrived to claim the land grant due to non-commissioned officers who served with the British in the American revolutionary war. In 1881 the family by common consent changed their name to the "old and true spelling of their name, to wit, Heine." By that time they were pillars in the Baptist Church, highly enough regarded for the bridge over the Millstream to be named the Heine bridge, and had sprouted distinguished twigs on the family tree.

The name change was puzzling. To revert after more than one hundred years from an Anglicized version of a name to the original Palatinate spelling made no sense. No one alive knew why, but digging around in old records provided a clue. In 1786, just three years after the Loyalists left New York, one Thomas Haney (who succeeded John Haney as corporal in the dragoon troop of the Queen's Rangers and probably was John's brother) was hanged in Saint John, N.B., for burglary. The family undoubtedly tried, a century after it happened, to erase the memory of a black mark on the family name.

As the first grandchild in my generation I was named William Colbourne (father added the "u") for Uncle Will and Uncle Colborne, a Presbyterian minister who dramatically departed this world at ceremonies marking his fiftieth anniversary in the ministry. It was hoped that the names would bring showers of dollars on the new heir to those names. Not so. Colborne left his surplus funds to Japanese foreign missions; Uncle Will left the interest from $1000 to Mother as long as she lived, which she has now been receiving for fifty-five years, the principal to be divided equally among her surviving children; that will mean $333.33 each when Mother goes to see where Uncle Will went; she delights in teasing me about my "fortune."

Uncle Will stories still survive in the family. He wasn't exactly mean but he sure was "close with a dollar." A lad who asked for a job reference in Saint John from "the squire," got the job, and later stopped Uncle Will to thank him, received a polite nod and a gentle request for reimbursement of the reference letter's stamp — three cents. Embarrassed, he fished out three pennies which Uncle Will stuffed in his little leather purse as he continued his dignified path into the village.

In an argument with my father about who gave how much to the Baptist Church, Father unwisely boasted he'd put in anything Uncle Will contributed. Next Sunday the usher was startled to see Uncle Will drop in a $20 bill (in the Maritimes in the 1920s they were scarce) and Father drop in another. Father learned long after that Uncle Will gave $80 a year to the church in four equal instalments.

My brother and I were wary about working for Uncle Will after piling wood in the shed all of a hot summer's day. Sent home to supper without the expected payment, we were disconsolate until Uncle Will's spare, bearded figure appeared on the verandah and called us back. He split an apple and gave us each half. We went on home even more disconsolate.

Uncle Will turned up at the local undertaker/taxi-driver/furniture dealer's barn one day to look at coffins. No one was dead; he just wanted to look at coffins. He poked with his cane, thumped top, bottom, and sides, then had one opened, stretched out in it, folded his hands, asked "How do I look?" and was assured he looked fine. He paid for it and was buried in it several years later at the lovely cemetery a few miles away where he lies to this day awaiting the time when "the trumpet of the Lord shall sound and time shall be no more" and where the view is even better than from his woodshed.

To jump forward half a century, in the family plot there, not far from Uncle Will's grave, I had a stone put up for Vivian and me, a black granite bench where a weary visitor can sit and admire the view. Names and dates are on three sides of the thick edges. Across the back is a line from the Rubáiyát of Omar Khayyám: "and, having writ, moves on."

The monument salesman wanted names and dates on the top, but I demurred. "Imagine some sweet young thing contemplating the view for an hour and walking away with 'HEINE' imprinted on her bottom. It's too awful to contemplate." He stared blankly for a moment, shook his head and murmured, "Ah, then would you just sign here, sir?" He seemed relieved when we left.

On a later trip to the Maritimes we mentioned our bench to friends who, at Christmas, put a note on their card: "On a visit to Norton we all drove to the cemetery and took turns sitting on your bench." Lovely thought at Christmas.

When the trumpet sounds and Uncle Will enjoys the resurrection in which he so devoutly believed, it's doubtful he'll be too happy with an inscription from verse about a non-Christian. But then, I'm not too worried; the trumpet will sound only for those who have been saved and I may not hear the call.

Uncle Will got me mixed up about religion because we went to the United Church in the city all winter and to Uncle Will's Baptist Church in Norton all summer. Sure was confusing; placid conformity in winter, hell and damnation all summer. Soured me on fundamentalists the rest of my life. I liked the Baptist hymns better though; they had a rousing beat. I can still sing "Will There Be Any Stars in My Crown" and "Where the Gates Swing Outward Never."

Teachers left no impression until grade nine in Norton, where the family moved into a summer cottage when Father's insurance business failed. The principal didn't have a chess partner in the village;

167

I learned quickly and thereby managed to move from wall to middle to window rows through the three-year high school curriculum.

Village life was dull. It was great for my younger brothers, who played hockey, baseball, and football. For me there was a great problem — few books. In Saint John at nine I'd exhausted the children's section and was reading that library over again (Tom Swift, the Alger books and G. A. Henty; the latter I still read from a personal collection). When I was eleven a kind librarian got me into the adult library, with more meaty fare — Dickens, Scott, Sinclair Lewis, and Mark Twain — and those long, wonderful history shelves, alternating with travel, biography, and science.

At Norton books were scarce, though some neighbours would loan them. When I began selling the *Telegraph-Journal* there was enough money to take the train to Saint John where the librarians ignored the rules and let me take books out of the city. It was tough reading four books in a week while making sure there was enough money to buy a ticket to return the books before having to pay fines.

Local boys were rough; I was a skinny bookworm. Several times they intercepted me like a pack of wolves closing in on a bleating sheep and beat the daylights out of me just for the fun of it. That didn't pall for them; it sure did for me. I spent a Saturday in the woodshed whittling out a maple stick which would fit down my pants leg. Monday, trembling in every limb, I headed for school and was duly intercepted. Fighting tears of desperation, I whipped out the homemade club and swung wildly in all directions. One boy limped for a week; another needed stitches for a head cut; a third had to write left-handed for a few days. I was left to my books.

At the cottage to which the family retreated during the Depression we burned wood in an open fireplace the first winter and struggled through deep snow to the outhouse. But we stayed together as a family, which was a considerable accomplishment in itself. My favourite place was the verandah, with glass on the west end against the prevailing winds. There from early spring to late fall I had a cot and read beneath the blankets far into the night — learning yards of the verse of Rudyard Kipling and Robert Service. I can still recite "The Shooting of Dan McGrew" and the "Cremation of Sam McGee" and, given a bathtub and a resonant chamber, sing a rousing version of "The Road to Mandalay."

One book is a vivid memory. The lady who loaned it obviously hoped it would be a warning of the terrible fate awaiting those who broke the moral code of the village. Outwardly strict, the place seethed with more raunchy behaviour than the Baptist fundamentalists let on — and undoubtedly still does. The impossibly thick novel, hard to hide under the bedclothes, featured a young squire of the manor house who steered a milkmaid to a riverbank and "there beneath the willow tree he had his way with her." It ended with the illegitimate offspring of the willow tree episode facing his wealthy and famous father and telling all, thereby ruining the scoundrel's career and causing his wife to die of shame and grief. Puzzled me at the time but a year or so later it suddenly registered what the rascal had done to the maid beneath the willow tree.

There wasn't much else to do — it was a major event when a travelling road show from "the Boston states" arrived in the village to play *Uncle Tom's Cabin*. I scrounged a quarter and sat entranced, particularly when little 'Liza, suitably garbed in white, expired on a white metal bed. Immediately lamentations broke out; 'Liza began to rise, or more accurately to be raised, still prone on an invisible wire strung from the lower left to the upper right of the stage, towards the gates of heaven. What brought a tear to every eye, halfway through her slow transition to paradise, was the pair of white feathered wings which sprouted from her back. Sure was impressive.

Despite being at the poverty line, there was little real work to do. I loved Mother dearly and didn't have to be bullied to bring in wood and pump enough water from the well for her to cook and wash, but it worried her terribly that her eldest showed so little interest in school. It took six years of war to persuade me there were advantages to a university education; all four of her children graduated from university one way or another, two through veteran's training schemes.

Before the war crashed in there was a year pumping gasoline in Saint John working for $10 a week and $1.50 commissions. That ended after a slugging match with the boss's son one morning in the garage basement. For the sheer pleasure of driving a car I chauffered the village doctor, A. E. L. Winsor. A Newfoundlander, he had sailed the Labrador coast as a boy of eleven in his father's fishing schooner; in his twenties he put himself through medical school working as a carpenter on Long Island. He was in many ways a surrogate father, unflappable, dedicated, wise beyond my understanding, and a fine companion whether we were skimming the gravel roads in the summer sun or struggling through winter snow drifts.

My most vivid memory is fighting through snow-blocked roads to reach a farmer ill with pneumonia. The doctor left a weeping wife with a bottle of pills, both of them knowing he could not get back and that the husband would die. Three weeks later, the roads cleared, we stopped to be greeted by a hale and hearty farmer. As we drove away the doctor had tears in his eyes. The pills had been a trial sample of sulpha; the "old man's friend," pneumonia, was no longer a winter killer.

Before that year was out war came. If it hadn't, with the doctor's encouragement and financial help, I might have applied for medical school. Instead, on September 4 George VI had a new recruit about whom he was destined to know nothing. A winter in Saint John, where an orderly-room job in the Canadian Dental Corps brought the dizzy heights of the sergeants' mess, was followed by volunteering for overseas. That was the cover story. Actually, the colonel wanted a typist who used more than two fingers and kicked me out. It had taken a little while to realize that while you volunteered to join, after that you did what you were told. Drafted overseas, I said farewell to tearful parents and boarded the *Duchess of Bedford*, but not before saying goodbye to Canada by being hauled to Ottawa for transhipment back to Halifax. In Ottawa, convinced there'd be no return (I don't know why but the feeling was there until the war ended), I went alone to the Château Laurier just to live it up once and was shown a table in the Canadian Grill.

The waiter was helpful, fully aware he had a greenhorn and a buck private at that, surrounded by officers from 2-T Louies to generals. He took an order for buffalo steak and asked about wine. Desperate, I looked down the list and tried the only recognizable word.

"Vermouth, please."

The waiter's voice carried over the conversation around us.

"With *steak*, sir?"

Late spring 1940, after a transatlantic crossing which scared the hell out of us because Italy had entered the war and the Atlantic was rumoured to be alive with Italian submarines, I was a private in the Second Canadian Division in England. On the first of many weekends in London, the Empire Rendezvous provided a ticket to see Anton Walbrook in "Watch on the Rhine" at the Savoy. It was another world, a dramatic introduction to theatre at its best and a long way, culturally and in miles, from a "Boston states" road show.

World War II killed some 80 million people. For hundreds of millions of other men and women who survived or who, like me, served but didn't see combat, the war opened entirely new worlds of art, theatre, literature, architecture, and the strange ways of men and women — as well as the reality of war. Every weekend and on leaves, sometimes without leave, London was a vast magnet — theatre, museums, art galleries, cathedrals, being entertained in English homes (through the Empire Rendezvous, where I was able to return the favour a couple of years later by escorting parties of Canadian and American soldiers through Westminster Abbey and other historic sites), and generally soaking up a culture which entranced me then and has ever since. And, of course, girls.

At last, book supplies were endless; even classical music became interesting despite an utter lack of understanding. When Ernest Bevin, that sturdy illegitimate workman who became Churchill's minister of labour, was in Aldershot to talk to Canadians about the allocation of manpower resources, there was a private among the officers. When Oxford offered correspondence courses in English literature and composition, I enrolled and hammered away on army typewriters by the hour; when Oxford offered two-week courses to Canadians on leave, the fleshpots of London took second place to beer, bread, and beef in the great halls of Oxford's colleges. And whenever possible there was travel, the beginning of the wanderlust which has taken me so many times to Europe, North Africa, the Middle East, the Far East, and all over the United States and Canada from the Florida Keys to the high Arctic. Then the range was more restricted, from Cornwall to the Moray Firth, from Dover to Glasgow, but it was a good start — criss-crossing England and Scotland by train, on army lorries, occasionally on a motorcyle pillion.

Promotion didn't come because slipping away to the far corners of the island on leave and neglecting to come back didn't sit well with the colonel. Not that there was much chance of promotion in a dental unit; zilch, in fact. Travel was broadening, however; there was an enthusiastic Scottish lass from Edinburgh whose mother worked nights as an air-raid warden. She (daughter, not mother) wrote forty-page letters and would be waiting on the station platform with two penny platform tickets — with the crowded trains of the day tickets were seldom checked on board. Scotland for tuppence meant money for pub lunches. And then there was a girl in London, the blond daughter of a blond English mother and a father who was the son of an English chief justice in India who'd married a Burmese princess — though as Kipling's soldier says about the girl he met on the boat going home, "I wouldn't do such 'cause I liked her too much ..." The Scottish lass in time chose a Canadian major; the London lass wrote only once after my return to Canada mid-war.

Escape from the army came when the air force began combing the army for potential air crew to replace the steady losses Canadian bomber and fighter squadrons were taking in 1942. Lt-Col. John F. Blair, a dentist from London, Ontario, was blunt about my leaving for the air force. No way. Why he was so adamant was a mystery because I certainly wasn't much use to him.

Until recently I had persuaded myself that when blank transfer application forms came through from the air force, I had waited until a Friday noon when Blair would be rushing off for a weekend in London with a girlfriend we called "Ducky" because her ass was so close to the ground. In this version I gave the colonel a thick batch of requisitions, reports, orders, and miscellaneous papers and hinted it was important to get it all off to division headquarters that afternoon. He signed everything with one eye on his watch, the other on his impatient brother officers waiting outside.

More than forty years later, however, researching an article on Canada's Access to Information Act, and being curious what various superiors in those war years might have written about me, I applied for all documents relating to my army and air force service. A month or two later a large parcel arrived with photocopies of scores of service records. Among them was an application for transfer to the RCAF signed by J. F. Blair, Lt-Col. A later signature in the pile of paper is quite different from his witness to and endorsement of my transfer application. Comparison of the application signature with my handwriting shows several points of similarity. Now I'm convinced that out of deep frustration with life in the dental corps, I didn't just slip one past the colonel; I forged his signature on the application. If so, it was a dangerously stupid thing to do; a court-martial would have brought months in the Glasshouse, the army prison where everything, even urinating, was done on the double.

Since receiving the mass of forms I've also taken legal advice and been assured that the statute of limitations ensures I cannot now be charged with what appears to be forgery. Good thing, too. In my mid-sixties the Glasshouse on the double would kill me in the first hour. My only exercise is acting as pallbearer for my fitness-minded friends.

When orders came through from the RCAF requiring me to report for examinations and a review board, Blair was furious. With the cunning rankers acquire when dealing with colonels, I assured him we'd discussed the transfer a second time and that he had agreed and signed. He enjoyed liquid lunches enough he couldn't be sure he hadn't. He had no way of knowing whether I'd got his signature by deceit or by forgery. There was no court-martial. In an attached form he said quite nice things about me, probably because he didn't want to appear to contradict himself. He would also have known that if I didn't make air force aircrew, I had undertaken to enlist again in the army and, given the shortage of infantrymen, that's where I'd have ended up.

It was a relief to get away to Scarborough for Initial Training Wing, then to an airfield near Leicester where my log book shows eight hours' dual instruction on a Tiger Moth before going solo. The

RAF having concluded from that performance it was worth sending me overseas for pilot training, they posted several thousand Englishmen to Canada and a score of Canadian army transferees to Rhodesia. The understandably angry Canadians, most of whom had been overseas for three years, gathered around my Manchester depot bunk to discuss the matter. I was delegated to call Canadian Military Headquarters in London and ended up talking to a most sympathetic major who promised we'd go to Canada if he had to bring us back from Rhodesia.

A week later the manning depot adjutant delivered a tongue-lashing for my having dared to go over RAF heads to CMHQ. I was to be court-martialled, returned to the ranks (as leading aircraftsman there wasn't far to go), and detained in barracks indefinitely. Having satisfactorily retrieved what he thought was his dignity, he ordered "you malcontents" to report next morning. After another lecture, we were marched to a waiting truck, driven to Liverpool docks, and loaded on His Majesty's troopship *Louis Pasteur*, which sailed next day for Halifax.

Homecoming in the middle of the war was most satisfactory. At the end of Commonwealth Training Schools there were pilot's wings and a commission. There was another hassle with authority when orders posted me for an RAF commission. The commanding officer was understanding and a switch was made, but the adjutant wasn't amused; probably in retaliation a posting came through to Trenton to become an instructor. No objection: England was wonderful but an egg a month for three years was tiresome. As required by the code of the day I showed enthusiasm when they said instructing was only for "a few months"; then overseas again. But there was a far better reason than food for welcoming an instructor's role; the girl I'd been seeing in Moncton and with whom I'd kept in touch while overseas, avoiding any mention of a Scottish lass and a London blonde, agreed a few months later to marry me. When we saved enough to buy a ticket, Vivian joined me in McLeod, south of Calgary. She spent the next year shepherding a couple of trunks with our clothes and few household possessions to a succession of rooms and apartments in Dauphin, Gimli, and Souris.

I never did get back overseas. The war was winding down in the fall of 1944 and few new aircrew were needed overseas. So I stayed a flying instructor on the prairies, acquiring complimentary log-book entries from senior instructors of which I remain rather proud.

The air force meant much more than the army. There was a glamour to flying that far exceeded clerking in the dental corps. Added to a commission, with substantially greater pay and perks, was the sheer pride of wearing coveted pilot's wings. We joked about cutting windows in our greatcoats so all who passed could see what we so proudly wore. Pride, however, was meaningless against the sheer glory of flight. The Harvard wasn't a Spitfire but it had a powerful engine, high wing loading, and many of the handling characteristics of fighter aircraft, which of course was intentional. It was the basic trainer for fighter pilots. The words of the young American, John Gillespie Magee, Jr., who died flying with the RCAF in England, are still vivid and moving:

> Oh! I have slipped the surly bonds of earth
> And danced the skies on laughter-silvered wings;
> Sunward I've climbed, and joined the tumbling mirth
>   of sunsplit clouds.

After the instructors' course at Trenton, it was off to the prairies, where fleecy clouds dotted skies, creating fantastic shapes around which the Harvard could climb, dive, twist, turn, and do "a thousand things you have not dreamed of." When there was no longer challenge in the sky we imitated more experienced pilots and danced along the deck, harvesting wheat with propeller tips, charging up narrowing ravines and, at the risk of court-martial, darting down prairie gravel roads towards an oncoming car until the driver, in sheer panic at the great whirling disc flashing near him, steered for the ditch and disappeared in a cloud of dust as the plane swept over with a screaming roar.

In time we could roll to the right 90 degrees, pause a second, roll another 90 degrees to be upside down, pause again, recover halfway and pause again, then complete the manoeuvre by rolling back to the horizon. More than thirty years later on a ride with one of the RCAF's aerobatic team, the Snowbirds, having boasted of my skill in the hanger before the flight, I was offered the stick with a question: "Like to try one of those four-point rolls?" First try wasn't too good. There was wobbling coming out and the nose was high on the horizon. Second time around was smoother and I came out climbing only slightly. Third time — no prize-winner but good enough to earn an appreciative nod and grin from the young pilot. The old coot he had as a passenger still had the ol' touch.

Pushing Harvards around the prairies wasn't as classy as the Tudor jets flown by the Snowbirds, but every minute was a joy while the war wound down in Europe and the Far East. The only serious interruption was a court-martial, not the one threatened by Colonel Blair nor by the RAF Manchester depot adjutant, but an honest-to-goodness one which kept me grounded for three weeks while the

RCAF mills ground exceeding small, determining punishment for an offending pilot. I'd taken an advance student up for a gunnery exercise; when the ammunition was gone, I told him to land at Weyburn relief field and send out the next student while ground crew rearmed the Harvard. By the time we landed, a snow squall was blowing and I wasn't keeping as close a watch on the student as I should. He managed to taxi into a galvanized steel fence sunk in concrete. His Majesty's aircraft was a sorry sight.

The student was in the air an hour later. As the aircraft commander, I was grounded pending court-martial, which involved my appearing before the air officer commanding, being asked if I'd accept his punishment, which I'd been primed was the smart thing to do, and was officially sentenced to a reprimand. Back to flying.

That weekend my brother Wallace, a pilot at a nearby navigation training school, flew over for a visit. He'd recently started up an Anson's engines inside a hangar (strictly against regulations) so the engines wouldn't freeze in the few minutes it took to push the aircraft out into the cold. Anxious not to be caught, he started out before the hangar doors were fully open — and sliced the wings off another of His Majesty's aircraft. He, too, got a reprimand from the AOC.

In the mess that Saturday night, Wally and I stayed well away from the AOC's corner. Mid-evening, an aide came over and asked us to join the AOC. The conversation went something like this:

"Good evening, gentlemen."

In unison, "Good evening, sir."

The AOC glowered at me. "I sentenced you to a reprimand this morning for damaging an aircraft."

"Yessir."

"And I gave you a reprimand last month for the same thing."

Wally nodded. "Yessir."

Pause.

"You're brothers, aren't you?"

In unison, "Yessir."

"Name's Heine."

"Yessir."

"German name, isn't it?"

"Yessir."

Long pause.

"Aha," said the AOC, turning to his officers, "sabotage."

When the laughter died down — ours was rather feeble — the AOC was all smiles.

"Sit down, gentlemen, and join me in a drink."

We got out of there as fast as we decently could, with a warm handshake from the AOC and a smiling admonition: "Please, gentlemen, try not to do too much more damage to our aircraft."

For weeks after, fellow instructors kept asking, "Hey, Heine, you just going flying or gonna sabotage another kite?"

The Japanese conflict brought one more hassle in the armed forces before George VI dispensed with my services. William Lyon Mackenzie King was anxious that Canada play its part in the Pacific war. For political reasons he decided those who were to be sent there to fight should sign an undertaking of willingness to be shipped to the Far East. It was a matter of pride to each station's commanding officer to have all his officers volunteer for the Far East.

I said the hell with that. Having volunteered in 1939 to serve "for the duration," I'd go anywhere anyone ordered but damned if Billy King could get off a political hook by that kind of nonsense. Once again I faced a furious CO. This one kept his record intact by posting me to Halifax for leave prior to being transferred to the inactive reserve (that is, discharged). That was fine. We had the summer in the Maritimes before making arrangements to take journalism at the University of Western Ontario.

In London there were three calls. First to the university, where Dr. K. P. R. Neville, then registrar, confirmed his one-sentence letter: "pack an overnight bag and come on up," and registered me as a special student. Without Grade 13 a make-up year was needed. It was a gracious gesture. Second call was to the *London Free Press*, where R. J. Churchill, then executive editor, promised me one night's work a week at $3 a night; not much, but in a month it was $12. DVA allowance was $80 a month, so $12 represented a 15 per cent increase in income. Third call, while still in uniform complete with wings, was on Colonel Blair, who was back from overseas. Confessing my deceit in England was met with complete indifference; I didn't stay long and never saw him again.

The first week at Western brought an hilarious confrontation with nineteen-year-olds on campus. They still indulged themselves with Frosh Week hazing, which included wearing a frosh beanie. Veterans returning to university were scornful and there were several petty incidents. My own brought little glory but great delight.

Accosted in a crowded hall between classes by three aggressive enforcers for not wearing my beanie, I was threatened with being carted down the hill for a dunking in the Thames. Teaching student fliers had not developed any commando killer instincts, and I had few to begin with. It looked as if I was about to be frog-marched to the river when two classmates came along. This pair, universally known as Mutt and Jeff because of their height, had fought across France and Holland with the Royal Canadian Regiment. Instantly grasping my predicament, they sauntered over.

"You having trouble?"

Wide grin spreading across my face, I allowed a dunking was being considered.

The frosh enforcers weren't as bright as they might have been. They took the approach that it was three to three and they were tough, too. That was a mistake. I stayed strictly out of it, partly out of sheer joy at watching professionals work, mostly because I chicken out in a fight. Jeff's foot flashed out. One of the enforcers doubled up in pain, flew back against the wall, cracked his head against the tiles, and slumped to the floor out cold. Mutt grabbed the other two enforcers by their shirt fronts and cracked their heads together. They stayed on their feet but their gaze was glassy.

"You OK, flyboy?"

"Yeah, thanks. Can I buy you guys a coffee?"

As we left, a respectful path opened up the length of the hall. Word got around; hazing of veterans faded rapidly.

University was hectic — a stiff course of subjects and, after the first year, full-time summer work at the *Free Press* and thirty hours a week in winter as well. We were also settling into a community, active in church and other activities, and enjoying a widening circle of friends. Four years later, after having worked virtually full-time summer and winter at the newspaper for the last two years of a four-year course, I graduated with low marks but considerable experience as a reporter, copy editor, financial editor, and feature writer.

There were no dreams of glory and none materialized. What did develop was a growing consciousness of an ability to put words together to express ideas and events to other people, and great pleasure in doing so.

For five years I covered the business and labour beats, learning a great deal about how corporations functioned in crisis situations (they often panic) and how labour unions manipulated their members, corporation executives, and the public. When the International Printing Pressman and Apprentices' Union was certified in the *London Free Press* press room, the publisher soon learned there was only one person in the plant who had any practical experience with unions — me. After a year of unproductive negotiation the union struck. Everyone else in the plant came to work. A week or two later the striking workers left town for other jobs provided by the union. Their departure was speeded by my approach on coverage of the strike. As the newspaper could not be expected to be unbiased about the matter, the company would state its case in a column and equal space would be provided for the union to state its case. After due warning, the first story ran with a blank hole in the page where the union had refused to appear. That jarred them. Next day the union leaders had their copy ready in good time. The first story included the names of all striking employees, their ages, and their previous year's wages. As they were for the most part in their early twenties and earning far more than the average industrial wage in London, they promptly lost the support of the city's other unions. End of strike.

After puttering about with a number of chores, wage surveys, and reorganizing the paper's delivery system, the next task was early planning for a new plant. I was encouraged by the then general manager, William G. Trestain, to travel the continent looking at other newspaper plants under construction or recently built, and, in time, to return to England for negotiations on the new presses to go in the plant. As with Arthur Ford, Bill became both mentor and friend. He could soak up an enormous quantity of information from paper; I wrote long reports on almost two-score newspaper plants. In all, preliminary work on the floor layout, negotiations with architects and engineers, contracts for construction and equipment, and supervision of the work occupied several years. With the building up and everything working well except the air conditioning, which meant little because my thermostat didn't register temperature extremes very well, I was at a loss for much to do, particularly since the publisher, a frustrated engineer at heart, took over the air conditioning problem and soon had it bludgeoned into smooth operation.

A year later I was negotiating with two publishers in the United States who wanted someone to co-ordinate building their new plants. (The *Free Press* plant had been on time and on budget.) There were many new plants going up and a vast array of competent architects and engineers to build them. What publishers needed was someone with experience in helping all the operating departments of a newspaper work out their space and equipment needs, then co-ordinating them so the architects and engineers would have something to work on. While these negotiations were going on, consultants were studying the *Free Press* organizational structure. I expressed blunt views. Most of all, the editorial side needed an editor to co-ordinate news gathering and the editorial page.

Arthur Ford had retired in 1962 at the age of eighty-two, after forty-two years as editor-in-chief. He was succeeded by John K. Elliott, who became an even closer friend of mine than his predecessor. In all the years in London, in or out of the newspaper business, I never heard an unkind word about John. He was a scholar and a gentleman and a good friend until he died. The stature of the man was never more evident than his departure as editor. He'd waited in the wings for years when Arthur Ford stayed on long past normal retirement, then enjoyed the editor's chair for only a few years. John's health was precarious (he'd had tuberculosis in the days when survival was uncertain and had since developed emphysema). After Arthur's resignation it was arranged that John, as editor, would be responsible for the editorial page and report to the publisher, while the managing editor ran the newsroom and reported to the general manager.

That worked fine until a consultant's report came in, a year after the building was finished. It recommended an editor be named to be in charge of all editorial content, news, and editorial page. I was asked to take the job. Though negotiations with American publishers to build their plants were well along, my heart was on the news side. There was a flaw in the offer — replacing John. Then I learned he had already been asked to step down because his health didn't permit him also to manage the newsroom. That took me off the hook; John being the person he was, he would hold no resentment towards the person chosen, nor had I been involved in his leaving the editor's chair.

Staff reaction was interesting. After some fourteen years in newspaper administration, few in the newsroom remembered I'd taken journalism and had been a reporter for several years. Among street staff there was considerable head-shaking. The managing editor, Ivor Williams, was gracious. His response was that "we're going to make you the best editor in Canada." That reminded me of Winston Churchill who, when he addressed the U.S. Congress, said that if his mother had been English and his father American, instead of the other way around, he might have got there on his own. I took the positive approach and assumed it was an offer of support. By and large with all staff it was.

There was one unpleasantness over which I had no control. Walter could be very definite when clear in his own mind about a course of action. My approach would have been to leave John in the large office he'd been using and take for myself a smaller office down the hall, nearer the newsroom. Walter would have no part of that; the editor must be in the editor's office and another office found for John. I was reluctant, but John understood. To ease the change I suggested coming into the office on a Saturday and, with the help of staff property workers, making the necessary changes. Vivian was in the Maritimes because of family illness. On the Saturday morning the phone rang in the office. It was Emilie Elliott.

"John and I thought you'd have a long and tiring day," she said. "We wondered if you'd have supper with us."

I managed to accept before choking up.

With that wonderful sample of a generous spirit — of two generous spirits — as a guide I began what must be one of the free world's most fascinating jobs, editor of a daily newspaper.

Though not carefully thought out and certainly not written down, the policies I followed for the next seventeen years were clear in my mind from the beginning:

For readers of the London Free Press: We should provide unbiased coverage on local, district, provincial, national, and international news. On editorial pages, offer informed opinion as much as possible by our own staff, given time and travel limitations, as well as from a variety of other sources. Make certain there was space for readers' opinions — all letters critical of our coverage or opinions were to be published.

For advertisers: We should offer courtesy as long as it was reciprocated; and provide coverage on news pages if newsworthy, but absolutely no shading of coverage or opinion under any circumstances.

For management: Whether finance, personnel, production, or marketing, we should give everything to which their specialty entitled them, but, as with the public and advertisers, allow no shading of content nor interference with staff efforts to provide news coverage. One senior executive's son got a three-month sentence for car theft. We published the story and, of course, the name and address. I got an after-the-funeral card with a note from the family, "Thank you for your sympathy and understanding." I still have it.

For staff: Well, it was a mixture of being tough and an old softie (sometimes the wrong response was offered at the wrong time). In the first few months as editor the chronic alcoholics were offered early retirement, a few months' pay to go elsewhere, being fired, or an end to drinking — cold turkey. Only one of several survived and, though much of what was done was strictly against company policy, I survived — probably because being fired in the first six months would be more of a reflection on the people who hired me than on me.

For most of the staff I had a benign view (few if any of them ever understood) which, in a conversation with the publisher, I once likened to owning a greenhouse. Reporters and editors (they'll react with raucous laughter when they read this) are like delicate flowers, sensitive to light, needing protection from disease, proper nourishment, adequate water, and shelter from wind, rain, excessive heat and cold, along with constant attention. My job was to see that no one cut a bloom (that is, a story before it was published); ensure that outsiders (people trying to manipulate news content) didn't break into the greenhouse and run it their way; give the plants nourishment (pay and other stimulants); as much as possible allow individual plants to flower in their own fashion; pull out a few weeds (alcoholics, incompetents, and plain lazy); and then let a thousand flowers (stories) bloom.

Walter thought that flight of fancy a bit ridiculous but restrained himself. Months later, discussing a newsroom problem, he said he'd been thinking about my greenhouse approach and that it made some sense. With a grin, he added, "not much, mind you."

To me, it was always a valid concept. It's not possible to tell creative people how to create. Writers like *Free Press* columnist Del Bell aren't manufactured; nor do they even need much encouragement. They are self-starters who become creative naturally, the way a seed grows if given light, heat, and water. It might help a little if their editor wrote effectively himself, or gave a little praise, but neither was essential. The newsroom was full of talent. Given support, creative people would create far more with minimal direction than with the boss dotting is and crossing ts for them.

During those seventeen years I blew large sums of *Free Press* money on extensive travel. As a line from a song in "Seventy-six Trombones" notes, you can't sell the goods if you ain't seen the territory. There were several trips to the Arctic, including a fascinating circle around the rim of Hudson Bay with the then NWT commissioner, S. M. "Stu" Hodgson; innumerable trips to Washington, the power centre (like it or not) of the free world; many visits to London; lengthy writing trips to Europe; a dozen or more to Cyprus, Lebanon, Israel, Egypt, Syria, and Jordan; and Far Eastern flights to Japan, China, Hong Kong, Thailand, Malaysia, Singapore, Indonesia. Most trips yielded an article a day.

It was a privilege to be in Vietnam as the war there wound down and spend a long weekend on an aircraft carrier (USS *Hancock*) in the Gulf of Tonkin; to be in Prague the week the Russians moved in; to be the first Western journalist to visit Greeks detained in the Dome Hotel in Kyrenia by the Turkish army which had invaded Cyprus; to spend several days in Dacca as the emerging new country, Bangladesh, was struggling in the aftermath of the defeat of West

Pakistan. These were minor exposures to danger compared to Southam's John Walker, who in his sixties walked into Afghanistan to cover resistance fighters there. For me, an editor in his fifties, these and other expeditions were excitement enough. Vivian wasn't consoled when I joked "there were lots of empty spaces between the bullets."

In my last several years, illness slowed me down considerably. It began with surgery for ulcers and gall bladder; minor surgery for a hernia; and then a major session again, intestinal surgery for diverticulitis. Despite looking distinctly gaunt and seedy, I got back to work each time.

In the end, it wasn't illness which led me to ask for an early retirement. I had been bypassed (rightly, because I couldn't read a balance sheet effectively) for the general manager's and later the newspaper president's job. Both went to Robert Turnbull, who'd handled production for many years and was an effective number-cruncher. Then Walter died of cancer in December 1983. Suddenly, early retirement looked very attractive. I waited quietly into the new year, then negotiated with Bob, who welcomed my initiative because he wanted to make changes, not all of which I endorsed, but which were inevitable anyway because my formal retirement was due in late November.

So mid-May 1984, quite by coincidence on the date thirty-five years before on which I had joined the permanent staff, I retired. For once the internal grapevine did not function and I made my own announcements. When all arrangements had been made (and the company was enormously generous), I told my long-time secretary at 3 P.M. The managing editor was briefed at 3:30 P.M. when a staff-meeting bulletin board notice went up for 4 P.M. It was standing room only as copies of a retirement memo were passed around. After answering questions for half an hour or more, I finished off a few details and left about 5:30 P.M.

As my wife and I were heading for the car park, a night editor caught up with me.

"Bill, here's a proof of a story about your retirement. What play should we give it?"

My grin was broad and genuine and my reply left him with an equal smile.

"I don't know. I'm not the editor any more."

In the morning when I padded out to pick up the paper the story was on page one, which was a play I wouldn't have authorized — if I were the editor.

Big Flap, We Got There;
No Flap at All, Anne Got There

Elgin County Municipal Council was a hard nut to crack. For years our reporter in St. Thomas had allowed himself to be fed whatever council members chose to tell him after they'd met in closed session. We didn't fuss too much because he was well liked and we got as much local news as we needed.

When he was replaced, new staff quickly began verbally banging on doors for admission to council deliberations. Staff challenged the county council at every opportunity; we wrote strong editorials insisting on the public's business being conducted in public; and I wrote plainly worded letters to council members. Finally, since the Ontario Press Council is a vehicle for complaint by the media as well as its more usual role of hearing complaints about the media, we presented our case to them. In due course a hearing was scheduled in St. Thomas but it was not very effective. Elgin County Council declined to turn up officially (though one or two sympathetic members did come and speak). The Press Council adjudication quite properly stated that public business should be done in public. The pressure had an impact. Before long the media covered Elgin County Council and the world did not come to a jarring stop.

The Lambton County Council had the same history of secret meetings. Our reporter, Anne Murphy, outwardly shy and with a gentle smile, had considerable determination. She turned up at a council meeting, presented herself as a delegation of one, and told her rural audience the score. We never learned just what she said, but to register on rural councillors who'd been running the county their way for a century or more, she must have been either persuasive or damned blunt. Probably she was both. Without a murmur, Lambton County Council voted to open its meetings to the public. Anne wrote a short story and that was that.

Reading it next morning I was both astonished and delighted. Here we'd fired away with every weapon we could bring to bear on Elgin County and were successful only after months of work. Anne did as much in an hour one evening. It was rudely suggested by my colleagues that maybe Anne and I should change jobs.

Artistic Talent Is a Nebulous Thing — We Back Our Critics in Assessing It

Drama critic Doug Bale's review of a London Youtheatre's play, *Leafin' Through*, drew an anticipated flow of mail condemning him for not knowing one end of a stage from another. As was our custom, we cheerfully published the critical letters because readers have a perfect right to disagree with the critics — and who knows, they might be right.

What many actors and actresses don't understand is that no actor or group of actors, audience, or critic can achieve the ultimate understanding of artistic truth. It may exist, but no one has achieved it. The function of critics is to express their opinion of the performance as honestly as they can, according to their knowledge of the theatre. The function is to inform readers who have not attended whether the performance is worth the price of admission.

Bale was and is a competent and indeed at times brilliant critic of the theatre. I didn't always agree with his reviews, but what one individual thinks of another individual's critical comment of a particular play isn't very important. What is essential is that the critic be free to express his artistic views without interference. Bale had that freedom.

As long as a critic was complimenting (which Bale did) or criticizing (which he also did) performances at a professional theatre like Stratford, his views were balanced by professional actors against opinions from other critics. The actors there were big boys and girls. They took their licks and basked in praise, as did most professionals, philosophically. That wasn't usually the case with non-professional theatrical groups and that's why we tried to avoid reviewing amateur events.

The young people who haunted high school, university, and summer theatre stages worked their hearts out on their experimental theatrical efforts, but they weren't professionals. Sometimes, however, they desperately wanted to be treated as professionals. Usually there was a telephone call or a visit to the newspaper insisting that we turn up and cover opening night.

Experience had taught us that those who perform are not ready to have us publish for all our 130,000 readers exactly what we thought about their efforts. What amateur theatre supporters really wanted was six to ten inches of pious pap, praising the efforts of young people for putting on the play, saying nice things about the costumes and sets, and carefully avoiding any indication of the critic's honest opinion.

The only aspect of a theatrical performance worth covering was, and remains, whether or not it was good theatre. If all we did was write publicity blurbs for the performance, we'd sell our 130,000 readers down the river. They wanted an honest evaluation.

Once in a while we were persuaded that an amateur event was so close to professional that we should review it. That was the case with London Youtheatre. I was assured everyone involved understood the function of a reviewer and, please, wouldn't we have someone there. We did. The flak began the next morning.

Don't misunderstand. I'm not complaining; that kind of reaction was one of the hazards of the business. But the rules stood and if high school or other amateur theatrical performances wanted our reviewer to take the same honest look at their efforts as he does at Stratford, Toronto, and Niagara Falls, they could call the city desk and ask if a review was possible. We'd do our best to write a fair assessment of the performance. But if we were just being asked to write nice things as part of a publicity blurb to sell tickets — sorry, that wasn't our bag.

Knock 'Em Down and Point 'Em in the Right Direction

A few weeks after the *Free Press* introduced a newsroom word-processing system, I was listening with one ear to the editorial conference and typing an editorial on the new screen. Turning to throw in a comment, I knocked the keyboard to the floor with a great crash.

Conversation stopped while I gathered it up and tested the keys and controls. "Isn't that astonishing," I murmured. "I knock it to the floor in the middle of an editorial, pick it up, hit the command key, and it just goes on writing the editorial for me."

Rory Leishman, a political scientist turned editorial writer with whom I'd had to be brutal in steering him away from academic language not suited to the daily press, has a devastating wit. He's also a thoughtful and effective editorial writer.

"Oh," he said, "that's not so astonishing. Some editorials I write, the editor knocks me down. I pick myself off the floor, he hits the command button, and I start writing the way he tells me."

Ah, the Mail: Fascinating as a Boy —
Even More So as Editor

As a teenager I moved from Saint John, then a city of some 40,000, to Norton, a village thirty-five miles east. It wasn't a traumatic experience, despite being deprived of movies, the "y," the library, and the exciting world of the sea around the harbour, because the village had its own compensations. Probably, in the long run, it was better for me; I have a nostalgia for several years in Norton greater than for the dozen years in Saint John.

It did leave me with an unusually strong attachment for mail, which came by train three or four times a day from Saint John and Moncton. Often I'd stand impatiently in the post office lobby, watching through the window as the postmaster sorted the mail, hoping for letters, magazines, or even junk mail.

His Majesty's mail was a link with the world I'd left. Each sorting had promise — an invitation to visit a relative; an answer to a coupon; maybe, oh great day which never came, a cheque for a short story laboriously pecked out with one finger on the family typewriter. There never was very much mail. What there was intrigued me.

It still does.

Now the flow is greater. Books; magazines; newspapers; company reports; government publications by the pound; publicity releases from charities, institutions, fund-raisers, hydro, telephone, and manufacturing industries; partisan publications from Arabs and Jews and from Indians and Pakistanis; press releases from Indonesia, France, Germany, Russia; and most welcome of all, personal and business letters from friends and acquaintances in Western Ontario, across Canada, and around the world. After years as editor it should have become boring, but it never did and now, retired, it still fascinates. Every day's mail is a new adventure, some of it thrown away, some of it skimmed, but much of it full of insights into and new associations with the complex world in which we live.

Frequently there is strikingly different mail, an envelope in the day's flow which delights or intrigues. (There are days when unhappy mail prevails, too, letters which are vicious, stupid, or even threatening.) Let me share a few fun ones, along with an oddity or two.

An envelope with a Japanese stamp brought this gem:

Dear Ontario Free Press,
How are you. I'm Japanese girl. I live in Tokyo. I want go to Toronto. But I have no friend, sponsor and not enough money.
If somebody give me bed and eat. I am very happy.
I hope introduce your newspaper to me.
Please give me good later.

There were a good many ribald comments about that "give me bed" bit. I've kept the return address from my lecherous colleagues, but I haven't replied — yet.

Then there was a printed letter from Maple Heights, Ohio, which began: "As Almighty God, I greet you."

A good many people over the centuries have believed they've talked with God, but there aren't many who've had letters from on high, certainly not via Canada Post. Reading on, it became obvious that this god had rather positive opinions about newspapermen.

"I want to extend my heart-felt gratitude to all the editors and publishers who have treated Us with generosity in the past. Many have published these letters in their gracious newspapers." It's clear where other kinds of editors and publishers are going. "A few despicable dastards had the audacity to vehemently doubt My Veracity; but as a few mangy curs hate Me, they shall also be hated with equal fervor." However, there's a hopeful note. "For those that Love Me, Love shall drown out all hate. Where true Love reigns, hate is forgotten and a true value of fellowship will remain." That's not a philosophy to be derided, of course. The letter ends with "Prayerfully yours," and "P.S. Please publish this letter in your newspaper."

One highlight from the past was a report from my man in Bangkok. Peter Jarvis, eleven years old, was the son of the first secretary of the Canadian embassy, W. M. Jarvis.

In 1972 I was in Bangkok for two nights, thoroughly enjoying a clean hotel and dosing myself with antibiotics to combat a fever picked up during a week in Calcutta and Bangladesh, prior to what were to be ten strenuous days in Vietnam. With the fever under control by Sunday, I phoned Jarvis, suggesting a late afternoon drink and a chat about the war in Southeast Asia. Typical of Canadians at overseas postings, he was quick to oblige and insisted on my going back to his home for dinner. And a delightful evening it was, too.

Peter listened to his father's questions about the articles I'd write during the trip, and asked one of his own: "Would any of those articles be published in Bangkok?"

I thought it most unlikely.

"Why?"

"Well, partly because the Bangkok papers don't see the *London Free Press* and wouldn't hear about the articles." I added modestly that maybe the Bangkok papers wouldn't like the articles anyway.

While his father and I talked, Peter was mulling that over.

"Maybe," he said, "I could sell them for you."

He was serious. On the spot we agreed that when all the articles were printed, I'd mail them to him. He was free to try to sell them anywhere in Southeast Asia. In return for his effort, he could have 50 per cent of the proceeds as his agent's commission. That's three times what literary agents get but considering the effort he'd put in for the sales he was likely to make, it seemed a fair deal.

Back in Canada a month later, I sent Peter the articles and a letter formally authorizing him to sell them at a 50 per cent commission. His father and I exchanged a letter or two. It appeared Peter was having little success.

I chuckled and mentioned to friends that my man in Bangkok was still trying. Well, he scored. He sold two articles to the *Bangkok Post*, at $15 each (considering the *London Free Press* could buy Walter Lippmann, when he was being syndicated, for $10 a week, Peter did rather well). When the *Post* pays him $30 he'll remit the remaining $15 to the *London Free Press*.

I'm tempted to write back telling him to keep the whole sum, but I know his father would say the boy should learn that a contract is a contract. Besides, the letter also said that now he's sold two to the *Post*, he's going to see if the *Bangkok Nation* will buy any of the other articles. If he peddles all twenty-eight articles from the trip that's, let's see, $420 and half of that is $210 — you know that eleven-year-old entrepreneur may be on to something.

See why I still find the daily mail so intriguing?

Brickbats, Bouquets, and Other Trivia

On a trip into the Northwest Territories with a group of teachers we were allowed off the cruiser to tramp around an island. A Byron teacher, Gay Murray, and I pretended not to want to leave the island, which generated much hilarity and suggestive comment from other teachers.

A few years later Gay brought her class to tour the *Free Press* plant. To tease her I told her class about our escapade. Much laughter and giggling.

Then came a letter from a young lad, Devin Hanes. "I sure had a good time and I'm sure the other kids did, too. Your stories were all very humerous [sic] especially the one about all those people on an island in the Northwest. Oh by the way what did Miss Murray and you do on the Island?"

Gay probably put him up to it. My reply was succinct.

Dear Devin:
You may be a little young for this, but from your letter and question, I'm inclined to think not. Therefore I'm sure you'll accept a bit of advice from a balding old editor — that a gentleman never kisses and tells. If you really want to know, I'm afraid you'll have to ask Miss Murray, who may or may not answer, but who has no reason not to.

Submitting a selection of six editorials to the Western Ontario Newspaper Awards, I was delighted to find myself a winner. Marjorie fished out the six editorials we'd sent in — and to my horror I recognized one of them instantly as not mine. My fault. A fast phone call to Ross Weichel, chairman that year, included an abject apology and a request the runner-up be given the prize.

An hour later the phone rang; they'd checked with the judges who made up their minds on three editorials, which did not include the one I'd not written. They were adamant the award would stand.

How to get out of that one? I invited all editorial writers, particularly the one who'd written the abrogated editorial, to dinner at the London Club — my treat for eight.

When time came formally to express my apologies, they broke up completely at my somewhat wry comment that the prize was $100; the dinner with drinks, wine, and brandy ran $227.

Served me right.

There's no covering letter attached to a twenty-page report by a student at Western on his in-depth interview with the editor-in-chief of the *London Free Press*, so credit can't be given. But the young man's perception of a newspaper when he arrived, as indicated in his report, was so different from when he left, I can't resist including portions.

> During the interview I was thinking along opposite lines as concerns the ability of the press to influence, and I still do, but maybe to a lesser degree ... [but] I think the interviewee truly believes what he is saying ... the interviewee has a healthy respect for the opinions of others ... and that the other's may prove to be more accurate ... [he thinks] that if you are going to take the flak, you might as well do it for what you think as for what someone else does ... he has a very definite sense of respect for the worth of others ... but respecting another person's opinion does not necessarily mean accepting it.
>
> Here his point is that either you explain your position to the other person so he understands and accepts, or you change your position until the other person can understand and accept it ... implicit in this idea is that the other person must be doing the same.
>
> He is always interested in making sure that people know why he is doing a certain thing, why he made a certain decision ... if he is honest ... the most that people can say is that he is wrong or is stupid, but [not] that he is doing something for anything other than good motives.

On the question of the power of the press, which I believe to be vastly overrated in the minds of most people, the young man ran up against a mental brick wall: "Either I believe in his honesty, or I change my way of thinking."

Sometimes our colleagues in broadcasting marched to different drummers. On one occasion they sent an unhappy memo to the publisher objecting to the newspaper "allotting so much prominent space to a promotion of our competitor CJBK."

Turns out we'd given ink to a CJBK bikini contest, which if it didn't meet the bare tits competition of the Toronto *Sun*, probably brought in a few readers for us and listeners for CJBK.

"If CFPL [the company radio station] has a bikini contest," I replied in a memo through the publisher, "I trust we'll cover it as thoroughly as we did for CJBK (or possibly the phrase should be uncover it)."

190

We had always, I noted, "taken the position that it was not in our long-term interest to down play our competition, nor to play up our other media outlets. We make an honest effort to assess everything which comes by our desks in terms of reader interest. If we are the subject of a monopoly inquiry some day, I want to be in the position of being able to testify honestly that we gave no favours to our company colleagues, nor denied any coverage to our competitors. The Kent Report merely emphasizes the propriety and desirability of that position."

There was no reply, comment, or reaction from anyone.

Combing through the 1975 report of the Ontario Arts Council, it was easy to pull out examples of the gross imbalance of awards to Toronto writers, artists, photographers, dancers, musicians — you name it — compared to awards given people in the rest of the province. So I wrote a scathing article, with frequent reference to a disease known as Torontitis, the symptoms of which, often seen in the *Globe*, the *Star*, and the *Sun*, are that if it doesn't happen in Toronto, it doesn't happen.

Weeks later came a charming letter from Ronald Evans, OAC's film and literary officer. "Bullseye! Your shaft, of course, hits us right where we live. My compliments, sir — it's a fine piece and fully justified."

Well, I'll be damned — almost, not quite but almost, made me wish I'd been more kind.

Ralph Palmer's dog, a Welsh Corgi, wrote a snarky letter about our discontinuing our afternoon edition, referring to "possible indignities on your pant leg" because "children [were] struggling through the pre-dawn chill" to deliver the paper no longer available in the afternoon. The dog today "had the opportunity of eating my dinner — on [a newspaper] — and was disturbed that most of the news in your day-old paper [was] CP fillers of dubious vintage." It was signed, "dictated but not read," Ralph Palmer, Esq.

I replied, "Dear Ralph: That's a doggoned good letter. Personally dictated and read."

Joe Barth, a dedicated supporter of the anti-nuclear movement, NDP candidate in the 1984 election, and a worker in the Divine Word Centre, London, came by the office one day with a delegation to see the publisher and me, asking why the centre wasn't getting more coverage.

We explained we looked at all material submitted, considered all events scheduled, and tried to publish and write about anything and everything we felt the public would be interested in reading. If they'd submit articles they wished to have published, we'd consider them and give those submitting the articles a prompt reply whether or not it met our needs and the public interest.

A few weeks later a news letter of the London Inter-Church Committee for World Development Education had a item by Joe in which he said "the publisher agreed to print anything we submit providing it is well written and readable." The qualification that material has to be considered to be of possible interest to the public was omitted entirely. My reply was more blunt than usual.

Joe, bless his heart, never listened — he was marching to another drummer. Maybe a better one, but different from mine.

From a lawyer in Toronto, Clayton Ruby, came a letter asking me to testify in a retrial of a case involving a gay magazine article titled "Men Loving Boys Loving Men." The idea was for me to speak to freedom of speech and freedom of speech in print.

"Unfortunately for your defence," I replied, that while the state does not have a place in the bedrooms of the nation, "the state does have a place in the nurseries of the nation ... and responsibility for the sexual inducements and relationships involving boys (and girls) who I take ... to be up to whatever age is considered by society or the law to the age of sexual maturity ... you'd find me not a very good expert from your point of view."

As a speaker at an American/Canadian conference at Campobello, the Canadian island home of President Franklin Roosevelt, I met Thomas Winship, the prestigious editor of the *Boston Globe* which, during his tenure, had won several Pulitzer prizes. After the conference he wrote that he had subscribed to the *London Free Press*: "It's about the best paper graphically I've ever seen, to say nothing of your solid and sophisticated content."

That went on the newsroom bulletin board with a note that Tom was writing about every reporter and editor on the staff.

Then, down to earth.

In the spring of 1984 I wrote an article suggesting in reasonably strong language that political and bureaucratic ossification had set in and that it was high time Canada had a new government. The heading was: "A Party Too Long in Office Burdens the Country."

192

Soon there was a letter from Robert Hubsher.

"I was utterly fascinated by the William C. Heine theory on ossification-in-office ... and wonder if this was a generalizable theory. For instance, The Theory of Institutional Ossification ... that any body (usually a human one) which occupies a particular space or position for too long becomes ossified ... such an ossified body must be removed from his/her office and replaced ... kind of like crop rotation for humans.

"Taking this theory and applying it to it's author's situation, I would suggest that William C. Heine be removed from the office of the Editor-in-Chief as soon as possible. His ossification is showing."

What no one on my staff knew was that I was planning an early retirement in May 1984. Though we cannot run all letters to the editor, this one was passed to me — no comment attached. With great joy I made certain it was published.

What remains a delightful thought is that the gentleman may well believe he was responsible for the departure of the ossified editor.

Chippy Editors Stay That Way Even After They've Retired

Maybe it had something to do with being released from the pressure cooker. In the first several months of retirement I banged off articles on widely different subjects which generated almost as much flak as during working years. It was, in a way, nice to be back in a hot seat.

One article savaged a Toronto police sergeant, Jack Press, over his testimony before the Grange Commission on Susan Nelles's arrest. Another blasted the then attorney general of Ontario, Roy McMurtry, for shopping for a jury to convict abortionist Dr. Henry Morgentaler. A third took delight in the Canadian Broadcasting Corporation having to prune expenses and suggested greater cuts were in order. And another saw no reason whatever why taxpayers should be helping to support people with incomes over $40,000 to bring up children or in their old age.

What had angered me most was Press's testimony that he was surprised by nurse Susan Nelles not registering surprise that police had come to her door. "Usually, people get quite excited when we knock on the door and say we're police officers," Press said. He told

Nelles "we believe you gave him [infant Cook] the drug" and at that point Nelles said she wanted to speak to her lawyer. What was most disturbing was that Press went on to testify he thought "if she had no involvement, then she'd be telling me about it in no uncertain terms. The fact she didn't protest, didn't assert her innocence just reinforced my belief [that she was guilty]." Earlier in the day, Press testified he had talked to nursing-team leader Phyllis Trayner, who had reacted quite differently. "She was behaving as an innocent person would — she was crying and upset."

My article continued:

And there you have it, a clear statement by a senior officer with 20 years' service testifying on oath that he had in at least one serious murder case decided which of two suspects he'd chosen to arrest on the basis that one of them remained calm and asked to speak to her lawyer.

Translate that attitude of a senior police officer into a personal situation. You've committed murder but think no one knows you're guilty. The local constabulary turns up and asks questions. On the basis of Press' testimony, now you know what to do. First and foremost, don't ask to speak to a lawyer — which is what any intelligent person would do — and above all don't stay cool, calm and collected.

The best way to handle such a situation is obvious. If you're a female, go into a fit of wailing and weeping along with vigorous denials — that's not to suggest Trayner's reaction indicates guilt; on the contrary, her reaction may have been, for her, as much an indication of innocence as was Nelles' reaction.

That raises a serious question. If Trayner had remained calm, cool and collected and had asked to speak to a lawyer, would she have been arrested along with Nelles?

If you're a male — don't mention a lawyer — you can talk to him just as well after you're arrested — erupt into a high dudgeon and call down the wrath of God on anyone who dares to suspect you of anything remotely resembling a dastardly crime ...

If this is the way Metro Toronto police force works, there needs to be a commission to consider that rather menacing situation — if Press' testimony reflects police attitudes, the role of Ontario's police forces has become sadly warped ... [an] arrest and charge should be based on the evidence gathered, not on an individual's reaction when told a charge is about to be laid ...

There's something desperately wrong with police work when a citizen's reaction to the threat of a serious criminal charge becomes a justification for laying the charge.

On the second Ontario charge against Morgentaler of performing illegal abortions, I wrote that McMurtry "was setting himself against centuries of law by refusing to accept jury verdicts on the abortion issue ... Three juries in Quebec and one (so far) in Ontario have refused to convict Morgentaler."

Jury verdicts, the article claimed, "reflect society's changing values," and quoted Manitoba's attorney general, Roland Penner, who noted that in the eighteenth century in Britain "200 crimes carried the death penalty." The noose was automatic for "stealing 40 shillings or more." Juries, said Penner, "began finding that the accused had stolen only 39 shillings," regardless of the value of goods stolen.

I cited a classic Canadian case, where a Halifax jury changed Canadian law and forced several magistrates out of office. Joseph Howe, editor of the *Novascotian*, published a letter charging that from the "pockets of the poor and distressed, [fines of] at least one thousand pounds are drawn yearly, and pocketed by men whose services the country might very well spare."

Howe was charged with criminal libel, which carried long jail terms as well as financial penalties. Civil libel involved only financial penalties. Criminal libel laws, furthermore, did not allow him to argue the truth of the charges; he could be convicted on proof he published the libel. Howe, theoretically, could do no more than use the supposed libel as evidence, the 19th century version of Catch-22. He spoke in his own defence — an impassioned speech to the jury of some six hours, charging that "these jobbing justices crawled in through this legal lubber-hole of indictment ..."

He was talking, of course, about freedom of speech and of the press. "I conjure you to leave an unshackled press as a legacy to your children." When Howe finished, the prosecution demanded a guilty verdict. Judge Haliburton improperly directed the jury to find Howe and his paper guilty.

The jury considered milord's direction for 10 minutes, then found Howe "not guilty," reinforcing once again the concept that both the government and the legal system are subordinate to the jury system. Before long, Britain replaced the Halifax magistrates and the provincial governor was recalled.

Appeals were not then and are not now allowed against jury acquittals in Britain. They are allowed, but should not be, in Canada. The results of these trials reflect a growing consensus in public opinion that abortion during the first several weeks of pregnancy is a moral, not a criminal issue ... as a mere male, I've concluded long since that unless I happen to have helped create a specific pregnancy, when for varying personal reasons I might try to persuade or dissuade the lady about an abortion, I'm hardly qualified to express an opinion on the issue. Yet since many males, not the least the province's attorney-general, seem to abrogate unto themselves the right to tell women what they should believe about abortion, I've no hesitation in expressing the strong conviction that every woman has a right to decide what use is to be made of her body ... To argue otherwise is to deny both female sexuality and the right of females to live their lives in these matters on their terms.

Of McMurtry's second trial for Morgentaler, I concluded that the "jury system was never intended to permit lawmakers and administrators to keep empanelling juries until they find one whose verdict fits their own prejudices."

That put the fat in the fire. Letters to the editor flowed in at a great rate, the majority from anti-abortionists, taking exception to any thought of juries "being above the law," and condemning my arrogance in daring to express an opinion on abortion itself — which of course is precisely what pro-life supporters are doing.

Universality of the old-age security pension and family allowance also generated reaction.

Ridiculing politicians who referred to universality as a "sacred trust," I pointed out both plans were introduced by earlier Liberal governments looking for votes (which is also the reason Conservatives now in power seem likely to retain them).

There's a nagging worry in the back of voters' minds about the consequences of loading $35 billion a year deficits on their children and grandchildren. Failing to get that deficit under control will keep Canada in deep financial trouble — and people know it.

The only thing sacred about old-age security and family allowance is the need to ensure that no one goes to bed cold, hungry or in need of medical attention ... if there's anything sacred ... it is society's responsibility to stop feeding federal funds to people with more than adequate incomes and to use the surplus partly to increase payments to those in need and partly to help reduce the national deficit.

It is vital, I suggested, "not to introduce a means test ... that's degrading and intolerable." It would be simple to provide that anyone could apply for and receive old-age security and family allowance, but that lines on the income tax form would provide full or partial repayment (plus interest) for individuals and families not entitled to benefits. "That would eliminate a millionaire aged 55 who marries or remarries and produces children being entitled at 65 to both old age security and family allowance (which has happened). That may be fun to boast about at the 19th hole, but it's no way to run a country's social services."

The article ridiculed NDP leader Ed Broadbent, who "came up with a classic bit of irrationality. 'All Canadians contribute,' he said. 'All Canadians should have them.' If he really believes that, he must find it hard to rationalize unemployment insurance, where all employed persons contribute but only those who become unemployed benefit." Another factor mentioned was that while more affluent beneficiaries pay tax on these benefits they're more likely to invest the money. More funds in the hands of those who need it would be immediately recirculated on food, clothing, and shelter, generating tax revenue.

"As usual, Jake Epp, health minister, put the issue simply. He said the government is seeking a more effective distribution of benefits. Right on, Jake."

The most common objection in letters to the editor to those views was that as the writer had paid taxes for years, he or she was entitled to an old-age security pension. Agreed, but not for those with total retired income higher than a cut-off line established by Parliament.

No matter, really. It's doubtful if any government, Tory, Grit, or NDP, would ever have the courage to rationalize the existing system.

And then there was the CBC. Those poor, deprived souls faced a 10 per cent reduction in operating costs late in 1984.

The article opened with a quote by Pierre Berton that if ever "Canadian culture needs support, it's now. Instead, it's being cruelly mutilated. The move to Canadian nationalism is deader than a dodo."

My article took on a sarcastic note.

There now. Singers, composers, musicians, authors and artists might as well hang up their vocal chords, keep warm burning musical scores, use half-completed manuscripts for job applications, and make a criss-cross of paint brushes to light the evening fire. Berton has spoken.

Margaret Laurence was even more incensed. "I'm absolutely enraged," she said ... [and she] worried greatly about the thousands of artists, writers and producers "who work behind the scenes," [and wondered] "what the cut will do" ... to the news makers, the film and documentary makers? (A little confusion there. Most journalists report news, they don't make it, but maybe the CBC is different.)

Out of 390 staff and contract positions in Toronto, "17 would be eliminated (that's jobs, not people) ... Proportionally, however, that won't hurt as much as the layoff of 100 to 194 out of 365 production workers by Bendix Heavy Vehicle Systems scheduled for early 1985 in London. There hasn't been a word out of Toronto about that upcoming layoff."

Then I unburdened myself with considerable enthusiasm:

Berton, Laurence and others seem to think Canadian society owes its usually self-appointed artists a living. Not so; those who produce discordant notes, unintelligible verse, a year-old desk blotter that passes as art, along with writers whose message escapes even the author, falsely hearty and erudite radio voices doing their best to make critics out of nonentities, and television personalities who could find air time only in the name of Canadian nationalism have been too long feeding at the public trough.

Even Berton has an axe to grind. A highly successful and commercial author (for which more power to him; would there were more like him), he's also a panelist on a CBC show, "Front Page Challenge." That show has long since exhausted viewers, even if it hasn't exhausted the supply of mysterious subjects for the panel's guessing games. South of the border the program would have been axed years ago. Now it may well be on the chopping block.

What the protestors mean, when you get to the bottom line, is that they are determined to do their version of Canadian nationalistic good to the Canadian reader, listener, and viewer — and to the Canadian taxpayer — whether or not readers, listeners, viewers and taxpayers want that kind of good done to them.

The executive director of the Alliance of Canadian Television and Radio Artists, Paul Siren, "put his finger on it when he said 'there's no point in having [a Canadian broadcasting system] without a Canadian presence, a Canadian identity. We might just as well have a conduit from the United States.' He spoke ... as if there was a choice over the conduit. There isn't."

Canadians have had a conduit from the U.S. for many years and would scream blue bloody murder if anyone tried to take that conduit away from them.

Most Canadians live within 200 kilometers of the U.S. border and most of those receive programs directly or by cable from CBS, ABC, NBC and PBS. If they find American crud distasteful (and there's lots of that) around these parts they can tune in to Global and CTV (which like their American counterparts are not immune to crud) along with TVO and CBC (which like PBS have many fine programs).

The CBC this year cost the taxpayer $906 million; another $190 million is earned in advertising revenue. That's $40 a year for every man, woman and child in the country. Like it or not, they pay. What's uncertain is how many Canadians think it work $160 a year for a family of four to listen to CBC-FM's energetically enthusiastic morning interviews with people only the interviewer knows, or to Knowlton Nash introducing "The Journal." (There are great moments on "The Journal," however, Prime Minister Margaret Thatcher putting down Barbara Frum among them.)

Canadian nationalism can't be bought like soap and lathered on thick. Canada's pride lies in its people and its grandeur lies in its vast spaces and natural beauty. Berton's histories, Laurence's novels, Bliss Carman's poetry, A. J. Casson's paintings, Maureen Forrester's voice — these and a thousand thousand other manifestations make up Canada's culture and Canadian nationalism. That nationalism doesn't have to be force-fed, like a goose having grain shoved down its gullet. In the long run, Canadian nationalism will do better on its own. That's how we survived 200 years of wary proximity to the U.S. — largely on our own. Given the ingrained attitudes of Canadians, that's probably a good way of surviving the next 200 years.

Oddly, there was little public response. Probably that was a result of what journalists understand to be a reality of public life — you'll hear if they object but not a word if people agree.

L'Envoi

Undoubtedly the kooks still called the *Free Press* but for a long time after I retired they didn't call home. Yet inevitably one did. With Vivian nearby working on the family balance sheet, and the ol' word processor generating yards of deathless prose, early one evening the phone rang. The voice was strident and bitter.

"Why do you publish all that goddam tripe in the ..."

When you've heard them all, it doesn't take long to recognize the kooks.

"Sorry, chum, I'm not the editor — go take your stupidity somewhere else" — and hung up.

He didn't call back.

Yet the call was helpful for two reasons: it confirmed the wisdom of my retiring and he must have passed the word. No kooks have called for months.

You know, I don't miss them at all.